Among the Russians

Among the
RUSSIANS

COLIN THUBRON

HEINEMANN : LONDON

William Heinemann Ltd
10 Upper Grosvenor Street, London W1X 9PA
LONDON MELBOURNE TORONTO
JOHANNESBURG AUCKLAND

First published 1983
© Colin Thubron 1983

SBN 434 77986 5

Photoset in Great Britain by
Rowland Phototypesetting Ltd, Bury St Edmunds, Suffolk
and Printed by St Edmundsbury Press
Bury St Edmunds, Suffolk

For Rae Sebley

Contents

The identity of many people in this book has been disguised. I am grateful to them for their candour, and sad that I cannot record their names to thank them.

C.G.D.T.

'Do you know who are the only god-fearing people on earth, whose duty it is to regenerate and save the world in the name of a new god?' '. . . the people of Russia.'

Dostoevsky, *The Possessed*

It would be a gross and pedantic superstition to venerate any form of society in itself, apart from the safety, breadth, or sweetness which it lent to individual happiness.

George Santayana, *Reason in Society*

1. Across White Russia

I HAD BEEN afraid of Russia ever since I could remember. When I was a boy its mass dominated the map which covered the classroom wall; it was tinted a wan green, I recall, and was distorted by Mercator's projection so that its tundras suffocated half the world. Where other nations—Japan, Brazil, India—clamoured with imagined scents and colours, Russia gave out only silence, and was somehow incomplete. I grew up in its shadow, just as my parents had grown up in the shadow of Germany.

Journeys rarely begin where we think they do. Mine, perhaps, started in that classroom, where the green-tinted mystery hypnotized me during maths lessons. Already questions rose in the child's mind: why did this country seem stranger, less explicit, than others? Why was it untranslated into any precise human expression? The questions were half-formed, of course, but the fear was already there.

Perhaps it was because of this that thirty years later the land glimmering eastward from the Polish frontier struck me as both familiar and foreboding. It flowed away in an undifferentiated calm, or rose and fell so imperceptibly that only the faintest lift of the horizon betrayed it. I saw nobody. The sky loomed preternaturally vast. The whole world seemed to have been crushed and flattened out into a numinous peace. My car sounded frail on the road. For three hours it had been disembowelled by border officials at Brest, and its faultily-replaced door panels rasped and squealed as if they enclosed mice.

Even now I was unsure what drew me into this country I feared. I belonged to a generation too young to romanticize about Soviet Communism. Yet nothing in the intervening years had dispelled my childhood estrangement and ignorance. My mind was filled with confused pictures: paradox, cliché. 'Russia,' wrote the Marquis de Custine in 1839, 'is a country where everyone is part of a conspiracy to mystify the foreigner.' Propaganda still hangs like a ground-mist over the already complicated truth. Newspapers, until you know how to read them, are organs of disinformation. The arts are conservative or silent.

Even in novels, which so often paint the ordinary nature of things, the visionaries and drunks who inhabit the pages of nineteenth century fiction have shrivelled to the poor wooden heroes of modern socialist realism. It is as if a great lamp had been turned down.

As for me, I was entering the country too impatiently to be well equipped. I spoke a hesitant Russian, but had read very little. And I was deeply prejudiced. Nobody from the West enters the Soviet Union without prejudice. I took in with me, as naturally as the clothes I wore, a legacy of individualism profoundly different from anything east of the Vistula.

But I think I wanted to know and embrace this enemy I had inherited. I felt myself, at least a little, to be on his side. Communism at once attracted and repelled me. Nothing could be more alluring to the puritan idealist whose tatters (I suppose) hung about me as I took the road to Minsk; nothing more disquieting to the solitary. All my motives, when I thought about them, filled up with ambiguity. Even my method of travel was odd. The Russians favour transient groups and delegations, which are supervised in grandiose hotels. But I was going alone, in my own car, staying at campsites, and planned to cover ten thousand miles along almost every road permitted to me (and a few which were not) between the Baltic and the Caucasus. My head was swimming in contradictory expectations. A deformed grandeur still hovered about this nation in my eyes.

So for more than two hundred miles between Brest and Minsk, I travelled in a state of nervous fascination. There was almost nothing else on the road: dust-clogged lorries carrying wood, cement, cattle; a rare bus; and once a truck packed with frosty-eyed Brueghel peasantry. Every twenty miles or so, in glass and concrete checkpoints raised above the highway, grey-uniformed police fingered their binoculars and telephones. The land was haunted by absences—no advertisements, no pylons, often no telegraph poles. The cluttered country of industrial Europe was smoothed out into a magisterial stillness. Grasslands, farmlands, forests. All huge, all silent. The eye could never compass any one of them. The forests, in particular, looked deep and unredeemed. They lapped against fields and roads in rich, deciduous masses of oak, beech, silver birch. This was Belorussia, 'White Russia', a state of rye and timberland which stretched half way to Moscow. The deadening pine forests still lingered about its pastures and stencilled every horizon in a line of coniferous darkness.

I gazed at all this with the passion of a newcomer, and scribbled it in a diary before I should forget the feel of ordinary, important things.

These first hours shone with a peculiar intensity. In the fields of potato and alfalfa, labourers moved through a soft July sunlight—men and stout women in headscarves wielding billhooks and pitchforks. No collectivized glamour, no tractors or combine harvesters intruded into the sodden ritual of their haymaking. Instead, where marshy fields elbowed through the forests, black and white cattle grazed in isolated herds, and troops of herons paced nonchalantly across the meadows.

After a hundred miles I stopped the car and lay on the verge among butterflies and lupins. The country was steeped in silence. In this limitless terrain, details of plant or insect shone with the exposed distinctness of things seen in the desert. A dragonfly clattered onto my knee. Bright yellow toadflax squeezed up between my fingers. They were obscurely comforting.

But I was conscious above all of the stunned desolation which seems to permeate these plains. It has to do, I think, less with their actual poverty—sandy soil, poor drainage—than with the inarticulate vast-ness of which they form a part. Without the nearness of towns or the presence of hills, the sky takes on a terrible passive force. Stand anywhere here, and three-quarters of your field of vision is engulfed by it, adding a pitiless immensity to the size of the land. The sun and clouds hang permanent and immobile in its blue. They curve above you like a Tiepolo ceiling. Everything beneath is exposed. The weather itself assumes a threatening, total quality, so that the earth can momentarily wither under a flagellating sun, and rain burst like a cataclysm. Above all, people—their houses, traffic, cattle—grow piti-fully incidental. The villages I passed generally stood far off the road—wooden cottages with asbestos or tin roofs pitched steep against snow. They were small, abstract—a civilization sketched puny in the fields, like a language I didn't know. Its people, it seemed, were not enclosed and nurtured, made private or different by the folds of valleys and mountains. They were figures in a landscape, living under the naked sky in the glare of infinity.

Driving eastward through this anonymity, I became obsessed by the sheer magnitude of the country I was trying to pierce. Larger than South America, two and a half times bigger than the United States, it extends half way round the globe and contains one sixth of the land surface of the whole earth. My own journey—eastward to Moscow, north to Leningrad and the Baltic Sea, south to the Caucasus and the Turkish border, back across the Ukraine and the Crimea—comprised only the historic edge of a mighty wilderness. If I traced an imaginary line eastward from where I was driving, it would move for more than a thousand miles over country nearly identical to this, where the altitude changes by no more than 980 feet until the Ural Mountains. Another thousand-mile line extending south-east would meet the black earth and grasslands of the steppes, which I would reach that autumn. But the Soviet Union here has barely begun. Eastward again the black earth pales into the deserts of Kazakhstan, where in summer the temperature may stand at 105°F in the shade for weeks at a time. For hundreds of miles the earth is tossed into dunes or sets hard as a parquet floor, and the rivers wind into landlocked seas or die of exhaustion across the sands. Northward, in the valleys of the Ob river, spreads the hugest lowland on earth—the mosquito-plagued lakes and swamplands of the West Siberian plain, while eastward again lies the forbidding heart of this whole continent: Central Siberia, bounded by the glacial waters of the Arctic Ocean.

It is these Siberian lands—ice-glazed, wind-stricken—which sit behind the inner eye as you drive east. They lend their invisible enormity to everything around you. While I was driving here at midday, their farther reaches were still plunged in night. In the far north—land of the reindeer and snowy owl—three months of winter go by without daylight at all, and the mean winter temperature is −60°F, the coldest of all habitable regions of the world. The rivers and the very seas freeze in corridors and oceans of ice. Even in summer the tundra subsoil is perpetually frozen, and the sun squeezes from the earth only a liquid mud, where bulbs flower in a fleeting gasp of scent. Across the wastes of southern Siberia, in a region huger than Canada, more than two and a half million square miles of stunted conifers, larches and birches surround rivers which are barely known—the Yenisei, gouging out a passage 3,600 miles into the Arctic; the Lena, which already measures twenty miles across in its middle course and floods 2,550 miles into a delta which is ice-choked even in August. The very girdle of mountains massed along these southern fringes echoes with un-reachable names—the Pamirs and the Tien Shan whose peaks are among the highest in the world, the Altai scattered with translucent lakes, and mountain chains still farther east which only peter out in the tiger-prowled heights along the Chinese border, and in Kamchatka's Pacific peninsula.

All this lent a majestic and dwarfing dimension to my journey. Already the country was cast in the mould of those imagined tundras and rivers. It was slow, impersonal and absolute. I could not help wondering what effect such isolation might have on its inhabitants—the lack of visual stimuli, of anything varied or unique in the landscape at all. Was the easy Russian submissiveness to God or tyranny, I wondered, the result of a people crushed by the sheer size of their land? Could it be that the meandering, mystical, rough-hewn qualities of the Russian psyche—Russian novels, Russian music—that the unwieldly immensity of Russian bureaucracy. . . .

But this froth of irresponsible questions subsided unanswered at a sign which said 'Minsk Campsite'. The place stood deep in pines and was insulated by ten miles from Minsk itself. Through the gloom I glimpsed little wooden huts whose pitched roofs reached to the ground. I walked to one marked 'Administration'. I had no idea what to expect. I had never met a Westerner who had tried to camp in the Soviet Union.

But by Russian standards these camps were all to be blessedly informal—no wardens, few administrators, no observable KGB (my troubles from them came in other places). A non committal and slightly lost-looking girl sat behind a desk with two pieces of paper on it: my first non-official Russian. She looked at me tiredly.

'Are you a group?' she asked.

It was a quintessential Russian question. I glanced down at myself. No, I was not a group. Solitariness here is rare, odd. It was not catered for. I found myself apologizing for it.

Then she said: 'You must be Mr Thubron. You're British.'

She checked through a folder and discovered my name on a telex. This ritual was to be repeated each night for more than two months, until the cold closed the campsites and forced me into hotels. I was invariably expected—and this foreknowledge struck me always with the unease of clairvoyance. I never quite got used to it.

But everything had been organized in London and on the Polish frontier. My route was prearranged and listed in detail, and was to be pored over by countless traffic police along my way. I had tickets for camping, tickets for petrol, tickets for hotels. But my technically accurate passport declared me a 'building company director' instead of a writer. I was, I think, unknown.

The girl looked at me uncertainly. In her enclosed face only the eyebrows seemed articulate; they flowed upwards strangely, as if stuck back by an icy wind. No Englishman had come to the campsite, she said, since . . . she could not remember. Her head bent down dismissively to her two pieces of paper again. But on this first night I was obsessed by the fear that the Russian people would remain as closed to me as their landscape was, and I started asking her about Minsk.

She did not come from Minsk, she said. She was wanly self-possessed. 'Tomorrow you may have an Intourist guide to yourself.' (Intourist is the travel agency which manages foreigners; it has links with the KGB.) No, I said, I didn't want a guide.

I wandered out into the camp. The only other foreign cars belonged to East Germans and Poles. It was the summer of the last Gdansk riots before martial law stifled Poland, but no word had reached anybody here. The Russians were intermingled with us in rudimentary tents and huts. The pine-scented darkness was filled with their voices and lights. The tents lay under the trees like dim-lit pyramids. Their warmth and glow excluded me unbearably. I made my way to a little café, which was shut, then found the washrooms; the lavatory seats had all been torn out. In the clearing where I parked, three old women were rummaging among the waste bins for anything left by foreigners: bottles, polythene bags, cardboard boxes. I spread a blanket on the bumpy mattress in my car, but I wasn't sleepy. A quarter moon hovered among the pines. Its unconcluded crescent seemed to symbolize the day. I felt a mingled elation and bafflement, as if every Russian—the very land itself—were the guardian of some secret from which I was ostracized. For the first time I was poignantly aware of my isolation. Was it possible, I wondered, to spend months in a country and yet not to touch it at all? Sheepishly I returned to the girl with the eyebrows and accepted a guide for next day.

Minsk, a city of over a million inhabitants, lies at the confluence of rivers no longer navigable. As early as the eleventh century it straddled the water-borne trade between the Baltic and Black Seas, and many different peoples—Poles, Tartars, Russians, Lithuanians, Jews— shared unequally in its wealth or despoilment. Eight times it was levelled to the ground. The Grande Armée of Napoleon razed it in 1812 and after the German retreat in 1944 there was little to be seen but a forest of brick chimneys whose houses had been dropped in ashes and whose inhabitants were living in makeshift shacks or burrows under the ground. One quarter of the whole population of White Russia—men, women and children—perished in the war.

Memories like these still haunt the earth of Minsk like a ghostly permafrost. Today's wide streets and modern institutes, its theatres and stadia—all the vaunted newness, the aesthetic monotony and social inhumanity (ten-, fifteen-, twenty-storey flat blocks)—all are ex- plained, and perhaps absolved, by the horror from which they sprang. Through dozens of these war-lacerated cities—Smolensk, Rostov, Kharkov, Simferopol, Kursk—I was to walk with the same equivocal feelings. I saw their necessity and admired the abstract achievement. But I wanted to close my eyes. Everything is planned on a titan's scale. The placeless apartment blocks, the dour ministries, the bullying monuments, have streamrollered over the war's ruin in a ferro-concrete tundra which is crushingly shoddy and uniform. Nothing small or different can leak between these sky-thrusting giants. Their size and conformity echo the blind stare of the plains.

'Minsk is the capital of the White Russian Soviet Socialist Republic,' intoned my guide—a young man dressed in an impeccable suit and categorical red tie. 'During the Tenth Five-Year Plan four million square meters of housing were built. Our university has eight different faculties, and with twelve other institutes totals 35,000 students; twenty-four secondary technical schools total 110,000 students. . . .'

I listened to him with the helplessness of the mathematically illiterate, who tend to judge a culture by whether the children look happy or the cats run away. But Alexander Intourist (as I silently named him) shared a trait which I came to recognize as profoundly Russian: he was hypnotized by size and numbers. He had recently graduated from language college, had completed his six-month training as a guide and was bursting with unimparted knowledge and statistics.

'White Russia as a whole has ten thousand schools, thirty universities and higher institutes, 130 secondary specialized educational establishments, fifty-three museums, 21,000 libraries. . . .' Figures tumbled out of him like the dry rush of a grain chute. He had been trained to answer all tourists' questions, and since I didn't ask them (he gave me no time) he did so rhetorically himself, and replied with a deluge of data. 'Are there new hotels in Minsk? Yes, there are new hotels in Minsk. On our right you see the Yubileinaya Hotel, which accommodates four hundred and was founded on the fiftieth anniversary of the White Russian Soviet Socialist Republic. The Planet Hotel holds six hundred. The conference hall beside it holds 180, able to listen to four different languages in simultaneous translation. What are the principal manu-factures of Minsk? The principal. . . .'

But I had long ago stopped listening to his words, and was watching his face. It was not that of a computer, but of a prophet. It was gentle, lean and fervid, bisected by a delicate nose and a loose-lipped, rather sensual mouth. Only in repose, I noticed, his heavy-lidded eyes lost their doctrinaire glow; then he would polish his spectacles nervously on a handkerchief, and his expression would show the faintly hurt, inwrought studiousness of the Jew.

It was not a face which I saw reflected in the people of Minsk. Before the Second World War half the population was Jewish, but they were scattered and decimated. Now, hemmed in glass and concrete, a desultory river of men and women commuted between placeless places with a look of stony dedication. I could discern in them, as yet, no distinct physical type at all. Like the Russian countryside, they seemed to be defined only by absences, by the demeanour of a people unawakened, their gaze shut off. They were like a nation of sleep-walkers. Small-eyed men in dark jackets carrying briefcases; soldiers with their caps shoved back from their foreheads; youths in poor-quality Polish jeans; hefty women with sensible hairstyles; old men, their shirts buttoned and tieless at the neck—they conformed, as if by conspiracy, to the Western notion of them: collectivized corpuscles of the state body. And there still clung about them the rough quietude of soil. They seemed not to be walking urban pavements at all, but trudging invisible fields.

By now Alexander Intourist was mounting to a new crescendo of statistics. We had driven past the Palace of Sport (serves 6,000) and the stadium (seats 50,000) and had arrived in one of those lunar zones of apartment blocks which surround every Soviet city. 'These are flatblocks of the fifties, the Stalin era, very decent,' he said, 'and over there are blocks of the sixties, even more beautiful, with shops below them. But in the seventies the system of mixing flats and shops fell out of favour, and we achieved blocks like the ones you see over there'—he indicated a cliff-like hulk of pale brick structures. 'Those are the most beautiful of all.' I glanced at him in case he were joking, but his face showed no hint of irony.

I understood then something which was to strike me again and again. The Russians do not see their buildings aesthetically, but symbolically. Certainly Alexander was convinced of the loveliness in these apartment blocks. But their beauty lay not in the concrete already cracking, nor in their brick and glass palisades rushed up to fulfil a quota in a flagging Five-Year Plan. It resided in the progress they embodied. It was national pride projected on utility. I was reminded obtusely of a Russian nun whom I had known in Jerusalem. All physical things, she said, were illusory; they were merely a shadow thrown by spiritual events.

We were moving toward Lenin Prospect into the heart of a city measured out on the clean slate of German destruction. 'Help the Motherland—Build Communism', 'Glory to the Communist Party of the Soviet Union'. 'The Ideas of Lenin live and conquer'—the only advertisements repeated and repeated themselves neon-lit above the rooftops or splashed across the walls, as if to din their purpose into brains armoured by defensive reflex. We passed the municipal design centre, glowing with a portrait of Lenin in phosphorescent lights, and debouched into Lenin Square. An ageing, ten-storey blaze of concrete spread across half the plaza—the seat of the Supreme Soviet of White Russia, whose powers are those of a mammoth district council.

'White Russia is a free republic,' Alexander said. 'It has a separate seat in the United Nations. It can secede from the Soviet Union any time it wants.'

I found myself staring at him again. Did he really believe this fantasy? (Anyone invoking the constitutional right of secession can face the death sentence.) But again his face showed no hint of cynicism or ambiguity. 'And there is its Ministry of Foreign Affairs,' he added.

'Where?'

'There.' I descried a pitiful attachment to the buildings of the city soviet.

I changed the subject. What of the church, I asked? It stood at one corner of the square, ancient and unlovely in the surrounding harshness.

'That? That's been turned into a movie-makers' club.'

I was beginning to be mesmerized by Alexander. The idealism of Communism was coursing through him as if this were 1917. He believed he lived in the perfect, the only society; yet he had no grounds for comparison at all. He seemed to be the pure creation of propaganda—a frightening mixture of naïvety and intelligence. I wondered if all Russians were going to drop this ideological curtain between us. But Alexander, perhaps, had redirected into Party dogma the fervour of a repudiated Judaism, and I never met anybody quite like him again. He loved to attribute every significant invention to the Soviet Union, and to Belorussia in particular. He repeated many hoary Stalinist claims— that a Russian called Popov, not Marconi, discovered radio; that Polzunov created steam-engines twenty-one years before James Watt. Potash fertilizer had been invented in Minsk, he said; and the first ice-creams had sprung from the sap of the Soviet birch tree, frozen overnight and tentatively licked by the inquisitive peasants of Belorussia. At some point, too, he emerged with the statistic that a cubic meter of Russian pine-wood could be made into three hundred men's suits—a beautiful thought, perhaps true, which often recurred to me on the Moscow metro when watching crumpled commuters.

As we drove down Lenin Prospect he fired off fresh volleys of logistics. He knew the numbers of dormitories rented out by the

Communist youth organization Komsomol, the new housing units per year and even their rents, the amount of hectares reclaimed for forestation in White Russia, the count of graduates from the pedagogical institute, then broke into an elucidation of Marxist economic theory. I listened to him in appalled hypnosis, until I had a fantasy that mounds of decimals and percentages were piling up inside the car, lapping against our chests. Yet his talk was also full of telling pauses and shallows, moments when his thoughts darkened and he would be answering the challenge of some imaginary questioner before emerging to denounce the threat in a fresh salvo of arithmetic. I think he had almost forgotten that I was with him. His gaze was fixed on his own clenched hands. A long fusillade of figures came clamouring out of him in defence of Marx's *Theories of Surplus Value*. But to my untutored mind he seemed merely to be engaged in a phantasmal civil war. He positively thundered with the drama of it all, charged in with quadratic equations, retreated before counterattacking quotients or dug in behind differential calculus, then sneaked up to deliver the coup de grâce with a vulgar fraction.

It was an awesome performance, at once dedicated, talented and futile. Somewhere he had picked up the British commonplace 'I can't quarrel with the statistics'—a saying which perfectly expressed him. In a moment of irritation I asked him why not (since Russian statistics are notoriously misleading) but he only winced at me, not understanding.

And it was in Alexander that I first heard the language of Soviet official sentiment. Certain words and phrases left his lips haloed in near-sanctity, and occasionally his talk became a positive blaze of these revered shibboleths. In this, too, he seemed deeply Russian, and intrinsically religious. As we approached the grey obelisk at the end of the Lenin Prospect, he announced: 'Here is the Victory Monument over the Hitlerites [Nazis]. It stands 41 meters high inclusive of the blazon, 38 meters if excluding. At its foot is the Eternal-Flame-of-Memory [the shibboleths always struck me as hyphenated] commemorating the heroes of the Great-Patriotic-War [Second World War].' He pointed out a small building hidden in trees, where the first congress of the future Communist Party was held in secret. 'The Party was united then,' he said. 'That was long before the Great-October-Socialist-Revolution [the revolution of autumn 1917]. Later the Party split between Bolsheviks and Mensheviks.' Then he added: 'The Mensheviks took up arms against the Bolsheviks, so they had to be eliminated.'

I no longer looked at him, because I knew that this lie had fallen from his lips with the same proselytizing certainty as the rest. He absolutely believed it. So I waited in silence as the past was falsified, feeling a mingled anger and hopelessness. Because instinctively I liked Alexander. Perhaps in his devotion to answers and absolutes, I found in him an inverted image of myself.

I turned on the car radio brutally for music.

That afternoon we drove out forty miles to Khatyn, where one of the largest memorial complexes of the war is spread through a forest clearing. The Second World War so haunts the Russian consciousness that no understanding of the country is possible without it. Between June 1941—when Germany launched a four-million-man *Blitzkrieg* eastward on a front 1500 miles wide—and the moment four years later when the shreds of those armies were tossed back over the Vistula to Berlin, the Russians suffered as did no other nation. Their military casualties were unparalleled in twentieth century warfare. In the first few days the dead immediately mounted to hundreds of thousands, and the civilian population perished like insects, almost unrecorded. In the siege of Leningrad alone nearly a million people died, many from starvation. Of Russian prisoners-of-war more than three million were starved to death, massacred or died from exposure. Every occupied city was half gutted. In Kharkov, for instance, the Germans found a population of 700,000. Of these they deported 120,000 for slave labour (such people were rarely heard of again); 30,000 were executed; and some 70,000 more died of cold and hunger. Here in White Russia the Germans murdered over a million men, women and children, and almost the whole Jewish population was annihilated. Villages suspected of supporting partisans were simply wiped out. In the vast extermination camp of Maidanek, near Lublin, an estimated 1,500,000 Russians and Poles perished in gas chambers and incinerators. When the Soviet Union at last awoke from her nightmare of suffering and revenge, she found her economy in ruins, with 2,000 towns and 70,000 villages utterly laid waste. Her dead amounted to over twenty millions.

Such facts go far to explain Russia's traumatized preoccupation with security. As we followed the road to Khatyn, even the continuing statistics of Alexander became forgivable. Through the fog of my thoughts I heard; '. . . 45,000 . . . the Eleventh Five-Year Plan . . . seven per cent. . . .'

But now I told him gently that this religion of materialism filled me with misgiving. I said that in my world, older in wealth than his own, trust in the value of material advance was faltering.

But Alexander attributed this to capitalist decadence. 'Where you come from,' he declared, 'people don't make sacrifices.' Whereas in his country, he added, the individual was still expected to serve the mass. He pointed out a village by the road. It looked clean and tended; an old woman was carrying buckets from the communal well, and a file of geese paraded along the verge. That village, he said, would have to be moved; it must be relocated to serve a collective farm, to serve the People.

I gazed back at the sagging silhouette of the woman. Wasn't that difficult, I asked?

Yes, but it was 'socially necessary'.

We drifted into talk about Israel. Alexander gave out a Party-line denunciation of Zionism, but I sensed a hesitation in him, and some demon made me probe him farther. I saw a chance, perhaps, to pierce his dogmatism and touch a human nerve. It is a measure of my irritation that I should have placed my attack so cruelly, saying that the Israelis had seized a land which was not theirs, by the insufficient right of religion and sentiment. I was speaking like an impeccable Communist. As I went on, his face puckered, as if I were stirring some conflict long buried. He grew lukewarm, then silent. His gaze took on its intense, self-consuming look, and he stared out at the woods as if they had suddenly become important. For several minutes I chattered on unanswered. He seemed to be turning his head away from me. Then at last, very softly, he said: 'I think the Jews should have a home. . . .'

For the first time I was smiling at him.

But we were nearing Khatyn now. It spread up the slope of a cleared forest, where a village of 123 inhabitants had been annihilated by the Germans. The site was not only dedicated to these few, but to all the 2,230,000 Belorussian dead, to the 209 towns ruined and 9,200 villages destroyed. In the car-park loudspeakers were relaying soul-searing music and exhortations.

Alexander, for once, fell silent, letting the place work on me. We walked up an avenue of concrete slabs, lined with begonias. Beyond, the huts of the burnt village had been traced out in grey foundations and ash. Every thirty seconds, in one of their gaunt chimney-stacks, a bell chimed with a desolate melancholy; while higher, covering half the incline, ranged a symbolic cemetery of 136 Belorussian villages destroyed and never rebuilt, each with a pot of its own earth on its grave.

As we wandered up the quiet slope, plunged in its ash and concrete ghosts, it threw out shadows which I was to encounter again and again at Russian memorials—not only of grief, but of something darker and less reducible. It seemed to me that those who came here—guided groups of sombre men, women clutching carnations—were not mourners, but communicants, and that this was a necessary pilgrimage into their atrocious past, a ceremonial opening of wounds. They were formidably innocent. They came here, I sensed, less in sorrow for the collective, unimaginable dead, than in a pantheistic tribute to the motherland—the scarred and holy womb which must never be desecrated again. The whole shrine-village emanated a sense of inflicted wrong.

In the evening light the slope was awash with enigmatic shapes and symbols: walls, gates, chimneys. At its foot, where the Nazis burnt down a barn crammed with villagers, the crashed roof had been recreated in black marble, and the colossal statue of an old man—a haggard, Shavian peasant with jutting beard and ghastly eyes—clutched in his gnarled hands the body of a boy.

'He came back to find his child in the ashes,' said Alexander. 'He was the only survivor.'

Higher up we reached a long, leaning wall pierced with niches dedicated to the dead of concentration camps and mass annihilations. Large niches commemorated atrocities of over 100,000 dead; small niches sufficed for less. It was dusk by the time we descended. The concrete cubes and squares gathered palely round us in a muffled hymn to the crucified and risen motherland. From the wasted chimney-stacks the clang of the bells fell on the twilit air with a blinding loneliness. We passed a place where three silver birch trees grew, and a memorial flame burnt in a pavement of black marble. These symbolized that one in every four Belorussians died in the war.

Yet all the time we had been walking here—among the graves of the vanished villages where nobody in fact lay, past the skeletal houses and avenues of remembrance—something was disturbing me.

This whole place kept resounding in my mind as an oblique lie.

Some two hundred miles to the east, near Smolensk, is the site of Katyn (the names are distressingly similar) where in 1943 the bodies of more than four thousand Polish army officers were disinterred by German occupation troops. They lay in rotting layers, twelve deep, dressed in full military uniform, and all had been shot in the back of the head. These men were murdered by the Russians in the spring of 1940, after the partition of Poland by Hitler and Stalin. But the Russians have denied it ever since, and their own people have been kept in ignorance that it ever happened. Finally, they alighted on this Belorussian Khatyn, and in 1968 completed its transformation into a patriotic shrine. Now the whole hillside is an orchestrated shout of national hurt, as if its fallen millions could drown out the Polish dead.

But when I asked Alexander about this, he looked genuinely puzzled.

'A place where Polish officers were killed? No, I've never heard of it. Who killed them?'

'The Russians accuse the Germans,' I said, 'but the Germans say it was the Russians.'

He stared at me. 'We would never do a thing like that!'

In his astonished eyes I saw the Russians' deep and perennial conviction of their purity. Hungary in 1956, Czechoslovakia in 1968, Afghanistan in 1979—neither these, nor any other roll-call of their inflicted empire, can shake a profoundly emotional belief in their own rectitude. Yet by Alexander's very unawareness, his government seemed to condemn itself.

'No,' he repeated, 'not us.'

In the following months it was at moments like these that the past seemed precious in its fragility. In Russia, I was starting to think, the suppression or distortion of history had persuaded a whole people of their virtue. Here at Khatyn the manipulation was of a peculiarly disquieting kind: for the most revered national symbols were not inviolate if the voiceless and sacred dead had been used to deceive and coerce the living.

The road from Minsk to Moscow followed a broad moraine, where glaciers had dragged out their track in the last Ice Age. But the faint scoop of the land was indiscernible, and its dead-pan expression of field and forest continued all next day. Here and there the long barns of state or collective farms stretched out in the meadows, and loose-knit villages were scattered along the road. Occasionally the terrain heaved a little, as if easing out of sleep, then relaxed again. A rise or dip of a hundred feet took on the significance of a hill-range, and gave views over an immeasurable country of intersplashed pasture and forest.

Yesterday had filled me with vague foreboding. Its dogma seemed to have leaked into the whole land, even the sky. Nothing here seemed to exist for its own sake. Everything was on the march. Everything was the victim of a Five- or Ten- or Twenty-Year Plan, which could snatch a man or a tree out of its own truth and bend it to social necessity. I felt a fugitive. The same power which had carved and quartered half the country into these giant fields appeared to have trampled out time itself

[14]

into robot certainties. I felt part of some decadent and long-repudiated naturalness.

Towards noon I stopped the car on the edge of forest. Birch woods thronged the roadside in a dense audience of silver trunks and thin leaves which dimmed and glistened under a filtered sun. I wandered in amongst them, then went deeper and deeper. There was no under-bush, only the dense palisade of birches, pale, abstract. The sunlight awoke glades and paths among them, slung with muslin spider-webs, and their trunks glowed with a parchment whiteness. The ground felt soft underfoot. Mosses, thick grass and a weft of mauve and yellow wildflowers covered the dark soil. The leaves of woodland strawberries were pushing up among the ferns, and the shadows were filled with early mushrooms. I was overcome by an extraordinary sense of home-coming. I lay down on an earth moist with molehills and decomposing bark, and gazed for long minutes at the ferns and bracken, at their beautiful and stressless permanence under the white trees. When I crunched the earth in my hands, beetles and ants in orange waistcoats trickled between my fingers and away over the ground. I realized how I had craved unknowing for these things which lived uncontaminated in their own nature. And I experienced a deep sickening of everything inflicted by human beings, my own kind. For an hour I lay and stared up at the sky, and listened to the few, socially unnecessary birds, whose songs rang out with a lonely, individual clarity through the woods. They touched the air with benediction. In the clearings around me bloomed pastel swathes of flowers filled with the moaning and delving of multicoloured bees. Larkspur, borage, St John's wort, white harebells—they grew in broken rivers and pools of colour, intran-sigently fresh.

It was late afternoon before I returned to the road. At first I thought that the only human object in the landscape was my own car: a lonely memory of the free world. I felt a foolish tenderness for it. Then I noticed a rusty Moskvich saloon parked in shadow, and a man sitting on the verge, munching bread. As I passed him, he looked up and said: 'Didn't you find any?'

'Any what?'

'Mushrooms.'

In the crowds of Minsk I had not consciously discerned any national type; but now I realized that I was looking into a typically Russian face. Nestled in flaxen hair and a blond moustache, it shone with an engaging rusticity. The cheekbones thrust up high, and the blue eyes settled their gaze on mine in candid inquisition. Volodya was a trainee

[15]

doctor on his way to Brest. He must have been in his early twenties, and was dressed with a Russian indifference to appearances.

'I thought you must be looking for mushrooms.' He offered me a chunk of malt-brown bread while I sat beside him. 'You find them here by thousands in the autumn.' And a moment later, in a way which I soon took for granted with young Russians, we were talking about everything under the sun, music, history, countryside. He longed to travel. The classical world had mesmerized him since childhood. He owned a few treasured volumes of Sophocles, and dreamed of columns fallen in the sea: of Athens, Tyre, Ephesus. But when I described these places I felt wretchedly privileged, and he began to look sad. He harboured an ambition to travel round the world, he said, but had never even been to Poland. 'It's hard for us here, you see. We may get permission for the Eastern Bloc countries, but beyond that. . . .' He shook his head. Then his face was glowing. 'Jerusalem! I believe that must be a wonderful place! I'd love to see Jerusalem . . . and all those strange cities. I'm not a Christian, but I think there's something rather beautiful about the life of Christ.'

All the time he was speaking I felt a shadow lifting from me and dissipating into the trees. It carried with it a haze of nightmares. Already they seemed ridiculous. This man's gusts of pleasures and hopes were a surety that the Russians were accessible.

'And Isfahan too,' he said. 'Have you been to Isfahan and Shiraz? And the ruined caravan cities of Afghanistan! They must have an odd fascination. [I remembered Alexander Intourist: 'Our forces are helping the friendly peoples of Afghanistan against foreign interventionists, who were exploiting the backward state of the country.'] In photographs the mountains there look almost unearthly, more beautiful than anything you can believe. . . . I've never seen a mountain, or even a proper range of hills. I planned to visit the Urals this year—but no money. So I'm going to the Carpathians. They're not really mountains at all, I believe, but still. . . .' He balanced a chunk of black bread on his knee. It stuck up like a hill. 'You see, we Russians are country people at heart. I've lived all my life in cities, and that's the only place for a good job. All the same,'—he turned his back on the road and stared into the trees—'I ache to get away sometimes, particularly in spring. You know our woods have a special smell in spring? It's partly rain, I think, partly the scent of pines. [Alexander Intourist: 'Pines must be used against pollution. The air is sterilized for three metres around any one pine.'] And in autumn, especially in birchwood clearings, the mushrooms come, with wild strawberries and gooseberries. In October you'll see whole families going out with baskets into the forests. Mushroom-picking is almost a disease with us. . . .'

I saw this later. To the Russians the wild mushroom has a peculiar mystique, and these expeditions lie somewhere between sport and ritual. They mingle the country-love of an English blackberry hunt with the delicate discrimination of the blossom-viewing Japanese. If Russia's national tree is the silver birch, then her national plant is this magic fungus, burgeoning in the forest shadows. It has sprouted up in Russian literature, even in Russian song. In one of the most poignant passages of *Anna Karenina*, I remembered, the learned forty-year-old Koznyshev goes mushroom-picking with the delicate orphan Varenka, meaning to propose to her, and both feeling their love; but instead they walk in fear and shyness together, talking of mushrooms instead of one another, and the moment passes for ever.

'Mushroom-hunting . . . I wish I could express it to you.' Volodya's face became filled with this obscure national excitement. 'It's like this. You get into the forests and you know instinctively if the conditions are right for them. You can sense it. It gives you a strange thrill. Perhaps the grass is growing at the right thickness, or there's the right amount of sun. You can even smell them. You just know that here there'll be mushrooms'—he spoke the word 'mushrooms' in a priestly hush—'so you go forward in the shadows, or in a light clearing perhaps, and there they are, under the birches!' He reached out in tender abstraction and plucked a ghostly handful from the air. 'Have you ever sniffed mushrooms? The poisonous ones smell bitter, but the good ones—you'll remember that fragrance for ever!'

He went on to talk about the different kinds and qualities of mushroom, and how they grew and where to find them—delicate white mushrooms with umbrellaed hats, which bred in the pine forests; red, strong-tasting birch-mushrooms with whitish stems and feverish black specks; the yellow 'little foxes', which grew in huddles all together; and the sticky, dark-tipped mushroom called 'butter-covered', delicate and sweet. Then there was the *apyata* which multiplied on shrubs—'you can pick a whole bough of them!'—and at last, in late autumn, came a beautiful green-capped mushroom which it was sacrilege to fry. All these mushrooms, he said, might be boiled in salt and pepper, laced with garlic and onions, and the red ones fried in butter and cut into bits until they appeared to have shrunk into nothing, then gobbled down with vodka all winter.

We sat on the verge for a little longer, talking of disconnected things. He was going to Brest, and I to Smolensk, and it was futile to pretend that we would ever meet again. This evanescence haunted all my friendships here. Their intimacy was a momentary triumph over the prejudice and fear which had warped us all our lives; but it could never be repeated.

Volodya clasped my hand in parting, and suddenly said: 'Isn't it all ridiculous—I mean propaganda, war. Really I don't understand.' He stared at where we'd been sitting—an orphaned circle of crushed grass. 'If only I were head of the Politburo, and you were President of America, we'd sign eternal peace at once'—he smiled sadly—'and go mushroom-picking together!'

I never again equated the Russian system with the Russian people.

Between Minsk and Moscow the roadside villages looked neat and artificial as toys. Built of planks or (occasionally) logs, with intricately carved window-frames, their cottages were fenced about with gardens of roses and hollyhocks. These villages seemed deserted and centre-less—rarely a church, never a café: only a desolate shop labelled 'shop'.

Some fifty miles beyond Minsk I crossed the Beresina river, north-ernmost tributary of the Dnieper. It is haunted forever by Napoleon's *Grande Armée*, whose retreat from Moscow in the autumn and winter of 1812 almost ended in annihilation here. For three days the chaos at the bridgeheads was utter. Soldiers, horses, heavy wagons and a confused mass of camp followers clogged the makeshift causeways or floundered drowning among the ice-packs of the river, lashed by Russian artillery. 'When they tried to climb up the sides of the trestles,' wrote the quartermaster-general de Ségur, 'most of them were pushed back into the river. Women were seen among the floating ice sheets with children in their arms, holding them higher and higher as they sank. When their bodies were under water their stiffened arms still held the little ones up. At the height of this ghastly scene the artillery bridge parted in the middle. . . .'*

Beyond the Beresina the tramp of Napoleon's ghosts grows thicker still. Of the six hundred thousand men who crossed the Niemen into Russia in the spring of 1812, barely one in thirty returned. Some had died in battle; but most were eaten up by the ravaging cold, the wind, the snow and the mournful, harrowing immensity of Russia itself. Their hair and beards were turned to icicles. Their inflamed eyes oozed blood instead of tears. Frozen and mad with hunger, they staggered off the army's course into the glacial pine forests and the

---

* *Napoleon's Russian Campaign.* Count Philippe-Paul de Ségur. Trs. J. D. Townsend.

[18]

waiting Cossacks. At night their camp fires were no more than icy splutters of light; the morning found circles of corpses around little heaps of ashes. 'We drifted along in this empire of death like accursed phantoms,' wrote de Ségur. 'Most of the men fell without a word of complaint, silent either from weakness or resignation.'

The roadsides, as I went, still seemed possessed by the memory of these dead, and by the shreds of Hitler's panzer divisions hurled back in 1944. The pitting of human armies against such a land appears an insanity. For its appalling, inert strength has eaten into the people too. The whole country is like a requiem. In its consuming maternity, its individual children drown; and all other nations become petty or irrelevant—they are far away. From her own people Russia elicits a helpless worship of belonging. She contains them with the elemental despotism of an earth mother, and they feel for her the supplicant's tormented tenderness.

The sheer size of the country has much to do with this, and with its shrouding strangeness. Wherever you touch it, you are conscious of a giant, alienating hinterland. You are always, somehow, on the periphery. Even in early historical times, people felt that the Black Sea shores passed northward into an echoing silence. The ancient Greeks confused the coastal inhabitants with a race living in perpetual mist at the frontiers of the world. Their knowledge petered out beyond the domain of the terrible Scythians, fading into rumours of a desert sub-continent inhabited by cannibals and gold-guarding griffins. But by the ninth century A.D. the eastern Slavs, who were to form the Russian people, were established and free between the Urals and the Dnieper; and it was through their heartland that I was now travelling.

This, above all, is a land of rivers. They wind among sodden fields and half-drowned trees—great motherly slugs of water crawling down to the Baltic, or tributaries of the Dnieper meandering hundreds of miles south. The Volga, the Don and the Dnieper all rise here within a few hundred miles of one another, and it was along their forest waterways that the early Slavic world grew up. They linked the Baltic with Constantinople; and the Vikings, riding their slow floods, carried furs and metals southward and dominated the trade routes all the way to the Black Sea. Kiev, Moscow, Novgorod, Smolensk all flowered in their wake. For a full century before the Norsemen were absorbed into the Slavic population, they guided the gleam of Byzantine traffic northward—jewels, silks, spices, Christianity itself.

Smolensk, which I reached that night, was just such a trading-town, but only the barrows of its tribal kings have survived from early years.

Morning showed a fortress-city mounded on a hill dark with trees. Beneath it the young Dnieper was coiled in a brooding, sky-filled flood. A florid cathedral shone in the mist, and the empty streets and squares were bathed in a feeling of permanent Sunday.

I sat under the city walls, eating a picnic lunch. Pram-pushing women with galleass bodies trudged past, and a student from the town's language college, noticing my foreign shoes, came up to practise his English on me. To discover a 'real Englishman'—and not an English-speaking Scandinavian or German—struck him as a great triumph. The city was dead, he said, there was nothing to do here except die. All the same, he showed me round.

He spoke in a dry counterpoint to the possessed babble of Alexander Intourist. 'This is the Smolensk Hotel . . . it's pretty awful . . . here's the stadium . . . I haven't a clue how many it holds. . . .' Ivan was twenty-three. He came from Grodno near the Polish border. His father was dead, his mother a teacher of psychology. His barbered hair and tended good looks were strangely un-Russian. A slight moustache undercut his fragile nose, and his lips were permanently cusped together, as if tasting something bitter. He carried a fashionable shoulder-bag and his mannerisms were nervously homosexual; in a Western country town he might have been ridiculed, but in Smolensk, I suspected, he was simply an object of puzzlement.

We wandered towards the Park of Culture where a monument commemorated the defenders of Smolensk against Napoleon. It was ringed by the graves of early Bolshevik leaders, but Ivan dismissed them. 'They're not important. I don't know who they are.' At the park entrance the city's board of honour announced the regional heads of factories and institutes who had won prizes or exceeded their output quotas. Their photographs gazed down at us with a hollow and illustrious fixity, as if responsibility had steeped them all in the same deadening brine.

Ivan sighed. 'Who wants to know these figures and percentages? It's all such rot. I can't bear to hear about them.' He glanced around. We were alone under the billboards. Their mute stare accused us. 'I tell you,' he added in his slight drawl, 'the young are the government's main problem here. There's nothing for us to do, nowhere to go. Of course the older people had to fight the war. They're more single-minded than us, grimmer.' He glanced up at the portraits, which went on exuding public worthiness. 'Naturally they don't like our music and clothes. But my generation is different, you see, less categorical. We find it easier to assimilate the new.'

We turned down anonymous streets. He emitted a continuous, pale frustration. 'There's something I dread, I must tell you. Every teacher and doctor in our country is sent away to some village in the wilds on a three-year term of work. That's all very idealistic, I know, and the old applaud it. But none of us young can bear the idea. We'd do anything to avoid it.' His face convulsed in an expression of bitter frailty. 'For three years you get boarded out with a family in a little room, and have to teach children who hardly know where Moscow is, let alone London. The Party's said that this way our villages will become like cities, but how will that happen? There are things a government can't do. . . .'

On the rooftops around us the repeated Party slogans—'Build Communism', 'Glory to Work'—seemed suddenly less like a shout of triumph than what I now understood them to be: a coercing plea for help.

We turned back along the hoary semi-circle of sixteenth century city walls. Their brick ramparts were slung between conical and polygonal towers, and rose to machicolated tufts of masonry like rotted teeth. I asked Ivan why he was attending language college here, and not in his native Grodno; but his face clouded.

'It wasn't allowed,' he said. 'There was some . . . scandal.' He stared up embarrassed at the battlements. Here, at Smolensk, four hundred miles off, the rumour of his offence had died away, or never arrived. 'I dream of living in Leningrad one day,' he said. 'The people there are cultured and gentle, and you can feel history pouring down on you like rain.' He opened his palms to receive an invisible downpour. 'Of course the old system which produced such things was evil, but the things themselves are beautiful, so beautiful. God!' He rubbed his eyes as if he wanted to weep. It was strange to hear the word God in the mouth of a Communist, but I often did. 'And half the palaces are reflected in the canals. You get them twice over! Moscow's all right, of course, but new buildings like that happen everywhere—they're all over the West too, I suppose. But oh, the old!'

Ivan wanted to find friends. We dived into a seedy apartment block, searching for a mathematics teacher whose flat number he had forgotten. We climbed seven storeys past padded or brown-painted doors with old coats and rags in lieu of footmats. Their bells didn't work or emitted a cacophony of buzzes, clicks and dings. Then the doors creaked open to cautious slits. Grandmotherly faces emerged under nests of grey or hennaed hair, and said *Net*; or young mothers with lumpish children turned us away. Behind each one glimmered a den of bleak rooms, relieved only by plants, a song-bird or the rare brightness of a carpet.

At last a tousle-haired man opened the door of a communal flat and burst into greetings. His tiny room was coated in peeling green wallpaper (a teacher's earnings are miserably low) and adorned with little but soiled paperbacks, a guitar and mounds of cigarette ash which lay heaped at intervals all over the floor, like the track of some ash-burrowing mole. But his flat was a Mecca for friends. Within minutes we were joined by a lorry-driver, whose pockets bulged with vodka bottles. This man dominated the evening. At the age of twenty-five he already looked a drunkard. Above his collapsed stomach and sagging shoulders his face showed a dissolute fleshiness. Little oily locks of hair splashed about bleary features. One after another he fixed us with a harmless, unfocused gaze—he was already drunk—then flicked a forefinger against his throat and clicked his tongue in the Slavic invitation to liquor. Finally he lifted two bottles high above his head, brought them to rest in tender ceremonial on an empty chair, then fell on our necks and kissed us in wobbling succession. Small glasses and tooth-mugs were produced from nowhere. The tousle-haired man seized his guitar. And in no time we were launched on a slow, Russian river of vodka-charged melancholy and half-forgotten songs.

A motherly-looking girl arrived, and the kissing started all over again. Then came a dour, square-headed colossus with drooping blond moustaches and Tartar cheekbones, who said nothing all evening, but lay against the wall looking like Ghengiz Khan, and finally slept. So we sat until far into the night, while the guitar-player remembered Western songs which he'd culled from records twenty years old, and the vodka gurgled neat down our relaxed and gabbling throats.

> *What we need is sympathy*
> *'Cos there's not enough love to go round*

The vodka bottles reproduced themselves as if by sleight of hand. Toasts flurried back and forth, or foundered into garbled oblivion. The drink's coarseness creaked and thundered round my head like a four-in-hand. 'Eat chocolate, eat chocolate,' whispered Ivan—it was all the food we had. I already felt unsure what would happen when I tried to get to my feet, or if I had any feet at all.

> *Half the world hates the other half. . . .*

After three hours we were all slumped about the furniture in postures of clownish indolence, and the lorry-driver was mumbling obscenities to himself, clasping the guitar-player round the neck and swivelling his gaze across the ample figure of the girl, who was seated a little prudishly (she wouldn't drink) on a cushion opposite. 'Drink too much, can't fuck a thing,' he apologized. But his voice was lost and abstract, as if he were addressing a chair or a star. The others grew angry with him; he wasn't behaving as he should with a foreign guest. Even through their alcoholic benignity, they felt ashamed.

'He's drunk,' said Ivan.

The guitar-player grew more sentimental with the hours. He sang in nasal English, the *lingua franca* of pop. Now and again his head nudged onto the girl's shoulder, and he kissed her soft neck. She laughed quietly to herself. Ghengiz Khan started to snore. The lorry-driver burbled new toasts to Ivan, who was swaying dreamily on his chair. The whole party was stagnating into nostalgia, but nobody could stop it. I gazed hazily round the room. It seemed to hold nothing but Western leftovers: guitar, jeans, song-books.

Ivan opened his eyes and questioned me haltingly about his language course. What did I think of Galsworthy? Of Walt Whitman? Had I read *The Importance of Being Earnest?* He knew nothing about Oscar Wilde. 'He was homosexual? I never knew that, I never knew. . . .' He derived a maudlin comfort from this, and kept murmuring and smiling to himself 'I didn't know.' But a moment later he focused me with a look of sheer loss. The vodka stumbled his words together. 'Is it true that you in the West allow it . . . between men?' He stared incoherently at the floor, and gave a sick laugh. 'But not here. Oh no . . . not here.'

The guitar-player had run out of songs by now, and was singing his own in faulty English.

> *A man about himself is still unsure*
> *A man cannot discern himself at glance*
> *He breaks up like an oak through forest floor*
> *And dreams and dreams. . . .*

He was going to Kiev soon; the girl would stay in Smolensk; the lorry-driver was a nomad of the road; Ivan must return to Grodno. The party already had a feeling of farewell.

'Grodno!' moaned the drunk, teasing Ivan. 'There's nothing there. Just old cigarette factories and barracks.' It sounded like a stage set for *Carmen.* 'Grodno's a piss-hole, I can tell you. But Smolensk is the centre of the universe.'

'He's from Smolensk,' said Ivan.

Theirs was a world of fleeting and unguarded friendships, scattered as they were by the vastness of the country and their differences of purpose. To me they seemed half dissociated from their culture, as if isolated on a bluff. The Western pop song had penetrated where Western ideology struck no deep root, and was expressing for them the private and estranged universe of the young, a universe which belonged not to their parents but was cherished as their own—waking beside an empty pillow, not being sure, going away, being unloved, un-everything.

By now the vodka bottles lay in an empty collage over the floor; the last dregs had splashed out of their tooth-mugs into our flaccidly open mouths, and we were sprawled among the chairs like bacchantes, fingering the glasses and grinning philosophically at the cracked ceiling. A gentle and absolving inertia was dropping onto us out of the night sky. Dimly, with a drink-sodden wonder, I recalled that only yesterday I had been afraid the Russians were inaccessible.

2. Moscow

THE ROAD APPROACHING Moscow must be the most heavily policed on earth. Beneath the concrete and glass checkpoints, which multiply as the city approaches, burly officers fret and strut, or swagger into the road's centre drumming their truncheons against their jackboots. The traffic slows to a servile crawl as it approaches them. They seem to embody a deep national insecurity. Within thirty miles of the capital the kerbs are lined with stopped motorists patiently explaining themselves. The roadside gendarmes, the police car drivers, the officers telephoning in the checkpoints, all seem to be participants in some fervid patriotic dance against an invisible evil. They had rarely seen a British car before, and often I glimpsed whole groups of them clustered in the glass checkpoints, staring at me like fish from an aquarium. I was stopped continually, my papers examined with a scrupulous and faintly bemused courtesy, then sent on my way. And as if the police were too few for this frenetic and sterile-looking labour, they were supplemented by posses of civilian volunteers in red armbands.

The outskirts came suddenly. Great white apartment blocks burst up from the skyline. Fifteen, twenty, twenty-five storeys high, they glimmered over the whole horizon, and were followed by others in pale pink brick, and by still others which lurched towards the road in monolithic piles hundreds of yards long. Stalinist neo-classical, the brick giants of the sixties, modern glass and ferro-concrete hulks—they covered the land with their desolate similitude. The anonymity of Minsk was intensified a hundredfold. The blocks loomed doubly high; the trees beneath them looked small and crippled as bonsai. Over the Moscow river, a distant tributary of the Volga, and into the city's heart, the planetary habitat thickened, as if its people had been packaged or broilerized for state purposes. Its chilling immensity became a hallmark, almost a distinction, and reached an awesome zenith in the ministerial skyscrapers which Stalin built in the thirties. Their gravity-defying height lent them a baleful ubiquity. Architectural Big Brothers, they shot up with a terrible vertiginous power. Forty, fifty, sixty storeys high (it became pointless to count), they inhabited the heavens with the mysterious naturalness of mountains: the offspring of early Manhattan skyscrapers and Muscovite fortress towers. Their summits seemed to recede into a supernal mist, tapering out at last in star-crowned spires, filled with an unimaginable Byzantium of civil servants. Bureaucratic citadels, archaic, defensive, they epitomized the public face of Russia.

Only a weft of trees sometimes mediated between the buildings and the passers-by below, where regimented parks lent a magisterial monotony to the sweep of prospect and boulevard. Between people and buildings a great vacuum seemed to lie—a space which in the West is thronged by restaurants, shops, cafés, pavement enterprises, all the private enthusiasms, love or grossness which we call freedom. But here there was nothing—only the sense of a deep division between the seen and the invisible, so that I became obsessed by the thought of the lives which the blank buildings hid. The shops were all gaunt and poor. I saw coiling queues for fresh fruit or a little meat. The identity of stores was reduced to 'Food', 'Culinary', 'Footwear', instead of the names of proprietors. The People, as Alexander had said, were the collective owners. Everybody owned everything.

The very streets seemed uncrossably wide. Starting across their tarmac, you feel you may be run over by a car still below the horizon. You have no rights. Pedestrian crossings merely indicate where you may pass; they give you no precedence over cars, which behave as if you did not exist. These are the least democratic roads on earth. The black Chaika and Volga saloons of government officials glide about them with impunity. A special lane down the centre is reserved for them, and their flouting of traffic rules is ignored by the thronging police, whose frenzy of officiousness reaches crescendo in the city centre. An uncanny tension reigns, which is more than the workaday strain of urban living. Just as the roads at Moscow's heart flow out in concentric ripples from the Kremlin, so this tension too seems to radiate from those secret and formidable walls, lapping outward to the suburbs and to the farthest confines of the Soviet Union itself, in ever-weakening but pervasive rings.

Driving in hypnotized circles around the city's inner boulevards, I was already judging Russia with romantic disillusion. The treatment of pedestrians or the privileges of officials would have seemed insignificant in another country. But Russia is haunted by absolutes. This country, after all, had dared to set itself up as the exemplar of the future, the lost paradise remaking; and I judged it automatically by the light of its own ideals. So every failure here was peculiarly wounding; it denied anew the possibility of imposing selflessness on men by any system. And my sensitivity to its dishonesties, I suspect, was in part a disappointment with all humankind, a self-accusing. This, after all, was the great experiment gone wrong, the Eden which became Babel.

Yet for all this I was conscious that these people still inhabited a different perspective from those in the West. However barbarously they may fall short, however corrupt their institutions and hypocritical their rulers, they belonged to an ancient spiritual extremism. They were still the rebellious children of their repudiated God, entertaining a vision, even in cynicism, of the consummate community.

I drove towards Red Square through streets clamouring with state advertisements: 'The Communist Party is the Glory of the Motherland', 'The Plans of the Party are the Plans of the Homeland', 'The Soviet Union is the Source of Peace', 'The Ideas of Lenin Live and Conquer'. Neon-lit, they straddled the skyline of offices and flat-blocks, and even—with a resounding clang of hypocrisy—the roofs of luxury tourist hotels. The blaze of Western commercial advertising—all its sense of choice and possibility—were echoingly absent. These Soviet slogans fascinated me. They were interesting less for their effect on the people, who told me universally that they never noticed them, than as a betrayal of their rulers' anxieties. Constantly they linked Communism with patriotism. It was as if they were trying to stoke the pallid fires of the Party, for which I had already sensed a deep-seated indifference, with the huge and potent furnace of Russian national feeling. Fancifully I experimented with inverting these slogans, as if this might reveal uncomfortable truths: 'The Party and the Motherland are disunited', 'The Soviet Union is the Source of War', 'The Ideas of Lenin are Moribund and Fading'.

Through the towering wilderness of central Moscow the people were pushing with the same patient obliviousness as those of Minsk. Even in summer they formed a relentless, rather private crowd. Not for them the chatter and nervous smiling of the Westerner. Their faces were slow and unlit. Clerks, soldiers, housewives—they seemed defined merely by their function. And even here they were only half urbanized, touched still by the heavy candour of the peasant, and perhaps by his cunning and opacity too. Yet I was aware of trickles and splashes of young colour, of talk and laughter unknown ten years ago. And archetypal faces emerged. I noticed the blond hair and moustaches of Slav folk-legend, the skin pulled sparely over a gaunt frame of cheekbones, the eyes a wintry blue or grey. Another face—it might

[27]

have been modelled on that of Kruschev—was collapsed in a counter-point of fleshy curves and circles, rounded cheeks and double chins, its lips thrust forward as if to graze the uprush of the big, pitted nose. Yet another face (I came to associate it with the KGB) showed a mysterious blend of the masculine and the infantile; in its heavy, round head the nose was a mere incident, the mouth a sterile bud, and the small eyes were submerged in a tundra of incoherent flesh, so that they seemed to be peering out through a crevice.

But most of the people belonged to no distinct type at all. It was the strangely unawakened expression which marked them as Russian. This look of wide, inchoate nature is, I suspect, ancestral. The same faces gaze out from the walls of Moscow's Tretyakov Art Gallery in some of the homeliest, fattest and coarsest-looking aristocracy of their time, whom even court painters could not flatter into beauty. The old, in particular, seemed the victims of their history as they trudged the Moscow streets. The bodies of a whole generation of war widows and war spinsters looked shaped only for enduring. But here and there the slimmer figures of young men and women presaged another era (the post-war generation, like that of Japan, looks down by several inches on its parents) and the subject peoples of the Soviet empire passed by in a sudden scent of mountain or desert—broad-faced Uzbeks in embroidered caps; the sombre, delicate features of Armenia; the black sparkle of a Georgian.

I merged with a tide of shoppers in the state emporium GUM, which faces the Kremlin across Red Square. This is a mazey nineteenth century caravanserai of shops, nearly a thousand in all. Ranged in three tiers and linked by balustraded bridges and promenades, they shelter under a glass and iron roof which sheds a jungle dimness on everything below. Perched in this Crystal Palace fantasy, and gazing down, I momentarily imagined myself looking on the polished ovals of Victorian top hats and spoon bonnets; but instead I saw the diligent Muscovites shopping—men in T-shirts and brown jackets, the flowered dresses of stocky proletarian women, war veterans with their medals sewn on their coats in faded ribbons. Among these crowds the rare Western tourist passed like a comet, so that I suddenly noticed the indefinable drabness, the sameness, of everybody else.

Shopping is the housewife's weariest chore. She is condemned to tramp a labyrinth in search of even simple artefacts. On an average day (it's been computed) she spends two hours in queues. In a single shop she may queue three times: once to select what she wants, once again to pay a cashier, and a third time to collect her purchase. It is like an

[28]

Alice-in-Wonderland scheme for full employment. The only readily available goods are those which nobody wants—all the spiritless, home-manufactured fittings which are dismissed as *brak*, junk. Muscovite women, and men too, prowl the shops on the lookout for anything of quality, their string bags or briefcases ready to receive the sudden arrival of Yugoslav boots or Polish bras. In a state-planned commercial economy, insensitive to consumer demand, availability is more important to the shopper than cost. So shopping becomes a nightmare game of musical chairs in which most of the players are left out. Anything un-Soviet is as precious and unexpected as a unicorn. The moment it appears, queues coalesce magically out of nothing, snaking down the streets on a wisp of hearsay. The sameness of life gives to the new an outlandish value—beautiful, different, snob.

The queues in GUM had the look of prehistoric insects. They moved with only the dimmest shufflings and heavings of their multiple feet; and like most insects they had no centralized nervous system so that the queue's tail did not always know what its head was gorging on. 'What am I here for?' said the last vertebra of a sixty-person centipede. 'I don't know. But it must be something . . . look at the queue!' Caught head-on in the torrent of such shoppers, I realized that theirs was not a job but a full-scale campaign, filled with precious triumphs and costly defeats. It was materialism at its most necessary, and its most heart-breaking.

I debouched thankfully into Red Square. Flanked on one side by St Basil's cathedral, on the other by the liver-red spires of the History Museum, it is, in some. ways, surprising—not regular at all, but sloping down erratically towards the Moscow river in a shining, grey-cobbled flood. Close to its centre, the mausoleum where Lenin lies embalmed attracted the most dedicated queue of all, winding many thousands long into obscurity; and opposite me, dominating the whole square in ancient foreboding, reared the walls of the Kremlin—a blank Russian face stubbled with irregular towers. In these brick battlements of a stoneless land, only the clock-crowned and star-topped Redeemer's Gate gave a narrow glimpse inside, flanked by policemen and by traffic lights perpetually red.

The Kremlin is the troubled heart of Russia. From across the brown flood of the Moscow river, its buildings emerge like a paradigm of her past. In front, the walls loom formidable and secret, staked out with prison-like towers and gateways. Although built by Italian architects in the fourteenth century, their size and archaism seem profoundly Russian, while within them, cushioned on a sombre cloud of trees, rise the multiple buildings of this schizophrenic land—the nineteenth century hulk of the Great Kremlin Palace with its endless stretch of windows, the classical Praesidium, the modern Palace of Congresses. But from the very midst of these, flowering on slender white necks of swan beauty, a golden cluster of Byzantine domes lifts its crosses to the sky. Nothing could be more moving and articulate as an architectural symbol of the country. The rationalism and balance of the West stand cheek-by-jowl with Byzantium; golden crosses shine among red flags and stars; and around them all, in ramparts and machicolated bastions, curls the disruptive genius of Russia's own dim forest world.

Even as I walked inside the Kremlin walls (open since 1958), I imagined some contagion crawling between Byzantine cathedrals and modern government palaces. It was as if the paranoid ghosts of Stalin and Ivan the Terrible were shaking hands across the centuries. The Praesidium of the Supreme Soviet, the Council of Ministers, the Palace of Congresses—impenetrable spans of marble or glass threaded by black ministerial cars—all seemed subtly infected by the Cathedral Square nearby, abandoned now except for tourists, but exuding an old dogma and opportunism.

Cathedral Square was once the soul of Moscow. And Moscow, as early as the fourteenth century, had the semblance of a capital. Although little more than a stockaded town at the junction of the Moscow river and the Neglinnaya (a tributary long since gone underground) it was the Vatican of Russia, seat of her metropolitan archbishops and premier princedom of the land. For some three hundred years its Grand Dukes bent before the Mongol whirlwind from the east and at the end of the fifteenth century, when the threat receded, the Muscovite tsar Ivan the Great was left lord of a united Russia and stood alone as spiritual and linear descendant of a now vanished Byzantium. Battlements of white limestone had long ago replaced the oak palisades of the Kremlin, and these in turn had crumbled away beneath today's circlet of brick. Pale stone cathedrals erupted in its centre, and city walls whorled outwards from its core. It was from this mediaeval Moscow—a glimmer of oriental domes sunk in a landlocked plain—that Peter the Great transferred the capital northward in 1712. And it was away again from West-orientated Leningrad, with its clear northern light, that the post-Revolutionary leaders reverted to the mother-city, as if transferring the seat of national consciousness from the head to the womb. Where Leningrad is surrounded by baroque palaces, Moscow is ringed with moated monasteries. The backdrop of Leningrad is the Baltic Sea, a grey eye on

Europe; that of Moscow is the umbilical hinterland of Asia, a world gazing on itself.

As you walk over the crinkled pink flagstones of Cathedral Square, the air grows foggy with imagined incense, and with the shades of those terrible elder tsars. Ringed by their draughty forests at the antipodes of Christendom, their reigns black with superstition and chaos, these sixteenth and early seventeenth century tyrants come down to us in a light eerily magnified and intense. Ivan the Terrible, Fyodor I, Boris Godunov, the False Dmitry—they process across the inner eye in a queue of ruthless autocrats or vacuous simpletons: religious, half-savage, melancholy-mad. Around their great square the white-stoned cathedrals lift in a ghostly choir. A four-tiered belfry, raised by successive tsars to 250 feet, towers in the sky with whole carillons of multi-toned bells. In the Cathedral of the Assumption, where the patriarchs and metropolitans lie buried, the tsars were crowned with a filigreed and sable-trimmed diadem which suggested Tartar khans rather than Christian kings.

But they inhabited these cathedrals with familiar ease. The two-hour morning liturgy broke over them like the waves of some benedictory ocean, while they deliberated with their councillors in the nave. This was their natural and exotic habitat. In its softly-domed interiors, among a liana jungle of hanging lamps and blazing copses of candles, their most secular and atrocious decisions took on the sanctity of gospel. All around them the God-focused eyes of the saints stared from frescoed walls or brooded in icons stubbled with uncut jewels, while metropolitans and bishops processed back and forth in a shimmer of Persian silks, and the incense rolled from the censers like celestial cannon-shot. Drenched in this soothing mist, the business of state continued in a dream or nightmare. Proscriptions, higher taxes, public works—all were sanctified in the stupefying fragrance. Momentarily, perhaps, as the tsar clasped in his jewelled hands the flower-shaped chalice of the Host, a decision to attack Poland or eliminate a too-successful boyar hung unconcluded in the bluish air. Then the cup's enormous calyx spilt into his mouth the absolving blood of Christ.

These men reigned, as their first Communist successors did, convinced of their divinely ordained mission, and of the degeneracy of other peoples. When they died they were entombed in the Cathedral of Saint Michael the Archangel, lying cheek-by-jowl in white sarcophagi. Above them on wall and pillar, their frescoed portraits still gaze with hieratic sadness out of an age both uneasily present and irretrievably remote. Their obsession with size is perfectly familiar. Beside the great belfry the hugest bell in the world lies useless and unhoisted, weighing over two hundred tons and splintered by too-quick cooling in an accidental fire. Nearby an elephantine cannon—the largest calibre barrel on earth—gapes northward in hollow megalomania. It was never fired.

Familiar, too, is the jingoistic disdain yet uneasy admiration accorded to foreign nations. Half Cathedral Square is the work of Italian architects, and the czars themselves were crowned on the ivory-pannelled throne of Western craftsmen. Yet at state receptions the tsar sat within reach of two jugs of water and a towel, with which he cleansed his hands after the touch of European ambassadors. Far into the seventeenth century his soldiers, mounted on unshod geldings, fought in dripping chain mail and helmets spired like Burmese pagodas, wielding poleaxes and six-pronged battle-maces or firing Tartar bows and arrows.

In the vaulted dimness of their chambers, imperial banquets proceeded with bucolic ceremonial. More than seven hundred nobles and ambassadors might feast off gold plate at one session, attended by a legion of servants who changed their apparel three times in the course of a meal. The whole court, with the baptised scions of the Tartar kings, sat at monastic benches in silk caftans or brocade and velvet coats lined with sable and polar fox. Avuncular beards gushed over cloth-of-gold stomachs. A gurgle of malmsey and Greek wine sounded in torchlit recesses. Then the boyars' greedy fingers fumbled for the knives and spoons which dangled unhygienically at their girdles, and the tsar himself would ritually poke the roast swan's meat and despatch succulent joints to those whom he favoured. Drunken oblivion was the end and purpose of all feasting. 'For making people tipsy is here an honour and sign of esteem,' wrote the ambassador of the Holy Roman Empire ruefully, 'The man who is not put under the table holds himself ill respected.'

Again and again, into the borrowed Byzantine forms of a building or a ceremony, something mysterious and illogical intrudes. St Basil's Cathedral in Red Square was built by Ivan the Terrible to commemorate his capture of the Tartar stronghold of Kazan in 1552, and belongs to a world of peasant woodcarving. At first I wondered if it were not merely a jumble of lunatic baubles. But it is, in fact, immensely complex, with a turbulent harmony of its own. Legend has it that Ivan the Terrible put out the eyes of the architects who conceived it, so that they should never repeat such a building. It emanates a mad brilliance.

The tent-like spire of its central shrine bursts upward clean through the canons of Western architecture, and around it the domes of eight smaller chapels are tossed into the air on a farrago of drums. It is less like a composite cathedral than a camp of Tartar yurts around the pavilion of its khan. The taller domes rise from angular turrets on a rumpus of buttresses, the lesser go twirling up in overlapping tiers of blind windows, then taper to stalks from which the cupolas explode into bulbous turbans topped by golden crosses. They twist and bounce and multiply in bursts of architectural merriment. Some are striated in barley-sugar clusters, others ribbed like cantaloup melons or coils of whipped cream, still others armoured in pineapple spikes, orange and green, red and white. It is the work of inspired peasants—a petrified juggling feat in which all the balls are in the air at once. Classical form is submerged by a rush of colour and detail. A hundred fanciful shapes and pigments jostle and yell. Yet all this sky-searching riot implies no unease, no Gothic hankering. Rather the cathedral is like some organic growth, a fantastical steppeland plant which is not reaching to the heavens at all, but is upside down—bulbs and roots waving in sky-blue soil.

Olga had lost her husband five years before, and lived with a bored daughter in one of those faceless apartment blocks which ring the northern suburbs of Moscow. A chance introduction from England led me to her doorbell, which I pressed with misgiving. She had dressed up to meet me: a squat, middle-aged widow. In my memory her face has now resolved into a few exaggerated landmarks—lipstick, spectacles, black cropped hair. Even at the time, her features struck me with the empty emphasis of a clown.

She had a problem knowing what to do with me. We sat in uncomfortable chairs at either end of a sideboard, and sipped thimble-fuls of brandy with genteel murmurings about life. By Soviet standards she had clearly once been rich. Her husband's collection of icons glowed on one wall in isolated distinction. The apartment she inha-bited belonged to a co-operative block—an unusual system. She would have paid for the ownership of her flat in three years' time, she said. But since her husband's death, life had been hard; now she worked in the local library—for money, and for something to do.

She was intensely nervous with me, as if I were posing her unspoken questions and embarrassments. Her painted toes wriggled in their sandals. Occasionally she would pick chocolate truffles from a box between us, replace them; or toy with some matches, but did not smoke. She was typical, I later felt, of a small minority of Muscovites who tried to live with Western refinement but had neither the means nor the aptitude. The whole apartment spelt a comfortless pretension. A strip of carpet dribbled down the room's centre between chunks of modern furniture, while a chandelier and some ormolued lamps lit the surrounding bareness with baleful affectation.

Suddenly Olga's nerves had spilt into her speech and she was asking: 'Do you think you were followed here?'

'I've no idea.' I felt mildly surprised. 'I don't think so.'

The blobs and splashes of her face were like a Morse Code; but indecipherable. 'I think you were,' she said. 'They follow every foreigner who's on his own. This isn't London.'

She went on to speak about England, where she had once been permitted to travel. She had loved London, she said, the department stores were a paradise. Then she stopped abruptly. 'But it's difficult to talk about.' Constantly her sentences would trail away into nothing, or suddenly end. Later I noticed this phenomenon in many of those who had been brought up during the Stalin terror. They were marked by unconscious fear. They would suddenly break off an innocuous conversation, leaving it to float into unspoken speculation; or they would interrupt themselves to say 'Of course this is only between ourselves' or 'But I could be mistaken.' I met a fifty-year-old journalist whose whole speech was littered by these reflex utterances, although he talked to me of nothing more perilous than his holiday on the Black Sea.

And now Olga said: 'I don't mean that I should like to live in Britain. Not at all. Your television's lovely, of course.' Her toes wriggled in anguish. 'But no, I wouldn't live there. It's too cold—the people, I mean.' She looked faintly confused. 'It's hard to talk. I can't say.'

Candour and secrecy coexist in many Russians. By second nature they may prevent their talk, or even their thoughts, from straying into danger areas; but the next moment they can show a countrified bluntness. 'You're going to Suzdal for a few days?' Olga suddenly said. 'Can I come with you?'

Was she serious? I never knew, for the next instant this question had drowned in a river of other talk. The diffident woman of a moment before had suddenly relaxed, and I was confronted instead by a hearty, child-like matron who was asking to go and look at my car in the park outside, as if we were partners at a village hall dance. Or would I drive it underneath her window when I left, she demanded, so that she could see what a Morris Marina was?

Now the truffles were tumbling into her mouth and she was talking about the dissidents she had met. Did I know M——, married to a

[34]

French actress? After a few collusive nods and winks, the names came pouring out. Had I met Y——, the leader of a disbanded Helsinki Human Rights monitoring group? She tossed back more brandy. Why on earth, she half shouted, didn't the Soviet Union cast up better leaders for itself? Kruschev, she declared, was an idiot, and Brezhnev a boor. 'Most of them speak the most *frightful* Russian, you know, almost uneducated. It sickens me to listen. . . .'

Within less than two hours she was by turns inhibited, vulgar, flirtatious, voluble and finally sad—a child of Russian nature. Whereas I was polite, hypocritical and emptily English. I could not like her at all. When I drove my car under her balcony and away, I glimpsed her Morse-Code face looking down at me, the reflecting orbs of its spectacles like the facial discs of an owl, high up and expressionless in the building's pallor.

Since entering Russia I had barely thought about the KGB. But a few days after seeing Olga, when I was visiting a known dissident late one evening, I double-checked that I was not followed. This time the door was opened by a forty-year-old man whose steep-browed face emanated something slow, patient and distantly hurt. Boris had been banned from his job as a university lecturer (dissidents are the only unemployed in Russia) and lived, I think, by the charity of friends and by free-lance teaching. The only luxury in his three-room flat was a library of scientific books.

We sat at a bare table. His auburn-haired wife set out little cakes for me, then relapsed opposite, resting her head on her bare arms, and watched us with the sleepy self-sufficiency of a cat. Boris talked in a husky, deliberate voice. I sensed in him that acceptance of affliction which gives to many dissidents who have suffered a gloomy stubbornness. They rarely sounded bitter. The retribution of the system might have fallen on them not from human beings, but from some blind, impersonal height—a force of nature as vast and deaf as fate or the Russian sky. Accused as traitors to a nation they loved, and surrounded by the narrow and universal patriotism of their own countrymen, they were doubly isolated. Few other countries on earth have the power of such ubiquitous damnation.

Yet the dissidents were never alone. A knot of friends surrounded them. This evening there was Nikolai, a pale, slight-built professor of languages. While Boris and Tanya often stayed silent and presented a punch-drunk obduracy to life, Nikolai was suavely animated, and seemed still unscathed. Even in appearance he and his friend were strikingly different. Above Boris's tall, kindly brows, a dust of light brown hair was softly receding. His face was drowned in its flesh. It gave out a muffled sadness and aspiration; it absorbed things like a quicksand, then returned to itself. But Nikolai's features were sensitized and mocking, silhouetted in a lank blackness of hair and beard, and lit by effervescent eyes. He looked like a pallid and cynical Christ.

I found them listening to the radio. They were waiting to learn the fate of a colleague, a priest who was facing trial, and were afraid that he might be forced into a public self-denunciation. We heard news bulletins, obituaries, the end of a play. They listened with bowed heads, afraid that at any moment they might hear the voice of a now unrecognizable friend. In the next-door room Boris's children awoke from sleep with faint cries. But the radio gave no word.

They were quietly relieved. To the dissident such 'confessions' are as meaningless to truth as the credo screamed from a mediaeval rack. But to Communism's public fantasy of faith, they are a grotesque kind of healing. The heretic is returned to the fold, no longer threatening the others by his separateness. The guilt or innocence of the flock scarcely seems to matter, provided it is united.

'A priest has a hard job here,' Boris said. 'In the country he may serve as many as thirty villages. People say our churches are only full of old women, and that they'll soon die out. But in the cities the congregations are growing. Somehow there's always another generation of old women coming along.'

'Where are their men?' I asked, expecting a pious solution in the war dead.

'Drinking, probably,' Nikolai answered. 'That's their form of oblivion. The old women take to God, the men take to drink.' He made a gesture of self-obliteration. 'Unfortunately it's easier to find a bottle of vodka than a church in Moscow. Some churches here look as if they're working, but in fact they're shut. The government restored them for the Olympic Games, and gilded their crosses to make it look as if they were active.'

Boris groaned involuntarily, and stared at his big hands on the table; Nikolai went on with a silky irony: 'Oh yes, our rulers have always worried about the Church. In 1974 a secret report was drawn up for the Communist Party Central Committee. And somehow it leaked.' His fingers waggled downwards in insidious seepage. 'Actually that's not surprising. The Central Committee numbers three hundred, and when you think of all their wives and daughters. . . .'

'And grandmothers. . . .'

'Anyway, this report dealt with bishops. It listed them in three categories. In Category One were those who supported the government's atheistic policies—imagine such a bishop! Category Two was indeterminate, and Category Three listed those who looked after their flocks and tried to keep their churches in repair.'

'The repair of a church—that's a delicate issue,' Boris said. 'You see, a priest often feels his bishop's too frightened to support him. As for those categories, they're probably a farce, since bishops can always bribe their government supervisors to depict them favourably. But a report like that shows how closely the Party oversees the Church.'

Nikolai chortled. 'Did you hear the joke about the bishop and the dissident? No? Well, a bishop meets a dissident who's just read the secret report. "And which category am I in?" the bishop asks in trepidation. "You're in Category One, among the atheists," the dissident replies. "An atheist!"—the bishop crosses himself fervently—"Oh, thanks be to God!"'

Tanya looked up through sagging eyelids and smiled as if at something she had dreamed. Boris said: 'All the same, the bishops are preserving what they can—even the Patriarch, who has to be a type of civil servant. I used to live near the church where he preaches, and—yes—I had the impression of a man of God.'

'In Category Two, I'd say!' Nikolai laughed impenitently; he was like a precocious boy who has run away from a bad school. But then he leant towards me, suddenly serious. 'The trouble with us Russians is that we're hopelessly religious. Of course Communism's a religion. It's never existed, in any country, as anything else. It has its own dogma, its own prophets, and even—ugh!—its own embalmed saint. What else is that Lenin mausoleum? It's pure paganism, or a throw-back to the relic-worship of early Christians.'

The analogies between Christianity and Communism, he said, were almost unending. Above all Communism shared with mediaeval faith its conscience-seated power and completeness. It resolved the troubling greyness of the world into a puritan black and white. Its heaven was the future forged by man on earth. Its god was the Party, whose service defined morality. But doubt one verse of its scripture, and the whole structure flew into fragments; faith demands submission. Like mediaeval Christianity, Communism precluded any fundamental speculation; its faithful walked in a blinding eternity of gospel. It was complete, dead.

'But in fact the average Party member is utterly cynical,' Nikolai said. 'There are only a tiny few who really believe—and those are mostly senile or very young. For the rest, it's just a career, a way of getting on.'

[37]

The feeling that Communism is a spent force had already seeped into me through—ironically—government advertisements. There was about them a ring almost of desperation, as if they were attempting a colossal confidence-trick on the people. For they were trying to equate the Party with that older, deeper Russian religion of the *Rodina*, the Motherland. Against this numinous and only half-translatable concept, the subtleties of Marxism-Leninism, with its vision of a nationless proletariat, broke in vain. 'We are anti-patriots', Lenin declared in 1915. But no people on earth indulge such a sentimental and subliminal patriotism as the Russians. It rises in them with all the unconditional love of child for mother. I knew White Russian nuns in Jordan who wept at their exile after more than fifty years of separation. Patriotism is Russia's heart and womb, whereas Communism is merely—and not always—its head.

'The Party's tapping nationalism quite consciously,' Nikolai said, 'because it's failed to drum up support for Communism. In my own lifetime I've seen an enormous growth of nationalistic ritual. These cults were very big during the war; then they faded, but now they're returning. They're like an attempt to replace Christian ceremonial. War memorials, you know, are our national altars. We're still building them thirty-five years after the war. I used to work almost within sight of the Tomb of the Unknown Soldier by the Kremlin Wall. It was only created recently, but now brides and grooms come to it after their wedding, as if it conferred some kind of sanctity on them.'

The countryside bristles with memorials, of which many are quite new—tanks and field-guns elevated on concrete plinths, mounds and circles of glory, eternal flames, sculptured heroes, obelisks, symbols, epitaphs. In every city callow-looking cadets of Komsomol stand guard in twenty-minute shifts at the monuments of a war which even their fathers are too young to remember. Teenage boys clutching sten-guns and Kalashnikov assault rifles goose-step (ironically) to and fro, and schoolgirls stand at knock-kneed attention on little wooden shutters, their hair bursting from under khaki caps in a froth of baby ribbons. These are the points of sanctity which married couples visit after their weddings. Shivering with cold, the thin-clad bride lays her bouquet at the shrine; the pair poses for a ritual photograph, lingers a while as if something else might happen, then drifts away. Such places are not really memorials to the dead at all. They are symbols of Russian regeneracy after the bitter humiliation of German victories and of German propaganda that the Slavs were semi-human. They are hymns and panaceas in stone.

[38]

'They are also useful points of unity for rallying our ethnic minorities,' Boris said, 'since we were all fellow-sufferers in the war. . . .'

Occasionally I sensed that Boris and Nikolai were flashing warnings or inquiries at one another, as if their talk approached invisible frontiers. After a while something made me ask: 'Is your phone tapped?'

Boris's laugh was more a sick cough. 'Not just my phone,' he said, 'but this whole flat.' He indicated the room's walls in two places. 'Here . . . and here. Oh yes, Orwell's books have come true in our country.' His gaze drifted across Tanya's reclining head and back to the table. He said: 'They're listening to us now.'

A sudden silence fell. Light rain was dropping in the dark outside; I hadn't noticed it before. For a moment we were all thinking of that other, unseen presence with us. I felt a naïve amazement at their outspokenness. Only long afterward, when I had myself been followed for days by the KGB, did I understand how hard it was to live a continuous lie, and with how passionate a sense of release a man casts off any feeling of guilt in the celebration of his own eavesdropped integrity. But for the moment my gaze hesitated between Boris, with whom friendship was an act of folly or courage, and Nikolai whose beard (I suddenly noticed) was faintly glossed with grey; and back to Tanya, whose very bedroom intimacies could never be quite holy.

'And you may be sure the KGB know about you too!' Nikolai's voice melted into a sarcastic sing-song. 'A Westerner in his own car! Alone, unmarried, and here for so long! That's not a foreigner they like, that's not a good foreigner!'

I answered—speaking both to him and to the unseen ear—that I found the police supervision of his monotonously passive countrymen to be inexplicable, and the numbers of police absurd. Their huge manpower, I suggested, would be better disbanded and employed in something more productive.

Nikolai stared at me hard. His restless lips and whitely tapering cheeks turned him more than ever into a mocking saint. Very distinctly he said: 'You are in error there. The government needs them. It needs the KGB too, they're the backbone. It needs them in order to stay where it is. *We're docile only because of them.*' He paused, as if to allow me (or the ear) to digest what he had said. 'The ordinary police are an easy tool. They're mostly young ex-National Servicemen, uneducated country lads. Their job earns a middle-grade salary, and if you're stationed in Moscow it carries citizenship with it and you can live here. So men join the force to further their status.' It seemed to me that the

Russians' intense desire for order assumed some fearful anarchy in their core, a profound self-distrust whose justification I could not gauge. But Nikolai continued deliberately: 'The Party's imposition of order is not neurotic. It is absolutely rational. If we had an election, only fifteen per cent would vote for this government.' He paused. 'No—less—*ten per cent*. Because nearly half our people believe in God—Christian or Moslem; and half are not ethnically Russian at all. You realize we are the only empire left on earth? And even those who are Communists are lethargic and disillusioned. This government has no base whatever.'

At last I understood him as he wanted: that tension and combat are built into the Party's very heart. It can never relax, because its fear comes first from within. Outside pressures are necessary to it in order to prevent the whole system from flying apart. So the age-old Russian nightmare of encirclement—from China and Japan, NATO and America—not only creates the Russian fear, but is created by it. War readiness is like a fever here: the aggression of a dangerous and insecure child.

These thoughts filled me with a cold helplessness. It seemed suddenly innocent ever to have hoped that the world was divided merely by some mammoth lapse of trust. When I said good-bye to Boris, I pulled him out of his bugged doorway and onto the landing. Was there anything I could do for him, I asked?

He looked at me with his fatalistic patience. No, he said, nothing. It seemed less a refusal of help than a statement of fact. I slid out of his apartment block by the back way, grateful for the concealing rain.

The queue for Lenin's mausoleum stretches several thousands long out of parkland gardens along the Kremlin walls, and shuffles across the grey loneliness of Red Square. In itself it resembles any ordinary Russian queue, neither more nor less reverential than those for bread or beer. It is drab, dogged, muttering. All along its line it is watched by police and uniformed KGB with a lingering scrutiny. But as it turns to face the tomb, a low ziggurat in red marble, it falls silent. People remove their hats, smooth down their hair. The aura of sanctity is suddenly intense and oppressive. This is the Holy Sepulchre of atheism. The youth in front of me was told to take his hands out of his pockets. The woman behind was ordered to stop talking.

Beyond the bronze doors, flanked by two guardsmen, sombre passages enclosed us. We descended steps down walls of black and grey feldspar, which sent out faint blue lights from their stone. We were never allowed to stop moving, and can have been in the crypt for less than a minute. Light fell indirectly high above, where the decorated walls showed jagged and violently red. My eyes strained in the gloom. I was moving below the head of a glass sarcophagus framed in gilded banners, then up a half-flight of steps circling around it. Four guards stood immobile below.

Lenin lay there bigger than I had imagined, the hair fairer, sandy and almost gone from his head. He was bathed in brilliant white light. Against his dark suit the face and hands shone vivid and isolated. The cheeks were touched by a faint stubble of beard, the eyes closed. He looked irredeemably unimportant. The skin glowed with a glassy, wax-like sheen, unmodulated, textureless. In the suit there was no sense of a body at all; the torso seemed flat, non-existent, the arms stiff and propped, like those of a mannequin. I understood why some Russians suspect this is not Lenin's body at all, but an effigy.

Almost before I had entered this presence, I was being moved out of it. I could only stare. The dead are not pitiful but changed, frightening. This was not, in any case, a face which I could gaze on with dispassion. History and the world's dilemma blew about it. I felt as if I were not looking at a man at all, but at an icon. Even the face, whose bumpy forehead and Tartar cheekbones were familiar from a thousand statues, had taken on the impersonal stasis of sainthood—neither living nor dead.

The tomb has been disturbed three times. During the Second World War, as the Germans advanced on Moscow, the corpse was evacuated eastward to the Volga. At least once the mausoleum has been closed while cosmetic repairs were undertaken to the body. And between 1953 and 1961 the embalmed cadaver of Stalin, whom Lenin had come to fear, was laid by his side.

But there was no time to evolve such thoughts. A moment later I had mounted into daylight and was walking along the graves by the Kremlin wall—Gorky, Voroshilov, Gagarin, Stalin now—some with busts in little iron-enclosed flower-beds, others modest wall-plaques with pots of plastic peonies below. They were fittingly simple. They lay in the clean-angled and uncompromising shadow of Lenin's mausoleum, and partook of that dark sanctity. The cult of Lenin seems to have stepped into some deep atavistic breach left open by a Christianity in retreat. It appeals to the same spirit in which people wept in panic and trampled women and children to death at the funerals of the tsars and of Stalin himself. It is part of the hunt for God. The megalithic gloom of the mausoleum reeks of it: a plea for immortality. And it is echoed, in a quieter way, by the hundreds of thousands of chapel-like rooms, filled with dusty photographs, which are dedicated to Lenin in factories and apartment blocks all over the country.

Yet this mausoleum had not the profound, almost organic sanctity of a true religious shrine. It was steeped in the anxiety of its own propaganda. Above all, it was an insult to the sobriety of Lenin himself, whose widow protested in vain at his embalming. Lapped in pharaonic glory, denied the decent privacy of death, he has become the victim of his own creation: a *coup de théâtre*. He is the most stared-at human being in history. Yet 'the cult of great men,' wrote Marx, 'is a bourgeois myth.'

After this my days in Moscow fragment in my memory. I cannot discern any pattern, but a brief week of kaleidoscopic moments and chance encounters.

One evening, pouring rain, as I drive into my campsite, a man comes floundering after me through wet grass and puddles, and signals me to open the passenger door. From his haggard face I anticipate trouble. Is he a harassed dissident? An informer? He throws back a cloud of dripping hair from his still-young face. But he has only one problem. 'Jeans.'

'What?'

'Jeans. Have you any jeans?'

In the fascination of young Russians for Western things, jeans are the *ne plus ultra* of the modish, cult and modern. They can be sold for eight times their London price. Yes, I had a pair of new British jeans.

'New?' His face fell. He had hoped I owned an old pair. He was too poor to buy new jeans at black market prices. He was married with one daughter, he said, and couldn't even afford a second child. He opened the door and prepared to plunge back into the rain.

'Take the jeans for their English price,' I said.

As he stared at me, his eyes grew watery with gratitude. Only later did I reflect that I was offering him the equivalent of a month's salary. 'Oh please, yes,' he said weakly, 'yes, yes. . . .' His fingers laced and unlaced under his neck like the forelegs of a mantis. 'Do you really mean that?'

I glanced at his stomach. 'I'm not sure they'll fit.'

'They're bound to,' he said, 'of course they'll fit. Of course. . . .' He seized them and dashed into a nearby camping-hut to change. A moment later he emerged encapsuled in jeans and gasping with triumph like one of Cinderella's ugly sisters who has fitted the slipper. Where the jeans began, his whole body tapered away like a tadpole's, while above them his chest bloomed in a monstrous burst of held breath and pigeon ribs. He looked terrible.

'Wonderful,' he said, 'perfect.'

Thereafter the demand for Western jeans accompanied my trip like an insidious litany. Their true value, pure *cachet*, was obscured by a haze of other, half-believed explanations. They didn't wear out like Polish ones, they didn't shrink or stretch. You could go to bed in them: they didn't crease. Whatever the reasons, they had nothing to do with politics.

'What can I do for you?' the man asked with his spare breath. 'I can get you Armenian brandy. Or do you have dollars? If you want a favourable exchange rate. . . .'

All spiritual and political ideals, it seemed, divided the world drastically; if it were ever to be united, it would be by jeans.

No, I had no dollars. The man struggled spider-legged away through the rain, leaving me struck by the illogic of things.

I find myself noticing the young, as if I were not among them. This process of ageing has its compensations: perhaps I am more objective. The young here were born into a happier world than were their parents. They have the softness of their selfishness. The old keep the grimness of their sacrifice.

I stare at girls and youths in the street, as if they contain a mystery. Their T-shirts fascinate: 'Michigan University', 'Lonely Art'. The faces above them bear symptoms of Western sophistication. Occasionally they drop pieces of American into their conversation like watch-words. 'Let's go'. 'Wow!' 'That's where I'm at.'

I queue outside Moscow's best-known Slavic restaurant, once the haunt of nineteenth century writers. Eating out in Russian cities is a battle, like everything else. After half an hour ignored in the cold, the queue starts protesting. But restaurant doormen are petty tsars; they grant or refuse entrance for arcane reasons. Several expensively-dressed couples push through unchallenged, and are acknowledged with servile nods. I wait an hour before gaining entry. No, I am not a group. From the magnificent menu of thirty-six dishes only one is available.

I engage in desultory conversation with the others at my table. They are in their early twenties. I guess that they enjoy the privileges of important parents; inherited advantages in education and jobs are a Soviet commonplace. They are friendly, candid and a little drunk. On radio, they listen to Voice of America (soon to be jammed) and the

BBC, they devour underground literature and frequent the black market. But they are secure. They look on politics with apathy, and scarcely question anything at all. They badger me for news of Western pop groups, but they don't understand Western freedoms. They know no other life with which to compare their own. If they were not gentler than their elders, I would be depressed. But even their materialism is an ugly kind of comfort.

On another evening I dine at the Arbat restaurant. It is very grand. Entry is by an unfathomable system of tickets which I had bought three hours before. I relax and stare at the clientele. Even here, in the hub of Moscow snobbery, it looks faintly rustic. The women hang their coats around their shoulders in the cold evening. At the tables of celebrating parties, littered with pressed caviare and Chicken Kiev, the diners are already flushed by the sunrise pink of vodka and pledging toasts with a foggy pomp which sometimes brings the whole party to its faltering feet. At other tables middle-aged officials murmur conspiratorially to each other, and wholesome young couples, with a look of pre-war Europe, are courting in gauche silences.

My questioning reduces the enormous menu to an available pittance. Meat is scarce this year. I rely on *borshch* and a powerful black rye bread, and later feel sorry for my chicken, which must have led a hard life.

I am surrounded by the upper stratum of Moscow society, in which Western vanities of class are replaced by those of bureaucratic rank, and it is sad to see it conform to cliché: heavy, hard-drinking, styleless. Only once a party of long-haired *jeunesse dorée* invades the dance floor in leather jackets and tight trousers. Some of them even wear frivolous military insignia, which is utterly un-Soviet. But the cabaret is about to begin, and the head waiter ushers them courteously away while a band strikes up on a garish dais.

Typically, the distinction of the evening belonged to this supremely physical cabaret—tumblers and acrobats and finally a balletic pair of extraordinary strength and stateliness. The man lifted his fragile-looking partner in aerial poses of miraculous ease, holding her up now by a foot, now by a hand, while she froze immobile like a bird in the spotlight, and the clientele went on eating its Chicken Kiev and fuddling itself on Georgian champagne.

One afternoon I wandered south over the loop of the Moscow river, where the Kadashevsky district begins. This area escaped the fire which gutted the city during Napoleon's occupation, and its stucco-fronted houses now meander along tree-darkened lanes in affable decay. Their doors burrow beneath street level. Their decorated window-frames are crumbling away. After the anonymity of the flat-blocks they reflect a life-giving diversity.

A public bathhouse loomed among them like a half-ruined factory. I was persuaded to visit it by jumbled feelings of griminess and curiosity. I don't know where the origins of this supremely Russian institution lie: probably in Byzantium, reaching back to Roman and Greek bath-houses, but perhaps also in obscure Tartar ancestors.

I undressed in a padded cubicle among a flotsam of shoes, bottles and drunken flies. An ancient colossus was already seated there, swathed in towels like a Berber chief. He had come for the afternoon with four bottles of beer, and grunted that there was no point in spending less than three hours in a bathhouse.

Thereafter the rooms succeeded one another like the circles of Dante's Hell. The tiled expanses of the tepidarium, ringed with stone benches, were pervaded by an insidious steam and filled with quiet, naked men. The Russian body is unlike any other. Hundreds of bull-necks, ponderous shoulders and nerveless torsos descended to a burgeoning delta of stomachs and thighs. The muscles were strong but passive. Their owners squatted and lumbered through the chambers in a miasma of friendly but neuter-looking flesh, plastic sandals and a phantasmal array of bath-hats.

I searched for a bench of my own. All around me men were scrubbing themselves or one another with the dedication of uncouth religious acolytes. They slopped water over their heads and backs, and soaped each other wholesale. Several were bending over like Victorian schoolboys about to be whipped, while others behind covered them from head to toe in suds.

Certain benches appeared to be traditional property. I mistakenly sat on one. A pale-eyed Goliath loomed above me. 'What are you doing on my bench, comrade?' It was the nearest to anger that I had seen in any Russian.

'I couldn't tell. . . .'

'You are not from here.' He stared at me incuriously. I moved away. He proclaimed after me: 'He is from somewhere else.'

A grumbling attendant was handing out *veniki*, bunches of birch twigs. With these the bathers set to thrashing their shoulders and legs, or flailed one another's backs with the vigour of flagellating penitents to muttered demands of 'More! More!' The air was filled with whirring and thwacking. But whenever they stopped, the brutal charade instantly collapsed. Then the *veniki* were tossed on the floor in sodden tufts. The skin of the flagellants, luxuriously tingling, was covered merely in a fragrant rash of birch-bark. They let out sybaritic grunts and burps. Their pores were opened, their flesh painlessly chastened, their minds touched with a pleasurable sense of atonement.

I entered a passage crossed by pouring water and indecipherable smells, then pushed through a wooden door into the third room. The heat hit me like a mattock-blow. My chest heaved but my lungs merely whispered feebly in its blaze. Only a ghoulish light crept through a window of clouded orange glass into the cramped chamber. The fire shuddered and sweltered through the air in invisible, breath-extinguishing waves. I made out a furnace booming in a clay boiler against a wall. Underfoot the tiles were scalding. Somewhere in the darkness above my head a voice demanded 'Throw on more!' until a man hurled water against the boiler walls, and the steam, bursting outward, seemed to extinguish the last wisp of air. I groped forward. Above me rickety wooden steps wound to an open loft, where men were slumped in exhausted stupor, or squatted on their haunches tickling each other's backs with birch twigs and murmuring together in the unbreathable air. It was the deepest circle of the inferno. All light, all sound, all movement were slowed into dreams and shadows of themselves. The air itself was the only real presence – a black and suffocating embrace. The Rembrandt light showed bowed heads and blobs and glows of incandescent flesh: the ultimate hopelessness. With each step of the stair as I ascended, the heat exploded in harder blasts. I reeled like a mountaineer at the top, then capsized among the mumbling bodies.

But the last stage of the bathhouse ritual passes by in a somnolent balm. All through the dressing-rooms lounge white-towelled ghosts celebrating their escape from purgatory. Their cleansed and rosy skin fills them with dronish well-being. For hours they loll in their cubicles gossiping about sport or women, munching dried fish and salami, downing mugs of watery beer. A clinking of bottle-openers releases a gurgle of smuggled-in vodka; voices rise and fall in clubbish collusion; and the seedy surroundings, littered (as are the older bathhouses) by the cracked statues and chandeliers of tsarist times, take on the surreal glow of a wrecked paradise.

Strange moment near the Arbat, one of Moscow's wealthiest thoroughfares. A big-boned young man and woman stand talking in the shadows. Suddenly the man lifts his fist and crashes it into her face. They continue talking. I stare at them, wondering if I am the victim of hallucination. The woman's face is unblemished; it wears a look of timeless endurance. Then the man draws back his fist again and slams it into her stomach.

'Comrade!' I call out incongruously. 'What are you doing?'

He turns and looks at me blankly. The woman's face wears no expression at all. Then they walk away, his arm around her waist. I am left staring after them, feeling as if I had interrupted some arcane mating ritual. I remember, too, reading from a sixteenth century manual of Muscovite etiquette. A husband should beat his wife lovingly, it advises, so that she will not be rendered blind or permanently deaf. I suppose I intruded.

I went to Children's World, the big toy store on Marx Prospect. Among the dense crowds a dangerous undergrowth of stout, pushing mothers elbowed its way at stomach level. Undemanding, unsmiling, uncrying, their children trotted after them. But the toys were bitterly expensive and so tawdry that I wondered how they could awake the imagination at all. War games were less common than in the West, it seemed—I saw only a few self-assembly rockets and tanks, and plastic soldiers which were mere wafers of men, unpainted. I searched for a smile among the soft toys and plastic dolls, but encountered only the compulsory grin of a frog. For the rest, their faces were cemented in expressions of Pinocchio idiocy.

But in the shop's centre the communal spectacle compensated a little for private paucity. A huge ship, crewed by two old men, a sick hippopotamus and a lame giraffe, lurched and revolved in an imaginary sea. And high on one wall, inside an elaborate timepiece, at the stroke of every hour a cuckoo rotated its plastic head, wooden figures patrolled out unsmiling from little doors, and the clock face opened two blue Slavic eyes which glanced circumspectly left and right, then closed again in sleep.

I returned late on the metro from the Bolshoi Theatre, whose banked tiers of crimson, cream and liquid gold were echoed in the 1930s glory of the underground stations. These are less stations than palaces: Augustan halls of jointed marble, and lordly floods of steps, friezes swagged in stucco banners and weaponry, or vaulted with mosaics. For a few pence you may ride here for ever. It is unnervingly clean and superbly efficient. At night the whole network is staffed by little more than women in red hats, who preside at train level in small

[47]

kiosks. The escalators flow fast down steep avenues of gilded neon torches. The platforms are chandeliered corridors.

I found myself climbing out at every other stop to stare at its Stalinist fantasies with mingled wonder and revulsion. Here, in the thirties, the luxuries of the palace were being consciously transferred to the people. Every station was different, and every line. I walked through steel and plaster Pantheons where paintings and bas-reliefs portrayed bucolic happiness on the collective farms, or flaunted a proud, unsmutted industry. The only other occupants of the trains were a few rural families travelling late to railway stations; they huddled on the seats with their silenced children, their string bags and bundles massed about them.

At one stop I stepped into a hall where stained-glass windows glowed with flower patterns in twilight tints. They filled the deserted platform with a weird, ecclesiastical gloom. It was here, set in mosaic, that I noticed the familiar slogan 'Peace'. But the word seemed to have shed its benign connotations and to mean something else. Although it hung on the lips of every Russian-in-the-street, and was uttered by him with perfect sincerity, it resounded as an instrument of Party propaganda with a perverted menace, shouted like a war-cry. And now here it was again, proclaimed in Stalin's Russia before the Soviet treaty with Hitler in 1939, before the partition of Poland, before the forced servitude of the Eastern Bloc, the suppression of Hungary and Czechoslovakia, the occupation of Afghanistan. 'Peace'. It glowed solemnly in the Gothic gloom of the station. I stared back at it. Peace, according to the Marxist-Leninist canon, could only come about when the world had ceased to change and had resolved into one system and one idea. Marxism itself, built on a Hegelian dialectic of opposites, drew its life from tensions and antagonisms; peace was merely 'a means of gathering together one's forces', as Lenin said.

I took the next train out.

Several times in Moscow I visited the ex-fiancée of an English friend. Lyudmila lived on the tenth floor of a high-rise flat-block with her bland-faced mother and her nine-year-old son by a broken affair with a foreign diplomat. She was attractive, for no perceptible reason. A pair of hesitant, grey and rather child-like eyes illumined her pale face, and her mouth was crammed with projecting or crooked teeth which manoeuvred her lips into smiles of oddly sensuous innocence.

She had given birth to her illegitimate son in the early seventies, long before the Soviet government discouraged abortion in order to bolster

[48]

the population. She had been confronted by the KGB and for a long time, I think, had lived through a private hell. Now, in the evenings, I would find her sitting on a wobbly chair with her legs tucked under her; sometimes she would close her eyes in mid-talk, as if she were weary or in perpetual meditation. The damp-streaked wallpaper of her apartment was lacerated by the child's graffiti; a barricade of cupboards and faded purple curtains partitioned the sitting-room from somebody's bed; and a grimy chandelier lit us outlandishly from above.

Lyudmila talked of her past life as if it were somebody else's. Even of mutual friends she spoke only with a remote and separated affection. 'I was unhappy for years after the boy's birth. I wanted to die.' Her eyes shut, as if testing the idea, opened again. 'I didn't find the world worth inhabiting at all. It was just a haze of people hunting for money, position, things. And I thought: what's the point? They were like children playing games.' She uttered this indictment in tones of faraway wonder, like somebody gazing at the universe down the diminishing end of a telescope. 'Sometimes I'm grateful to have been born in Russia,' she said. 'If I'd lived in a better society I'd have believed myself free. I would never have discovered the reality inside me. But instead I was born into this hell, and was forced to discover my own peace. Perhaps, in the end, we're lucky here. . . .'

It was easy to guess the nature of her refuge. On the chair where she was sitting her legs had buckled into the lotus position, and through her bedroom's doorway, jarred open by the boy's bicycle, I saw the photograph of an Indian guru whose garlanded head and wrinkled paunch presided over the Slavic chaos with bizarre serenity. In front of him she had placed a little vase of flowers.

For her the 'real' world had dimmed to an asylum of the lost. It had become unbearable and she had rejected it, had rearranged it in the tranquil Buddhist patterns of wholeness and incorruption. She looked on its striving, she said, with increasing alienation and faint surprise. All that was irrelevant.

'You see, all the time life—reality—is not in these battles and struggles at all.' She picked up an apple which her cat was patting across the floor. 'It's everywhere else. In the trees around us, in the earth. Truth is in this apple, for instance. The apple is purely itself. And we're surrounded by such things, but we don't see them. . . .'

It was all perfectly familiar, the neo-Buddhist litany. What was extraordinary was to find it here in Moscow, in the heartland of pragmatism. The cult of meditation was new in Russia, she said, but it was quietly growing. 'They say here that there's only one right way. But right and wrong are meaningless—figments of mind. What *is* lies above morality. Look at this cat'—she cradled the oblivious creature between her thighs, then held it up to me. 'Do you see why I like it? This cat is itself. It's uncontaminated by human beings. And birds too. In spite of revolutions and politics, the birds sing. . . .'

I remembered the birds in the Minsk woods, but said teasingly: 'I thought bird-songs were territorial war-cries.' I stared at the cat without envy.

But she did not listen. She was, in her way, as certain of her truth as an early Bolshevik or an Orthodox bishop (Category Three). Often silences fell between us. Much of the time I felt that she was not in my company at all, nor I in hers. She would close her eyes for long, still minutes, smiling crookedly. It was as if she were swimming under-water—her sustaining habitat—and rose only occasionally to a strato-sphere whose harsh air she could not breathe. I must have moved strangely in and out of her subaqueous world. I don't know how she conceived of me. She only fixed me with the mild, half-focused gaze of a dreamer, and although she spoke so much of happiness there was in this look something witheringly sad and lost. Once she murmured: 'I can't talk to adults, I can only talk to children,' and once: 'I don't know who I am.' And she was still afraid: afraid that my car might be noticed outside her apartment block, afraid to be seen in a restaurant with a foreigner.

In retrospect, she amazed me. Her mysticism, in its denial of the material world, was the purest negation of Communism I ever met. It was also, of course, her way of coping with her brutalized past. She believed herself liberated by it; I felt that it had killed her.

It was, however false or true, the ultimate protest.

3. Early Heartlands

T HE WHOLE SKY was filled with rain that August—rain which sieved down in gusts over the roads, blew between the cliff-like apartment blocks and whirled and howled across the fields. It swelled those remote tributaries of the Volga which dawdle down from unnoticeable uplands north of Moscow, and followed me eastward in thinning gasps, then faded away. I drove through the rain-polished light of an invisible sun. A hundred miles east of Moscow, near the town of Vladimir, the sky cracked open into floating lakes of blue, and I entered the watery plains of the Zalesye, the 'Land Beyond the Forests', a country of flax and potato farming. It looked gentle and poor.

These lands became the womb of a new Russia in the twelfth century, after the southern princedom of Kiev lost its hold. For seventy years Vladimir itself assumed the mantle of Kiev, before Tartar invasion ravaged them both. The town's heart is mellow and intimate. It covers a long headland above the valley where the Klyazma and Nerl rivers meet—a green mound blossoming with domes. Many ages of building are sprinkled here—low-built houses in commingled stucco, brick and stone. The drums of a twelfth-century fortified gate loom in the main street, and ramparts of grass-glazed earth heave under old trees.

Vladimir became the premier city of Russia when Andrei the God-Fearing, Grand Prince of Kiev, established it as his princedom and relegated the first and glorious capital to second place. Already, for many years, people had been drifting away from Kiev towards the bleak woodlands of the north. Here, in Russia's new heartland, arose the cities of her future: Vladimir, Suzdal, Novgorod, Moscow. The trade-softened world of Kiev, which looked towards Byzantium and the Mediterranean, was never to recover.

Andrei was an austere, half-Turkic tyrant. But he left Vladimir beautiful. He built the Assumption Cathedral, as lovely as any in the land, and commemorated his first son, killed in battle by the Bulgars, with a tiny church of near-perfect proportions, dropped like a stone tear on the banks of the Nerl. But in 1174 Andrei was murdered by his nobles in collusion with his wife. His body was thrown to ravening dogs before being retrieved by his court jester. Then, in that familiar tradition by which the Russians revere their powerful rulers, however monstrous, he was canonized and entombed in his great cathedral. His murderers were hunted down, and their corpses, sealed in tarred coffins, were set afloat in the marshes of the Nerl, where they may still be heard groaning on winter nights.

Andrei's successor Vsevolod—called Big-Nest on account of his myriad children—is remembered in Vladimir for the Dmitriyevsky Cathedral. Tall, almost windowless, it echoes the austere beauty of Andrei's Cathedral of the Assumption nearby. But whereas the walls of the Assumption rise stark in the glow of their stone, those of the Dmitriyevsky are carved with a seething cacophony of beasts and men. Lions with mask-like, furious faces, rampaging horses, peacocks, demons, eagles—a whole oriental bestiary scrambles and swarms round the windows, dangles between the half-columns, writhes up the dome. High in the pale masonry, Alexander the Great is carried up to heaven by a herd of griffins; King David fingers his harp before an Orphic cluster of listening animals, and I dimly discerned Hercules at work on the Nemean lion. On another wall Vsevolod Big-Nest presents a newly-born son to his family, which attends him in a Soviet-looking queue; while all about them clamours a tempest of vomiting dragons, double-bodied lions, tree-chewing goats and symbolic lambs.

But lower down, the storm is suddenly stilled. Between the half-columns apostles and prophets stand on little cushion-shaped clouds or have levitated to the tops of sculptured trees. They are emblems rather than men. They dangle censers and hold up texts. Together with the pagan hurricane above them, they form a microcosm of the universe of their time: past and present, dark and sacred, seen and unseen.

The nearby Cathedral of the Assumption produces an utterly different effect. For two and a half centuries, until long after Vladimir's power had passed to Moscow, this was the foremost cathedral in Russia, where her Grand Dukes were crowned. Poised on the plateau's edge, it overlooks a jig-saw of forest and pasture, where sluggish rivers creep and wander. It is built in the same living white limestone as the Dmitriyevsky, but is grandly beautiful. Its walls rise clean and un-earthly to a gold efflorescence of domes shaped like the helms of Slavic warriors. To north and south its seamless façades are decorated only by a few carvings of sleepy lions and women, which look out enigmatically over the rain-soaked valleys. Sheathed in white and helmeted in gold, it emanates a kind of Parsifal purity.

I peered inside, where groups of Russian tourists were walking. Over the walls and arches a dreamlike population of painted saints and angels kept pace with them. Some had almost flaked away; others had paled to silhouettes. Hovering on soffits or banked along the choir, they touched the air with a moribund glory. The darkness was filled with the lifting of their faded hands and crosses, the rush and flutter of their wings. Troops of avuncular and half-vaporized prophets congregated blackly on the pillars or marched along the aisles in indecipherable procession.

A whole cycle portraying the Last Judgement was painted in 1408 by the incomparable Andrei Rublev—the Duccio or Fra Angelico of Orthodoxy—but its colours were all but drunk away into the plaster. A tourist guide harangued his group beside me. 'Look up there! See how recognizable the faces are! It shows that Andrei Rublev was a man of the people, clearly. . . .'

Russian patriotism demands that the great pre-Soviet countrymen be enrolled as honorary Communists. And now here, even, was Rublev—pious monk and iconographer—being gathered in among the chosen people of Marxism. The group stared up at the surge of the righteous hurrying to heaven in an undemocratic richness of robes. And it was true that the frescoed faces were human and woundable, with small Slavic eyes and barbered beards. Composed during the slow recession of the Tartar onslaught—once laid on Russia like the flail of God—they belong to a time of new confidence, when men felt that the denizens of gospel, or even of heaven, might look like ordinary humans.

Of the Last Judgement the guide said nothing. The group merely gazed up with the same wizened, incurious eyes as the blessed. Under the central arch a blemished Christ swam almost faceless in a mandorla of blue. If you stared up long enough his eyes emerged slowly to meet yours as in some worn-out palimpsest, but were strangely restive, the face nested sadly in a fleece of sallow hair and beard. But beneath him, on the rise of the vault, were gathered the aristocracy of heaven. Apostles and evangelists cradled open books and lifted their fingers in nervous benediction, while massed behind them, their haloes overlapping like the scales of some tarnished but gorgeous serpent, a crowd of androgynous angels turned its heads this way and that in silent converse. They seemed less a heavenly host than a clutch of courtiers gossiping together in imperial antechambers. Only far below them, at the foot of one pier, a single archangel survived to trumpet the glory of God in a clatter of half-obliterated wings.

As I gazed up at those declamatory prophets clutching their infallible books, I was reminded inescapably of their descendants. Lenin, Kalinin, Kirov—in half the squares of the Soviet Union their baggy-trousered figures are silently shouting. Lenin's statues, in particular, have sprung up like weeds wherever those of Stalin were torn down. Gospel-bearers of the later faith, their iron fists are closed over scrolls and bulletins. In these men the old Russian belief in an apocalyptic history continues: history with a divine purpose, a beginning and an end. They are the initiate, the bearers of fire from heaven. The directives and warnings of Christian gospel are replaced by the insights and sociological lumberings of the Communist Manifesto. But the message is still sacrosanct. There is no middle path. At the great Internationals anathemas flew, heretics were excommunicated, orthodoxy redefined. The very language was Christian. Lenin, in a moment of high repudiation, accused a colleague (the philosopher Mach) of 'betraying materialism with a kiss.' Sometimes it seems as if nothing has profoundly changed at all. It was Marx who said that 'the tradition of all the dead generations weighs like a nightmare on the brain of the living.'

But the greatest treasure of the Assumption Cathedral is not here. The twelfth century icon called 'Our Lady of Vladimir', the most revered in the land, was taken to Moscow's Kremlin as long ago as the fourteenth century, and has come to rest in the Tretyakov Art Gallery. The ancient choice of this 'Virgin of Tenderness' as the pallium and figurehead of all Russia can be no accident. The Russians inherited from Byzantium two utterly different iconic conventions. In one, the *Hodegetria*, the Virgin and Child confront the worshipper in hieratic and unrelated glory; she is the unearthly Queen of Heaven, he a precociously adult Child enthroned on her lap. But the Russians rejected this too-intellectual formula, and instead fell in love with the less common but warmer *Eleousa*. Here the Holy Child—a swaddled infant—curls his arms about the Virgin's neck and presses his lips to hers, while she is a mother of sorrowful, dark-eyed tenderness, whose head inclines to his in a gesture of stately adoration.

This image of motherhood plucks a profound chord in the Russian soul. It pervades Soviet nationalism with its mystical invocation of the *Rodina*, the motherland, and reaches back, it seems, to a time long before Christianity, when a primordial Great Mother ruled these pagan woods and plains. This Mother was faceless, perhaps nameless:

an all-engendering womb. Through the animistic worship of her nature—trees, pools, fire, stones—she enveloped her worshippers with a passive omnipotence. At the coming of Christianity, it seems, she was tamed and christened in the *Eleousa*. Icons, churches, feast-days were poured into her lap. Her common and beloved name is not the 'Holy Virgin' (the virgin saints are almost ignored by the Russian Church) but *Bogoroditsa*, 'Mother of God', a word filled with soulful power. And her ancient pantheism is perhaps responsible for that passionate attachment to icons, relics, chalices—all the kissed and supplicated paraphernalia of the house of God—which still pervades Russian Orthodoxy. The dialectic of Byzantium and the legalism of Rome are equally far from this peasant adoration. To many Russian Christians a church is above all a treasury of objects in which divinity resides, just as divinity once dwelt in plants and stones.

The pre-Christian goddess lent a deeply fatalistic character to the society which she imbued—a fatalism personified in the *rod*, the ancestral clan. After his earthly life a man expected no personal resurrection. He was merely a link in the divine continuum of the *rod*—a fleeting moment in eternal time. Drowned in the ubiquity of mother earth and in the authority of the departed, his own personality was still-born. Even late Byzantine writers observed the passive conformity of the Slavic people.

The *rod* found a back door into Christianity in the spring feasts of the dead (still celebrated in graveyards with occasional orgiastic outbursts) and in liturgical echoes of the pagan funeral banquet. It is not surprising, then, that Russian Christians came to conceive of themselves as a vast *rod* whose father was the czar. Here, perhaps, lie the deeply regressive roots of Soviet collectivism, of the recurrent yearning to regard their leaders as divine elders—'Papa Lenin', 'Uncle Stalin'. In this land of surviving patronymics, perfect strangers may still be addressed as 'brother' or 'uncle', as if the whole Russian world were tender with the intercourse of relatives, or fraught with an orphan's fear.

That evening, as these heresies ramified through my mind, I turned north towards the little town of Suzdal. The suburbs of Vladimir vanished in unexpected factories and flat-blocks; but Suzdal, where no building over two storeys high is permitted, showed nothing in the darkness but cottages and the silhouettes of crotchety windmills.

For a few years early in the twelfth century, Suzdal succeeded Kiev as Russia's foremost city, then succumbed to the power of Vladimir.

Morning showed it furled along the banks of the Kamenka river, a town untroubled by any later pretensions to greatness. Its early, wooden basilicas and palaces have long ago burnt down or rotted away, but all through its streets, and scattered in its fields, seventeenth and eighteenth century churches stand in pairs—a low one for winter worship, a tall one for summer. Ambling south along the river, I passed one of these architectural marriages almost at once. Beside the church of SS. Cosmas and Damian, a voluminous octagon built for summer, his barn-like wife, the Bogolubskaya, stretched her long, winter body, capped by a curious dome. These Russian domes are not the all-embracing canopies of western Europe or Byzantium, but little more than the finials of decorative towers—small announcements, as it were, of something important beneath. Nestled under this demure hat, Bogolubskaya sat smugly beside Cosmas on their mound, he with a green roof, she with a brown.

After days of wandering the sterile geometry of Moscow, I plunged along the marshy coils of river in boisterous spirits. Grasses and dew-soaked clover lapped against my shins and drenched my feet. Sometimes I stopped to luxuriate in a hazy sun, while all about me a myriad frogs in green battledress plopped and spatted among reed-filled pools. The Kamenka river, in the strange Russian fashion, had gouged its banks steep in the west but smoothed its eastern shores into shoals. I followed it with indolent delight. High on one bank the wooden cottages were waking to the morning. Framed in their elaborately-carved windows, old people stared out with the quiet plenitude of icons. Misted in lace curtains or cut off arbitrarily by a bank of potted plants, their dreaming faces scarcely noticed me. Theirs seemed a slow and trusting world, where dogs never bothered to bark and tortoiseshell cats sauntered up to rub themselves against the legs of strangers. No traffic sounded; only lisping rain, desultory birdsong. Sometimes, when a door was left ajar, I peered into the scenario of a nineteenth century novel or folk-tale: wood-fenced courtyards stacked with winter logs and crowded by white chickens and roosters, while rooms beyond gave disconnected glimpses of shawls and samovars.

I made my way along paths muddy from storm, by ramshackle orchards and gardens of phlox, hollyhocks, stinging nettles. Steep above the river the faded defences of the Spaso-Yerfimievsky Monastery loomed in creaking brick ramparts and wonky towers whose roofs were gaping now. A tide of moss poured over the crenellations and dribbled through the loopholes. For quarter of a mile, towers and walls tottered along the river bank together in grim senility, while beneath them the bed of the Kamenka river was half-abandoned and sown with vegetables. On its far side the green domes and fortified walls of other monasteries cluttered the banks and distant meadows until their onion spires died out in mist. Here, almost alone in Russia, the old relationship persists between church and dwellings. No tenements obliterate the sky. The towers and belfries lift in consecrated tyranny above all else. The land is like a dream of Holy Russia before the time of Lenin or even of Peter the Great—a God-haunted, mystical, enclosed, poor country, which gazes on itself in tended gardens and domes—beautiful, charmed and unjust, spread along its river in a feudal sleep.

Into this peace, on the eastern bank, the fourteenth century Pokrovsky Monastery strikes a warning bell. Here many a repudiated Russian princess was forced to take the veil by her bored husband, including the consort of Ivan the Terrible and the first wife of Peter the Great. Early in the sixteenth century, the childless tsaritsa Solomoniya, repudiated by her husband Vasily III, was incarcerated here when he married the Polish princess Helen Glinskaya. But no sooner had Solomoniya assumed nun's habit than she gave birth to a son. To this day nobody knows what became of the child, heir to the empire of All Russia; but his mother, fearing for his life, was said to have smuggled him from the convent, proclaimed him dead and staged his funeral. For four centuries the matter rested. Then, during excavations in 1934, a tiny sarcophagus was found beside Solomoniya's tomb. Instead of a corpse it contained a pearl-embroidered silk shirt, which was wrapped around the rudimentary dummy of a baby.

The centre of Suzdal, crowning the Kamenka in a ring of earth ramparts and scattered gates, was filled by another maze of churches: churches with needle spires and painted domes, single cupolas and clustered ones, churches plain or gabled like the peaked *kokoshnik* headgear of mediaeval women, churches lordly and domestic, silver, white, black, green, renewed, decaying. They rose in their pairs like parables of Christian marriage: the tall sanctuaries of summer and their winter spouses. Even in the centre of the town square the belfried Voskresenskaya accompanied his stand-offish wife, the Virgin of Kazan. There were morganatic marriages and incompatible ones, chic couples and dowdy twosomes and perfect love-matches. They continued far beyond the walls in fields and clearings. A pair of dwarf chapels sat high above the river, divorced by a ravine. And a complete wooden church, built in 1766, had been brought from the country and reassembled—a lonely bachelor from that village world of timber whose pagoda-like turrets and snow-deflecting, witch-hat spires were perpetuated in the architecture of stone.

In front of this church I encountered a notice-board and a sign which read: 'Dear Tourist, if you wish to commemorate your name, write on this board and not on the monument. The administration guarantee to preserve your name out of the public funds of the museum.' Never was the instinct for scribbling lawless graffiti so punctured! But there, sure enough, the tourists had obediently inscribed their names and cities: 'Yuri from Leningrad', 'Natasha from Klin'. I realized then that I had not seen a single spontaneous graffito in the Soviet Union: not even a simple love message, let alone anything sexual or political. Watching the wooden-faced families of tourists trickling round the church, I suddenly longed to hear an argument or the yell of a recalcitrant child.

But not a mouse squeaked. Grass-filled spaces spread a halcyon quiet through the town. Its greatness had ebbed as Vladimir super-seded it, and has leaked away ever since, leaving it lovable and unimportant. The thirteenth century copper doors of its cathedral, damascened in gold, come from richer, more imperilled times; but their inlaid figures, darkened now, still glimmer with life, while the campanile is hung with aged bells which chime and ding whenever they feel like it.

I crossed the Kamenka southward. Far away, over cattle-strewn pastures, the florid nineteenth century church of SS. Flora and Laura, massed under a flurry of silver domes, had contracted a mésalliance with a dumpy little eighteenth century basilica. And all along the river, back to the shuttered and leaning towers of the Pokrovsky Monastery, these churches continued. The feel was of a world unchanged. White goats munched in cottage gardens, and fishermen were wading through the marshes, where families of domestic geese nested. But when I approached some old women to ask them the name of a nearby church, they stared at one another with pursed lips. 'I don't know,' said one. 'How should I know? That's all finished now.'

In the whole of Suzdal only a single pair remains open for worship.

I thought then how the near-closure of Russia's churches—by 1939 their active numbers were reduced to about a hundred—must have thrown a huge spiritual caesura into the lives of ordinary people. Even today, in milder times, only 7,500 remain open in this vast land, barely one seventh of the pre-Revolutionary figure. In Suzdal it is easy to imagine the emotional impact of their loss. Aesthetically and physically the churches once dominated every Russian village, filling the air with the gold propaganda of their crosses: the serenity of eternal law.

Small wonder that the usurping creed had to mimic them. All through Stalin's reign public buildings subconsciously strained for religious effect, and frogmarched into service half the paraphernalia of classical paganism. Municipal and Party offices shouldered their way skyward on fluted porticoes. Wedding-cake Corinthian and prestige Doric abounded. Plaster garlands tumbled and swung, urns slopped, cornucopia gushed. Railway stations proclaimed the new age of the Machine in bursting domes and walls afloat with bas-reliefs. No matter if the plumbing stank, it was the effect which mattered. Nowadays young Russians snigger a little at these monstrosities (they were denounced by Kruschev). But such buildings have become a part of Communist history. They are fervent, primitive. They seem to belong to an innocence irretrievably gone. Their very trust is weirdly touching. They are exemplified most perfectly by the derided statues which adorn them—statues whose physical proportions, like those of ancient Greece, symbolize spiritual energies. But on these Communist plinths and pediments stand no Praxitelean Zeus or Aphrodite, but the working Artemis or Hercules of another age—mattock over shoulder, hammer in hand: the apotheosised ordinary man. The paradigms of this time are the firm-faced land-girls with men's limbs and mothers' breasts, blacksmiths and road-builders. The symbols they hold are spades and scythes.

The wreath and the lyre are gone.

Driving north-west through light rain, I turned towards that other great Muscovite principality, Novgorod the Great. It lay more than three hundred miles north on the Leningrad road, which was a typically Soviet two-lane highway, indifferently surfaced and thick with lorries. Towards evening a red, watery sun emerged on the skyline, the rain cleared and I found myself driving along a causeway over the Volga. I stopped the car and gazed. A great swollen calm of river, grey under the grey sky, it wound among marshy islets with the majesty of a whole lake or sea on the move. Even this far inland, seagulls were wheeling above it with harsh cries.

The Volga shares something of the numinous mystery of the Nile, and of those other great historical rivers—the Euphrates, Indus, Ganges—which heave through the deserts and jungles of Asia and a child's imagination, so that from a first glimpse of them there arises this sense of their being already known. In such a way, perhaps through some folk-tale or poem long since unlearnt, the Volga stirred in me a memory of Slav and Viking traders, and of all those huge rivers—the

Dnieper, Don, Dniester—which bend in liquid blades of civilization through Russia's forests down across the dark centuries into the dawn of northern Europe. All rising close to one another in the glacial watershed west of Moscow, their trade was once linked northward by porterage to the rivers of the Baltic, and flowed southward to the fringes of the ancient world: the Don and the Dnieper to the Black Sea, the Volga to the Caspian where the old Silk Road passed. Thus they formed a corridor across the whole width of Russia. For two thousand years they joined the north to the sunlit orbit of Greece and Rome, Byzantium and Venice, and on their broad, softly-flowing backs carried silks, jewels and spices in exchange for furs and slaves. Where I sat on its bank, the Volga already measured hundreds of yards across, but moved on for another two thousand miles to the Caspian. Nothing about this sluggish womb of a river, neither its green shores nor its grey waters, betrayed that it was polluted by the toxic effluent of hundreds of factories.

By nightfall I arrived at the campsite of Kalinin, and was assigned a tent-shaped hut among shrubs. A coach of Australians was parked in one clearing, some Belgians in another. Beside our village of wooden tents stood a modern restaurant where I hogged down two bowls of the meat soup called *solyanka*, and a dance-floor on which the town's young gathered in the evenings. The moment the band struck up they rose from their tables in unison and began solemnly to dance the twist. There was an extraordinary quality of sameness to them. They jigged and bounced with utter unabandon, applying themselves conscientiously to the ritual of being young and modern. Many of the girls danced together in sad-seeming circles. They looked like English girls of the fifties, prim and untried. I watched them for a trace of Western ferment. There was none. The moment the band stopped they left the floor like a regiment, suddenly laughing and smiling, as if relieved.

I wandered back to the campsite feeling depressed. A drunk had befriended some of the Australians, and was trying to reach them with a bottle of vodka. But only campers were allowed in, said a policeman at the gate. 'Fascist!' bawled the drunk. At that the policeman's temper broke and he lumbered after his quarry into the darkness, trying to hit him with a folded raincoat.

As I walked through the gates a tall figure took advantage of the policeman's absence and slid in beside me with two cans of beer. Sasha was a schoolmaster, a teacher of mathematics. He was gauntly handsome, his face crowned in wiry black hair and touched by a slight moustache. A pair of scrutinous and restless eyes, together with the bony, thrusting movements of his body, emitted a suppressed frustration. We drank the beer together in my camping hut.

Sasha simply wanted to talk, to pour out his anger with the world around him and the poverty of his place in it. Things in his country were becoming worse all the time, he said. For seven or eight years now the economy had been sliding back. He spoke in embittered bursts. There were towns only a day's journey from Moscow where you couldn't buy a scrap of meat, fish or fruit. Salaries had been almost static for eight years, but prices had soared. The present leadership were just nonentities, he could barely remember their names.

Three or four times he sprang up and wrenched open the hut door. Each time only the night air, suddenly cold, blew in on us. 'I thought I heard something. Didn't you hear it?' For a moment he would glare out on the rectangle of black shrubs and faded stars, then slam the door to with his foot. Each time I felt a sense of wonder at the risks he knew he was taking, and at the value set on these explosive moments of human exchange. Since Alexander I had not met a single Russian who was happy with the system. Haunted by memories of wartime famine, it was the food shortage which was on everybody's lips. Even in Moscow the only meat I had seen was sausages, scrawny chickens and the ubiquitous tinned fish which Muscovites say is inedible. The failure of the economy—some called it decline, others stagnation—was the stock-in-trade of guarded conversation; so was the dismissal of the leadership as privileged nonentities.

Sasha was one of those, increasing now, who looked back with nostalgia to the reign of Stalin. 'Kruschev was wrong to denounce him. Stalin was a strong man, a great man. And who was Kruschev? Just a buffoon.' Sasha was almost too young to remember Stalin's time: either its low standard of living or its terror. He simply cherished the idea of power in his rulers, because their strength would be his strength. His was the old Russian yearning for a tsar or a god, for somebody to impose discipline on the nation's ancient anarchy and indolence. It was perfectly familiar. When Stalin died a whole section of the populace was seized almost by panic, like children left undefended; and a contemporary English traveller wrote of Ivan the Terrible that 'no prince in Christendom is more feared of his own than he is, nor yet better loved.'

I said bluntly that Stalin was a monster.

'But we need him,' Sasha insisted. 'We need that strength and order. Have you seen the stickers of Stalin on people's cars? Well, they're increasing. Maybe people don't actually want another Stalin, I don't know. But it's a way of protesting against today's regime.'

We heard footsteps in the grass outside. He jumped up and jerked open the door. This time the night was blotted out by a fat, chestnut-haired girl who looked in on us with amused eyes.

'Akh, it's only you, Vera. Come in.'

She bounced down on the bunk.

'She's nice,' he said.

His frustration continued in softened, disconnected sentences while he looked at her. Beneath his condemnation was an implicit envy of Western Europe, which he had visited in a supervised group six years before. He looked across at the girl. 'But it's no good my trying to explain to *her*, for instance. She's never left this part of Russia. It's impossible for anyone who hasn't been outside to understand.' She smiled blandly back at him. Every Russian who had visited the West was afflicted by the contrast, and by the hopelessness of transmitting it. 'Better to see once than to hear a hundred times,' they used to say. But few of them wanted to leave for ever.

Sasha's intolerance of what lay around him was rooted in personal wretchedness. He earned barely enough to feed his wife, whom he did not love, and his two small daughters. 'Sometimes I supplement my income by unloading wagons at night. That way I can earn thirty roubles in eight hours—that's a week's salary as a schoolmaster! Doctors and teachers are paid like dogs here. I told my wife I was unloading tonight and wouldn't be back until morning.' He pushed a cigarette into the girl's lap, letting his hand rest there. 'I stay with my wife for the sake of my daughters. If you don't get away sometimes you go mad. So I have these nights out—unloading wagons ... with girls. ...'

The divorce rate is appalling. A third of all recent Soviet marriages end within one year. Explanations for this cite drunkenness, cramped living space and the need for wives to work. But every case I encountered complexified these categories or turned them irrelevant. 'I was blindly in love with my wife,' Sasha said, 'but we were completely different. Her family, you see, were in the medical profession, dentists. They kept to themselves. But mine were real workers' people. My father was a tanner, open-hearted as the day, and our house was always full of people coming and going. [The class distinction was a subtle one: a dentist earned less than a tanner.] My father knew I'd be unhappy. He died soon after our wedding. I think it killed him.'

Sasha's high-wrought features had hardened; he was looking to me

[62]

for sympathy. But I was imagining his wife, a schoolmistress, returning from work to collect the children out of nursery school, going back to an empty house, feeding them, coping. The vaunted equality of Russian women is a mirage.

'Yes, it's harder to be a woman in life than it is to be a man,' Sasha said. 'We think more about ourselves.' He did not look as if he meant to change this.

We talked about other things, and laughed at politics—his world's and mine—in which neither of us trusted. Then he got up to go. He was taking his daughters to swim in the Volga early next morning. 'I told my wife I'd be back by two o'clock.' But it was only midnight. Vera got up with him. He squeezed my hand as he left. 'You're not like an Englishman at all,' he said. 'You're more like a Russian!'

I accepted this gratefully for its spirit, with its overtones of spent inhibition, and watched him and Vera disappear up a pathway. There were plenty of empty huts.

In my own the mosquitoes were whirring back and forth like helicopters. I massacred them with a folded copy of *Izvestiya* and spread out my sleeping-bag on the wooden bunk, remembering Sasha with warmth. These intense, subterfuge-ridden conversations, snatched in camping-huts or tiny flats, had about them a feel almost of redemption. In them I sensed a weight of fear and suspicion, unconsciously carried all my life, lifting from my shoulders with the ease of a natural event, of something rectified. Then I would realize by the depth of my pleasure how profound the fear had been. All the while, in the asking and answering of questions, it was less the facts that mattered than the human touching, the translation of an abstract people into flesh and spirit.

This ambassadorial glow accompanied me next morning while I strolled about the town. Kalinin was once an imperial staging-post between Leningrad and Moscow, and spread along the Volga with a jaded neo-classical distinction. It was Sunday, and thousands of white, sunbathing bodies turned the riverbanks into beaches. In the Park of Rest and Culture old women were selling red and white gladioli—but Rest was interrupted by loudspeakers pouring out political harangues, to which nobody was listening, and Culture was confined to an outdoor theatre where nothing happened, its seats filled by families staring at its stage with a common expression of emptiness. A board of honour and an avuncular portrait of Lenin presided in the dusty gardens. At a line of outdoor tables middle-aged men were playing chess. Nearby, in a stadium of bumping-cars, the small boys were not shouting and crashing into one another, but circled round and round in a studious and polite ceremony of avoidance, and there was scarcely a noise. Soon the speeches from the loudspeakers were superseded by the marching paeons of a male choir. Archaic, drenched in patriotism, they exhaled a chilling martial bumptiousness and mission. Together with bass folk-songs sung in mock-Chaliapinesque, they were the standard fare for Parks of Rest and Culture, and they pervade my aural memories of Russia in a cold leitmotiv.

I joined a crowd around a group of little girls. Immaculate in frilled dresses and white socks, their hair ballooning with ribbons, they were kneeling round a playground and chalking pictures on the tarmac. The subject of the drawings—it was a competition—was 'Peace'; and the judges, a trio of friendly-faced municipal officials, were being lobbied by possessive mothers. The girls were very quiet. They drew their pictures with the same look of demure solemnity as that with which the small boys avoided one another in bumping-cars. In the corner of each they inscribed their name and age.

I stared eagerly at their compositions, as if to peer into the mind and heart of a whole generation. They were heartbreakingly similar. They portrayed the symbolic Olympic bear Misha—all round ears and cuddly torso—under the slogan 'the Olympics means peace.' A few auxiliary cats and flowers completed the stock of fantasy, and above each picture the five- or eight- or ten-year-old child had inscribed 'Peace' or 'Peace to the World'. They had drawn nothing truly their own.

An elderly man with whom I had spoken before took me gently by the arm. 'You see these,' he said. 'You must understand now how much we want peace. I hope you will go back to your people and tell them.'

Looking into his childlike eyes, I couldn't doubt their sincerity. But I went on gazing at the pictures, hoping for I know not what. Perhaps I was perverse in finding something empty and frightening here. But these designs had not even the naturalness of stick figures or a box house. They were merely taught phrases and symbols, all alike. These children, I felt, might equally well have inscribed 'War', for they were drawing only the government's temporary requirement. They were perfect tools, pure reflections. They were morally neuter. I wanted to tell the man that imbued obedience was the enemy of peace, and that while these white-stockinged innocents were chalking their bears on the tarmac of Kalinin, Soviet gunships were murdering Afghans in the Hindu Kush.

But by now the children had meandered back to their parents or stood in meek groups, looking at the work which they thought was theirs. As I watched their clear faces, I felt a muffled despair. It seemed as if a whole generation were being anaesthetized before my eyes. A single precocious girl had chalked down something different. Her picture showed a bomb escorted by grotesque, top-hatted Americans, whose button eyes squinted above overfed cheeks, crammed with cigars. Above this was inscribed another current state slogan 'No to the American Neutron Bomb', and at its foot 'Drawn by Anna, aged nine.'

Half visible in drizzle for miles ahead, the road dipped and tilted over the light breathings of the plain, pushing to Novgorod through a vista of pastureland and rain-faded forests. I had arrived within sight of the city's lakes, and the first, watery bloom of domes beyond, when a young woman tottered off the verge into the middle of the road and stood with downcast eyes as if embracing death. When I stopped she came and tapped faintly at the car door with her ringed fingers. She was not suicidal but sublimely drunk. She wanted a lift into Novgorod. My passenger seat had been flattened for camping, but she climbed into the back with a wilting bunch of flowers, and twined her arms about my neck as we drove. The arms were soft and slender. But she herself did not possess even the interest of ugliness; she seemed oddly unformed (although she was twenty-two), her eyes callow behind their spectacles. Her talk was a breathless and musical ramble. 'I'm drunk,' she said, without shame. 'But I can show you the way. I'm a crazy person, I ought to tell you. I'm unhappy, that's why, or so my parents say.' She began fondling my ears.

'Where's your boyfriend?' I asked.

'He doesn't write to me. He's a fighter pilot. In Poland. I worry. Oh God, I worry. Where's your girlfriend? Are you alone?' She inspected the car with bovine turnings of her head, as if one of the seats might yield up a woman. Then she returned to my ears. 'I'm so glad I met you. Where shall we go? My parents have just got a new flat. I don't know whether they'll be there or in the old one. . . .'

Framed in my driving mirror and in a limp horseshoe of hair, her bespectacled face presupposed some species of louche and highbrow siren. As we entered Novgorod, she pointed out the sights, her fingernails alternately disinterring and embedding themselves in my shoulders. 'That's the Church of St Somebody . . . and there's the headquarters of the KGB . . . heh-heh . . . I'm not really drunk, or am I? . . . and there's old Lenin. . . .' She gestured ahead with a wavering arm. 'I used to work somewhere over there . . . I still work sometimes

[65]

. . . and sometimes I make love . . . Turn to the right here. . . . Let's try the new flat.' She lowered her spectacles over her chin and pinched her eyes. 'I hope you don't mind me . . . I'll never see you again after tomorrow, I realize that. . . .'

We reached the flat through a rear courtyard, where men were playing backgammon under ragged trees. These huge blocks are a busybody's paradise—we were raked by a crossfire of inquisition as we entered—yet often neighbours do not know one another's names, and the old communal village life finds its grave here. I was relieved to meet the girl's two brothers, struggling with a hillock of unsightly furniture and books in the entrance. She stumbled along the corridors. By Soviet standards the apartment was spacious, and she crooned at the thought of having a bedroom to herself, where previously the whole family had slept in one room.

When I tried to leave, she stared at me with a vague sadness, then begged to be taken to her old flat and sat resolutely in the back of my car again. The tears began to roll down her cheeks and into her mouth. I didn't know what to do. Sexual puritanism here is allied strangely to this peasant frankness, which can be both rude and touching. Many young people, especially, live in a violent chiaroscuro of public prudery and private licence.

Then a Lada saloon drove up beside us. In it were her parents: a stony mother and a bald, bullet-headed father with authoritarian grey eyes.

'That's them,' she said. Her voice had dwindled to a miserable hush. 'They're angry because I'm in a foreign car.'

They were. In the back seat a formidable pair of grandmothers added their Gorgon stare to the barrage of accusation, until the whole car resembled some livid and scandalized hydra, which said not a word. I went up to them to talk, but they stared absolutely through me at their neurotic daughter with a terrible suppressed fury and shame.

And now the girl was beside me. 'Mother'. She knocked with her fingers on their car door as she had on mine. 'Mother. . . .' Trembling, she thrust her straggly bouquet through the quarter-open window. Her mother snatched it and tossed it behind her. The girl turned to me. 'I'll see you tomorrow,' she slurred. 'Good-bye. I think you're so . . . so very. . . .'

She was, I thought later, the most contemporary Russian I had met. She could have been any member of the West's lost young. And Novgorod that evening seemed to sympathize with her, bleakly conscious of its poverty. People were few and hurried in the streets. The voids in the landscape appeared to have intruded into the city, exposing its inhabitants as to some brutal public gaze. Roads, buildings, squares—everything was bigger than the citizens were.

The old town keeps a tended, antiseptic beauty. It is restored, cleaned, petted. The Volhov river cuts it in two. On the west bank the kremlin, its princely heart, erupts from dense trees. On the east a constellation of churches marks the old merchants' quarter. Novgorod, like half these north-western towns, grew up as a trading-post between the Baltic and the Black Sea, and was ruled by the haughty democratic spirit of its *Veche*, an assembly of leading citizens whose parliament, guarded by an octagonal tower, still stands on the river bank. A practical, earthy spirit pervaded the town almost from its beginnings. 'Lord Novgorod the Great', as its citizens named it, was the only republic in Russia. 'If the prince is bad—into the mud with him,' they said. The churches which sprinkle its riverbanks were built not by lords, but by trade guilds. At its height the population stood at four hundred thousand.

The earliest surviving letters of its citizens, jotted down on birch-bark in the fourteenth century, are typically pragmatic. 'Order to Gregory: I've sent you a bucket of sturgeon.' 'Greetings to Father and Mother: When you've sold the house, you can go to Smolensk or Kiev. Bread is cheap there. . . .'

Even its icons betray it. Those of Vladimir and Suzdal, its rivals, are pervaded by a cool, patrician lyricism; their colours are lilac-brown and silver-grey, and their painted prophets seem to be participants in some celestial ballet, choreographed in Constantinople or in paradise. But Novgorod's icons are robust and emphatic, filled with the joy of life. Powerful scarlets, yellows and vivid blue-greens predominate. They are at their most typical when exemplifying action. These are the icons of peasants: warm, sensual, nationalistic. Their Virgins and apostles keep their feet on the ground, and might drive a hard deal; and one suspects that the real stock-in-trade of their shrewd-eyed saints is not human souls, but flax or carpets.

I imagined the features of these canonized shopkeepers reproduced among the modern inhabitants. But it was a different face which looked through my windscreen as I was bedding down in the campsite that evening. Circled in a golden halo of hair and beard, its brown eyes inspected me with a questing puzzlement. I opened the door and the gently leonine face peered in. Its expression was one of mingled diffidence and trustingness.

'You're the Englishman?' Vadim spoke fluent English. He was an

[67]

engineer from a sordid-looking factory nearby, whose guarded gates were plastered with slogans for harder work. He had heard that an Englishman had arrived in Novgorod, and he was anxious for books. Had I, by any chance, the novels of James Hadley Chase? Well then, Dickens or Lawrence. . . .'

'I can't get English novels here, and our own are hopelessly dull.' He settled himself in my car and plucked two bottles of vodka from his pockets. 'Here, let's get drunk. Got a cup?' We swilled alternately from a plastic mug balanced on the hand-brake between us. 'It's coarse stuff,' he said. 'I don't like the taste, I like the oblivion.'

So we started to drink. Vodka—that colourless innocence! It's the curse and liberation of Russia, a self-obliterating escape from tedium and emptiness, from interminable winter nights, and the still longer, darker nights of the soul. It is drunk in furious, catatonic debauches, with the full intention of rendering its drinkers virtually insensible. Bottles are always tipped dry, glasses drained at a gulp. Drunkenness accounts for over half the motor accidents and almost all the murders in the country. It has accelerated infant mortality and drastically reduced the life expectancy of men, whom it lures from their work and leaves crumpled in the doorways of every city in the land. As early as the ninth century, it is said, when the Russians were choosing which religion to embrace, they repudiated teetotal Islam with horror. 'Drinking is the joy of Russia,' declared their prince, 'we just cannot do without it.' And travellers since the sixteenth century were astonished at how the Muscovites seized on alcohol as on some suicidal sport, how state banquets ended with the whole imperial court collapsed under the tables, and how people dropped dead of drink in the streets.

As for me, in no time my head was misted to a beneficent blur on weightless shoulders; my voice became the woodwind section of an orchestra tuning up for symphonies which never took place, and my vision contracted until it encompassed only the cherubic face of my host, which started to gyrate slightly around his sad, brown and still puzzled eyes. We talked about Western pop groups, of which I know nothing at all. Yet I dimly heard myself holding forth on Pink Floyd, The Rolling Stones and several groups which I must have invented. We drank to them all.

Once only Vadim's talk strayed into politics. He said that the Moscow leadership was hopeless, moribund.

I pricked up an inebriate ear. 'Why?' I asked.

'All this propaganda,' he mumbled. 'It makes you puke. Equality! I tell you, there are people living round me who are all but millionaires

[68]

. . . four or five of them. . . . By the way, you know that black American group. . . ? These millionaires don't get rich on salaries, of course . . . they're all in some underground business, selling stuff on the black market. . . . Let's open the other bottle. . . .'

After three hours I drove Vadim back to his home through the dark. I was criminally drunk. I fumbled along the road with mole-like caution, concentrating on the weak-looking blobs thrown by my headlights. Beyond these were only my own and the night's darkness. My head was a gaseous bubble floating in nothing. Praying not to encounter the police, I dropped Vadim two streets short of his house, as he wished. Talking with foreigners was permitted, he said, but not liked. Novgorod was very provincial. We arranged to meet the day after tomorrow, and he vanished shakily into the blackness.

All next morning I lay stretched out with other drunks in the parklands round the town's kremlin. Vodka is said to bequeath no headache to its victims, only a painless anaesthesia, but my head throbbed and filled my eyes with lead. From time to time I would heave them open and gaze across to the long, blistered fortress. It rose from an embankment now deep in shrubs and grass, and circled above a marshy moat filled with butterflies and yellow flowers. Squat wall-towers with witch-hat roofs and mean, barred windows stiffened the hoary circlet of its walls, which curled for a full three-quarters of a mile, enclosing the inner city above its steel-bright river. On the eastern bank the churches of the merchants' quarter bubbled up in a fantasia of wasp-wasted globules and cones, tubular turrets, onion cupolas and spires; and my vodka-dimmed eyes discerned the gutted arcade of a seventeenth century market—a last memory of those lantern-hung booths and multicoloured awnings which once illumined the spices and slaves of Novgorod fair.

A sadness haunts these buildings. They stand in rank grassland, locked and boarded up. Frescoed saints still brood about the walls of the Church of the Transfiguration, but are faded to shadows, their mana gone; and the narthex of St Nicholas Church has been turned into one of those 'atheist museums' so common between the wars—an abusive history of religion culminating in the poster of a black bat of a priest, who holds back his flock while the rocket of modern Soviet technology shoots past them to the moon.

Inside the kremlin the eleventh century cathedral is empty too. Its frescoed Christ gazes down with a lost sweetness. And in the vaulted chambers of the Palace of Facets, glowering with murals, the proud republic of Novgorod met its end. Absorbed by the risen power of

Moscow in 1478, its independent spirit was chained at last by Ivan the Terrible, who slaughtered sixty thousand of its citizens and invited its leading boyars and clergy to a banquet in the palace, where they were massacred in mid-orgy. By the seventeenth century the populace numbered barely two thousand, rustling like ghosts in the shell of a half-forgotten city.

But the most impish fate of all has befallen the Church of the Intercession, glued against one of the kremlin towers. The day before I left for Leningrad, Vadim proposed we meet there for supper. It had been turned into a restaurant. A maze of stairs and storeys twined church and tower indivisibly together. Embalmed in the monastic aura of rough-hewn benches and wrought-iron candelabra, the diners were slopping down *borshch* and *solyanka* where once the incense-blue spaces had thundered to the cherubikon or (if they were in the tower) to some less holy language.

Vadim was nervous. He had booked a table in a shadowy annex, and hoped we could talk unseen. 'I expect people will think you're an Estonian,' he said, comforting himself. Estonians were gaunt and tall like me, he added, and they spoke bad Russian.

For a while we shared the table with the family of an electrician from Baikal near the Mongolian frontier. They had never been to European Russia before, and the restaurant's sophistication cowed them. A lethargic little boy seated opposite asked me to return to Baikal with them and go bear-hunting. This proposal drew a shame-faced rebuke from his mother, who crushed each bubble of initiative as it surfaced through the child's melancholy. 'Don't touch the cutlery . . . Elbows off the table. . . . Don't scratch your neck. . . . Bear-hunting, how *could* you? . . . I'm sure the comrade gets plenty of hunting as it is. . . .'

Vadim was relieved when they left, and suddenly ordered a carousal's worth of drinks: Georgian white wine, brandy, several fruit juices and a jug of mead. He looked as if he were settling in for the night. 'So the vodka hit you badly?' he said. 'Next time you must drink a little more in the morning. It takes away the headache.' He tugged thoughtfully on his panoramic golden whiskers. 'Vodka can cure most things, but can kill you in exchange. We call it "The Green Snake", I don't know why, and drunkenness "the White Fever."' He stared up at the ceiling. 'Do you know this is the first time I've been in a church? My wife wanted a church wedding, but they'd have kicked me out of Komsomol for that.'

Two hours later the mead and the wine were finished, and the brandy gurgling musically in and out of our glasses. Vadim's cheeks were lit by a sunset flush, but his eyes stayed lost. He began to complain about the system. These jeremiads were familiar to me by now. They rang with a deathly boredom and disillusion. No rebellion, no vision. Their cry of hopelessness fell into a world as stifled and changeless as the Soviet earth. Nor was any change expected, although these dirges belonged, above all, to the young. It seemed to me that half the nation's energies were draining away in bitterness or drink, or were never awakened at all.

'Talk of bureaucracy!'—Vadim laced the thought with an instant slug of brandy—'Have you seen our Palace of the Soviets in the main square? Looks like a mountain and houses thousands of administrators, where five would do. We've got ten bosses to every one worker!'

I mumbled something about change.

'Change! How can anything change? Even in elections to the local soviet, which don't mean much anyway, there's no real choice. The two or three candidates are already selected. In theory you can complain about them, but you'd have to go up to a little curtained booth, and everybody would see you go. And of course the KGB would be there.'

This sense of a jungly and unconquerable bureaucracy reaches down to humble levels. An Asiatic stress on the prestige of position has pervaded Russia for centuries. Behind a million desks and shop counters the faces of ensconced bumbledom look up at you—or do not—and clear little spaces of authority around themselves by momentarily refusing service.

Perhaps the mania for supervision is the reverse image of a natural anarchy. I remembered what Nikolai had said in Moscow: that without constraints, the system would fly apart. Only the previous evening I had witnessed a scene which seemed to occur in shadow-play, so noiselessly and totally was it smothered. While walking along one of the town's boulevards, I saw three vans converge on a corner. A minute later eight or ten factory workers were being thrust inside by police and auxiliaries in red arm-bands. Their movements, as they vanished, showed only a dogged resignation, except for one tall man who shouted something inaudible to me and was at once seized by both wrists and hustled after the rest. Farther down the street I saw other police vans imbibing other victims. A minute later they had gone, leaving me with the uncanny feeling of having woken from a dream. The boulevard, meanwhile, had emptied. The only witness left besides myself was a lame roadworker; but when I asked him the cause he merely said 'They're taking them off in scores,' and turned away. But for a few eerie seconds a gap had opened in the placid surface of the everyday world, then closed again. It was unexplained: a Kafkaesque dumb-show. Victims and persecutors had seemed to collaborate together, so silently and inevitably did it pass. Such moments are sinister for their secrecy. They will probably never be reported.

'It's true that we learn to read between the lines of our newspapers,' said Vadim, who knew nothing of the incident, 'but how can we know if even the lines aren't there?'

Later, before we parted, and perhaps regretting his own long *cri de coeur* over his country and his city, he suddenly said: 'But I love Novgorod more than anywhere else in the world. Our people are mostly good here, you know, and I think we lose something by leaving. Years ago I had a girlfriend who married a lorry-driver from Amsterdam, and emigrated. The first time she came back to visit us she was homesick. But later she returned with her nose in the air. Oh God! She'd taken a slimming course and lost kilos! She'd been a big strong girl before, and now she looked like a ghost—a sort of artifice, I can't explain. She thought we were all mad to stay in Novgorod, and she gave us expensive presents as if she pitied us. But I looked at her and I thought: how strange, what has happened to her? She wants us to become like her, but is she better? What is she?'

He poured out the last of the brandy. I too could imagine the girl, her homely peasant looks fined down to mimic European manikins, her Mongol cheekbones rouged to Western colour, her mind and emotions grown more circumspect: less rude, less slow, less candid (but it was only a guess). I too doubted if she were 'better'. Appearances and material things still seem to interest the Russians only in some shallow part of them. Objects may be acquired with bitterly-won time and money, but will be given or feasted away with scarcely a thought in a burst of exuberance or a maudlin lapse. They exist in the service of feeling or of friendship: it is a proud and primitive state. And when I looked at Vadim across the bottle-strewn table—the meal must have cost him three days' salary—he too seemed still to belong to this peasant aristocracy.

But now it was late. The doorway behind us showed a cold quadrangle of stars. We toasted the people of each other's countries for the last time, and stumbled out into the whispering grass and meandering footpaths of the kremlin.

4. Leningrad

LENINGRAD IS LIKE no other city in Russia or on earth. It seems to reject the half-Asiatic hinterland on whose rim it hangs, and to have exchanged this troubled parentage for the grace of eighteenth century Europe. On the northernmost limits of the ancient Byzantine world, it lies like a pale and beautiful question-mark. In 1917 the Bolsheviks repudiated it as capital, and it is touched now by the sad, patrician glow of an Istanbul or an Alexandria. However important its present, its past seems to saturate it. Bathed in the lost harmony of Europe, it symbolizes the paradoxical leaning of Russia towards the West, spurred by an atavistic dread of China and a centuries-old longing for civilized recognition.

Whereas the streets of most old Russian cities radiate out from a crumbling or vanished kremlin, those of Leningrad echo the centripetal grace of its canals. As I drove in deeper, its office and apartment blocks gave way to a glimmer of nineteenth century mansions, seedy and blemished now, along the outer waterways. Then, in an ever-tightening rhythm of alternate water and stone, the city's heart came beating round in its saddened splendour. All the way to where the Neva river wound beneath a rank of water-reflecting palaces, and the Gulf of Finland opened to the west, canals and avenues succeeded one another in long, shining arcs of ever-increasing beauty.

Leningrad ineluctably has been called the Venice of the North. In fact it resembles Venice little more than Paris or London does. No Mediterranean warmth overhangs the measured glory of its canals, but a clean, unenchanted Nordic light. Palace follows palace, terrace follows terrace, with the impersonal radiance of a Bach cantata. All is cool, balanced, spacious. Under a coldly luminous sky, the thousands of quiet dwellings line the waters without appearing to partake of them. Even in summer the fogs and ice of the Neva seem to pervade the streets. These mansions reject any charm of southern ornament or light, and hold their place by elegance of proportion alone. Here and there the curve of a pedimented window or a lightly-moulded frieze

[73]

breaks the stone serenity, but all the rest is a soft interplay of chromatic squares and rectangles. Their colours are wintry pale—gentle and reticent in the summer sunlight, as I first saw them: pastel yellows, ochres and oranges. The quays and pavements beneath are shod in pink-grey granite, and the bridges reach over the canals in single spans of handsomely-wrought iron, forged with winged heads and long-redundant coats-of-arms.

All through the city's heart it is breathtaking. From across the river the palaces shine with an unspoilt, eighteenth century refinement. It seemed a crime to motor here, but for a while I drove about in blithe exhilaration. Trams and concertina-like Hungarian buses wobbled along the streets; but often the ways were half deserted. In every other lane my car would hit a heaving slipstream of cobbles. Open manholes gaped without warning in the middle of the thoroughfares, and twice I nearly dropped the car into one. Every street was a long, seductive ambush. Tram-lines erupted like swords from their cobbled beds; and once I almost crashed into one of the black official limousines, bullying its way down a road's centre.

But the city was not built for cars, and the next day I lapsed into a directionless roaming. Soviet Leningrad faded away and I indulged a dream of tsarist St Petersburg. The treacle-brown waterways, the granite pavements under my feet, the street lamps with their embossed bases and politely dangling brackets, filled me with the balm of an old and recognizable world.

Yet increasingly I realized that the city was, in its way, profoundly Russian. In its vista-hung perspectives and its avenues breaking into lake-like squares, in the endless frontages of institute and palace modulated by battalioned columns and flanked by enormous, almost unpeopled gardens, the size of the land itself seemed to boom and resound like the sea. The yellow brick of modern Moscow seemed realigned into expanses equally enormous, whose characteristic pale yellow stucco could be as forbidding and remote as a Stalinist sky-scraper. Then as now this impersonal vastness was the public face of Russia. Its voice, if it had one, intoned an unmistakable *Net*. And all the canals and looking-glass mansions, in their courtly but firm way, were saying *Net* too.

Even then the prestige of size seemed to mesmerize the nation. Buildings became symbols. Along the 25-acre parklands of the Field of Mars, a Palladian salient of barracks sweeps for literally hundreds of yards. A mammoth 768-windowed crescent of imperial offices encloses the southern façade of the fifteen-hundred-roomed Winter Palace.

The nearby Admiralty, on whose site ten thousand men laboured in the time of Peter the Great, rises to a height of almost two hundred feet. St Isaac's Cathedral is more than half as tall again, and once held congregations of thirteen thousand, while that of Our Lady of Kazan was built as the third largest cathedral in the world, to rival St Peter's in Rome. Such buildings, I think, once occupied the same place in the national heart as do today's Bratsk High Dam or Kama River Truck Plant. They belong to the gigantism of a people troubled, in their most secret selves, by fears of inferiority—a nation which centuries of Tartar domination held back from Europe.

St Petersburg itself was founded by the eruptive energies of a man furious to catch up. Almost single-handed, Peter the Great heaved his country out of its mediaeval sleep and hurled it into the scientific age; and although he only accelerated a process already tentatively begun, and left his revolution insecure, Russia was never the same again. He overhauled the army and created the navy—his passion—out of nothing, developed industry tenfold and recast the entire administration, producing a new technical and professional élite. The whole nation was set to work. Its noblemen and gentry were tied to government service for life by being conscripted into a meritocracy graded into fourteen ranks, starting at the bottom.

So the old aristocratic order ended. But from this new 'Table of Ranks', it seems, there developed that stultifying snobbery of grade, that corrupt bureaucracy obsessed with petty formalities, which has oppressed the country ever since. It is perhaps the Russians' very inexpertize at such work, their disinterest in everyday data, which has translated them into this unwieldly officialdom. Bureaucracy has multiplied precisely because they are so bad at it. Marx wrote that under Communism the state itself would wither away; but here it has proliferated and ramified like stinging nettles.

Peter the Great had no patience with such dilatoriness. In fact he had no patience with anything. He blew gale-force through his country's past. Nothing and nobody escaped him. He modernized its orthography and calendar and forced his upper classes to abandon their lapping beards and ankle-length caftans for Western dress, sometimes shearing off their hair and sleeves himself in a frenzy of urgency. He commanded their secluded wives to appear at court thrust into Parisian dresses. 'They all sit as though they were dumb', remarked an ambassador, 'and do nothing but look at each other.'

As for St Petersburg, it was a pure creation of the emperor's will. Raised on stone and wooden piles among the marshy islets of his newly-conquered bridgehead on the Baltic, this 'window on Europe' became a base for Peter's infant navy and a self-consciously Western capital. Exposed to sudden floods and sunk in a lacework of streams, its birth was a nightmare. Peter drove on its builders like a flail. They were marched here in tens of thousands under armed guard from all over the empire. Shelterless and half starved, thousands died of dysentery and scurvy, or were swept away by flood. They deserted in hordes. But thousands more were marched up to replace them; and the nobility, who hated the site, were forced by imperial decree to live and build stone houses there. 'On one side the sea,' moaned a court jester, 'on the other sorrow, on the third moss, on the fourth a sigh.'

Peter himself supervised his capital's creation from a three-room cottage, which was later enshrined in a stone shelter by Catherine the Great; and his modest summer palace, its rooms friendly with Dutch tiles and stoves, still occupies the gardens which he peopled with statues transported from Rome and Venice. Under the towering shadow of oak and plane trees, these sculptured gods and demi-gods, Greek heroes and Roman emperors, pose and lounge and slumber on their plinths in all the graceful prolixity of the ancient world. If there is a true Park of Rest and Culture in the nation, it is perhaps this one, for the classical pantheon kept open house, and tolerantly enrolled whatever extra gods came along. Even now the abstract postures and secret smiles of its statues do not caution the passer-by into lipservice, like the bitter ideologies which followed them. Burly workers on holiday, portly ladies in astonishing hats, children, *babushkas* (grandmothers), old soldiers, all go past unsolicited, or stop to examine the statues like people striving to read a foreign language.

Peter the Great, predictably, engaged in pagan tippling here. Visiting gentlemen and their ladies might suddenly find themselves locked in, then be whirled up by the czar and his cronies in an obligatory drinking debauch of Bacchic enormity. For this awesome wild beast of a man could tolerate little court life, and no ceremonial at all. Impetuous, coarse, hugely physical, he surrounded himself with gifted foreigners and upstart Russians, shipwrights and proletarian mistresses, and eventually married the daughter of a Lithuanian peasant. On all these, mindless of their age or sex or rank, he would shower hugs, blows, kisses and tears in a blinding rainbow of emotions. Ungovernable fits of violence would set him smashing the faces of his advisers with a cudgel or bare hands, or hurling them to the floor and kicking them in a paroxysm of impatience. His voracious fascination with practical crafts pitched him into the sciences of gunnery and engineering, fortification, stone-masonry, metalwork, woodturning, paper-making, leatherwork, etching and engraving. He was driven on by a ravening, barbarian intelligence. He made his own boots, his own furniture, his own boats. Yet his handwriting was appalling and he could barely spell. The official regimen of his reign was filled with a counterpoint of patriotic object-lessons and grotesque horseplay; blasphemous religious ceremonies mingled with Roman-style military triumphs, dwarfs' weddings, titanic firework displays, public flagellations and beheadings, open debauches, prestigious ship-launchings, furious drunkenness.

In the Winter Palace sits an extraordinary lifesize waxwork of the emperor, moulded by the Florentine Carlo Rastrelli. The clothes it wears, perhaps even its hair, are Peter's own, and its face, hands and feet were cast from wax impressions immediately after his death. It is an outlandish, threatening figure. The man himself seems to confront you. Propped tense and upright in its chair, the great gangling body—he was six foot, seven inches tall—appears on the brink of springing up. The intemperance of a Vesuvius infuses his whole frame. The strangely delicate hands agitate on the chair-arms; their fingers seem to be drumming. His clothes of blue and gold have faded now—appropriate to a man happiest in darned stockings and shabby coats whose pockets he stuffed with state papers. His lanky shins end in small, oddly slender feet. The whole body projects a weirdly mingled grossness and delicacy.

But stranger still is the emperor's face, for this, too, is in almost unbearable suspense. Its cheeks are unindented, sickly yellow, and his dark brown hair hangs disordered. From under strongly-marked brows the slightly dislocated eyes shine with paranoid intensity. The whole countenance is listening, straining to understand, but barely able to delay the primitive explosions of the body. The features and neck seem on the point of being convulsed by the ferocious tic which preceded his anger. All the gaunt strength of the frame, the manic stress of its limbs, the small, intolerant mouth, attest a brilliant and half-evolved savage, suspended between the will to comprehend and the passion to act.

Such a figure hints that the Westernization of Russia, even in its reformer, went barely skin-deep. And the impression lingers. In 1698, while already championing European civilization, Peter took part in the inquisitorial torture and beheading of rebels, whose flayed backs were roasted over slow flames and whose corpses were hanged in hundreds around Moscow's gates and kremlin. Even as St Petersburg was rising from its marshes in the borrowed panoply of Athens, he had his own son Alexis beaten to death for conspiracy. His subjects enjoyed no true

[77]

rights at all. The emperor was an autocrat, and Russia his personal estate, just as it had been the estate of Ivan the Terrible more than a century and a half before, when an English ambassador wonderingly contrasted Russian servitude with the sturdy rebelliousness of his own countrymen.

Some sense of underlying rusticity in the life of St Petersburg troubled the more acute Western visitors always. At its best it showed itself in bursts of informality and frankness, as in those annual balls to which noblemen and peasants were invited equally—'the Emperor in gold and jewels elbowed by his lowest born subjects,' wrote an astonished Englishwoman. Those who were not dazzled into blindness by the endless banqueting and polonaising, by the rolling of four thousand carriages and the masked balls for twenty thousand guests, noted that the Russians' French dress was not matched by French suavity, that wife-beating was universal, that the children were rickety and the aristocracy, in Macaulay's words, 'dripping pearls and vermin.' An Anglo-Irish lady wrote cruelly in 1805: 'Have you ever seen a clumsy, romping, ignorant girl of twelve years old with a fine Parisian cap on her head? So seems to my eye this imperial realm.' She gave Russia five or six centuries to catch up.

The same witness wrote, more darkly, that the Russian despotism corrupted morality by equating good and evil merely with favour and disgrace—much as modern Communists may conceive of service to the Party. The crabby Marquis de Custine left a picture from the nineteenth century which resounds with the unhappiness of the twentieth. Fear of the truth, he said, was ubiquitous. The past itself had become undiscoverable. Thought was a crime.

Reminders of old cruelties touch the beauty of Leningrad with a sombre caution. In the red bulk of the Mihailov Castle, a forbidding confection of granite and stone honeycombed with secret passages, the half-mad emperor Paul was throttled by noblemen in league with his son. Near the north bank of the Neva the island-fort of SS. Peter and Paul lours across the river. Its ramparts and bastions march faceless into the water, while above them one of those golden spikes which the Russians love gleams in the air like a poisoned rapier. Under its cathedral's dome the later tsars and tsaritsas lie in cold, desanctified splendour, entombed under white sarcophagi nailed with gold crosses. They are neither reviled nor revered. Only round the grave of Peter the Great a vase or two of red and white carnations withers. The fortress dungeons held all the early revolutionaries: Bakunin, Pisarev, Gorky; Dostoevsky too. Peter the Great's son was killed here. Outside its walls

[78]

the five leaders of the 1825 revolution were incompetently executed. ('They can't even hang a man properly in Russia,' groaned one, as he fell to the ground with only his legs broken.) Now the dungeons are a Soviet showpiece, where delegations from Cuba and Gabon tramp and shiver and make notes of whatever their guides are telling them. All the imported and native architectural beauties of St Petersburg—the inspired flamboyance of Bartolommeo Rastrelli, the neo-classical groupings of Rossi—cannot quell a rankling unease, a feeling that too close behind this European harmony the darkness of an older Russia looms unresolved.

Through the slightest of introductions my days in Leningrad were warmed by an exuberant couple who adopted me with proprietorial completeness, fed me, got me drunk, guided me, washed my clothes. Lucia and Anatoly both worked in theatre administration. He was fifty years old, half Armenian—a plump, ebullient man whose face was usually crumpled in a look of benignity. But his eyes, set deep in their warm wrinkles, were intelligent and faintly irascible, and when he spoke to business colleagues over the telephone, his voice sharpened into unrecognizable authority. Lucia was much younger than him, and beautiful. Fair, regular, hers was a classic Russian face. Her blue-grey eyes shone far apart and her cheekbones stood Tartar-high. She came from an old Leningrad family. Before the Revolution her grandmother had attended the Smolny Institute, the school for young noblewomen founded by Catherine the Great, and had survived afterwards as a teacher. Some heritage of sophistication clung about Lucia. She was perfectly conscious of her beauty. She was tinged, too, with a Chek-hovian boredom and dreaminess, and was faintly contemptuous of much that lay about her, as if she instinctively measured it by a Europe which she had never seen.

She and Anatoly lived in a nineteenth century apartment house in the city's centre, four storeys up magisterial stone steps with elaborate iron banisters, dark and filthy now, the windows cracking. Their three-room flat looked down into an echoing courtyard piled with crates. The living-room was monopolized by two huge beds raised on blocks of wood. The curtains were gossamer thin. Heavy furniture stood about, its drawers crammed with worn blankets, pillows, books. A budgerigar perched dumb in a cage. There were no carpets, no ornaments, no pretence at decoration at all. The Russian aesthetic sense seemed to have died with Lucia's ancestors.

This was nothing unusual. Everyone I had met lived in the same

[79]

discomfort. The strangeness lay in the outward sophistication of the couple—they dressed elegantly and owned a Volga car—and the wretchedness of their home.

'This was how the poor used to live,' Anatoly said. 'But we're all poor now. One day we'll get round to painting the place, but we've no time.' He glanced up to where a jagged crack split the ceiling. 'Getting hold of a builder needs an all-out campaign in Leningrad. The best hope is to find a man moonlighting from his job. I'll probably repair the place myself.'

That first evening, as we stared down into the resonant courtyard, I imagined that they were satisfied and slightly privileged. Their Volga saloon gleamed below us beside my dust-glazed Morris. I gently probed them. Was it an embarrassment, I asked, if their neighbours noticed they were entertaining a foreigner? But Anatoly shrugged this away. 'Maybe in somewhere like Novgorod people get afraid. But here they're used to it. Anyway, we don't know our neighbours.' He lapsed into silence. From out of the darkness came sounds of splintering glass and shouting where (he said) the police were probably breaking up crowds around a drink shop open after hours. I muttered something about the numbers of police in Leningrad.

'The more police there are, the better,' Anatoly said bluntly. 'Without them we'd never have any quiet.'

Lucia prepared a supper which was even more costly in time than in money: tongue, black caviare, smetana, cucumber, champagne. She had also procured seats for the Kirov Ballet, which had extended its season into late summer. Such tickets were gold-dust. She and Anatoly obviously wielded *blat*—influence, 'clout'—which is more important than money and which becomes a weapon in the hands of almost anybody from a doorman to a marshal. Jokingly, tentatively, I said that half the Kirov stars—Nureyev, Makarova, Baryshnikov—had defected to the West, and that I'd be interested to see the other half.

'It's better that we lose those stars,' Lucia said, 'and that the world gains them.' It was an extraordinary remark for a Russian, to whom the outer world is so shadowy and their own so passionately loved.

Surprised and still formal, I murmured that I hoped the West and the Soviet Union were drawing closer together; it was good that we should grow like one another. Yet it seemed to me that the new forces arising in Russia—all the separations of wealth and privilege—were precisely those which coarsened the West, and that our richer freedoms scarcely counted here at all.

'Grow like one another?' Anatoly laughed, then said very calmly: 'It's

[80]

better only that we should grow like you.' Either this remark or the champagne uncorked a river of sorrows from him. 'We had a golden age in Kruschev's time—then the axe came down in 1968 after the invasion of Czechoslovakia. And we've never recovered.' He turned the radio to the forbidden Voice of America as if in revenge, and settled back in his chair. 'Do you know that some lunatics here even want the Stalin days back? If that happened, Lucia and I wouldn't be here at all, and you wouldn't be sitting with us. As for television and radio, God knows. . . . Even now our only way of getting at the truth is often *that*.' He cocked an ear at Voice of America, which was jammed a few days later. 'Our newspapers preach at us as if we were kids.'

Many Russians had learnt to interpret the news in their own way. An instinctive mental sieve separated the facts from the trappings. From sheer boredom rather than disbelief, they ignored the turgid editorials of national self-congratulation, which painted a Marxist universe of class conflict, Capitalist conspiracy and a Soviet Motherland encircled by enemies. They tended instead to read the little news items: pure, important facts, and they took it for granted that big news often went unprinted, just as it had in tsarist times. In their own lives, after all, they practised the same techniques. With automatic double-think, they used one language to express their opinions in public, and quite another among their close friends. However much ordinary people might accept the general tenor of propaganda (and they did), and whatever their ignorance of the West (and it was profound), they found it hard, on some deeper or emotional level, to hate the individual. The concept of the West might be abhorrent, but the Westerner himself was human and susceptible, and the Russians' open nature embraced him, at least in my experience, with an immediacy which was the more touching because it flew in the face of everything they had been taught.

Among the educated a growing disillusion with the leadership had turned people more sceptical of the media still. 'Do you know,' Anatoly asked me with mock solemnity, 'the collected works of Brezhnev? Yes, six or seven volumes full of political hogwash. As if we didn't have enough. . . .'

'You've read them?'

'I?' He looked quite angry. 'Do you take me for a fool? I wouldn't touch them. *Nobody* buys or reads them.' He dismissed the subject with an admonitory flourish of the champagne bottle. 'No, I'm reading something else, published in *samizdat*—underground literature, you know. It's called *Animal Farm*, by a man named Orwell. . . .'

The last of the champagne splashed into our glasses, easing us into

[81]

drowsiness. Lucia was giggling to herself at the thought of Anatoly reading Brezhnev. 'Guess who it was,' he said, 'who wrote that a censored press corrupts its government and forces the people into living private lives?' He puffed up a cynical cloud of cigarette smoke. 'Marx.'

Next Sunday I went through deserted streets to morning liturgy at the Monastery of Alexander Nevsky, Leningrad's oldest religious foundation, whose eleven churches and four cemeteries lift in a baroque fanfare at the end of Nevsky Prospect. Along the winding paths old women were begging alms from churchgoers, or wandered under the trees to gather herbs, crossing themselves from time to time to exorcise their theft. A faint smell of incense clung about the graves and lingered in the sky. Tchaikovsky was buried here under the maple trees, and Borodin and Mussorgsky side by side; Rimsky-Korsakov lies under a fat, Celtic-looking cross, and Dostoevsky beneath a bed of crimson begonias.

Incense billowed through the cathedral doors and drifted in the cavernous nave like the breath of God. Everything inside glittered and swam in a miasma of intensified colour, where priests and acolytes and the limned saints of a hundred icons inhabited the same universe of mystery and hope. I felt as if I had strayed into the illuminated pages of a mediaeval psalter, or as if a trapdoor had opened in the plain, material world to which Russia had condemned itself, and dropped me into this other, secret stratum of its soul.

The congregation packed rank on rank against the railings before the iconostasis. It must have numbered over a thousand. Most of the people were old women, some minute in size, all cowled in head-scarves. But I saw groups of young men too, and girls on their mothers' arms. Beside me a bearded student was bowing with the fervour of a desert anchorite; not far away stood three army officers and an airman.

But nothing seemed farther from the ancient religious roots of Russia than the eighteenth century glamour of this cathedral. The saints did not stare from their panels with the grave stillness of Byzantium, nor lurk behind their candles in flickering zones of fire, blackened by the kisses of the faithful. Instead, the nave unfolded about the congregation in an elegant counterpoint of pilasters and fluted columns. The painted prophets and apostles postured in gilded frames or processed across the iconostasis with archangels of Renaissance beauty and earthliness, while high above, a Pantheon-like dome surmounted the chancel in a coronation of light.

[82]

But this aura of religious theatre is half appropriate. The Orthodox rite itself is like a rambling and timeless mystery-play. For more than thirteen hundred years scarcely a syllable of its liturgy has changed. It proceeds with a leisurely pomp which is infused by the victory of a resurrected God rather than by the guilt and tension of alienated men. Its mood of intimate sorcery was all about me now. Through the fog of incense and filtered sunlight the sturdy priests, lapped in a flood of black beards and dalmatics, came and went with the glitter and solemnity of wizards, while from a gallery behind us the dying tones of the choir filled the nave with their antiphonal sadness.

In a side-aisle, lying in an open coffin, an old woman awaited burial, her feet couched in flowers. Dressed in embroidered peasant gown and scarf, she seemed comfortably ensconced among the congregation, many of whom were as pale as she. All through the liturgy they crossed and recrossed themselves in rippling commotion. Then they would move about the aisles as if at home, buying candles, chewing bread, kissing favourite icons, their frames, their feet. They would gossip in corners, then assemble with old friends to murmur condolence around the coffin, saying how nice she looked. A familiar and easy-going reverence embalmed every act and enrolled the whole congregation— living and dead—into the household of God. Sometimes an old woman, bent double in her shabby overcoat, would creep among the gleaming priests to perform some cherished office: the placing of a lectern or a stool. Then, at one of those points of unruffled climax which pulse like waves through the liturgy—the Triple Great Blessing, the Entrance of the Book or of the Host—half the congregation would stumble to the floor, touching their foreheads to its stone.

This deep, communal spirit of the Orthodox Church is not exclusive to Russia. Its essence can be felt at any country liturgy of Greeks or Christian Arabs. But it serves and prolongs the ancient Russian instinct for *sobornost*, 'togetherness', and was inherited in the tenth century with all the calm of a completed journey. For Orthodoxy arrived in Russia with its theology already petrified. Intellectual strife had faded from it. It was a family, a tradition, a womb—far removed from the vigorous dialectic of the Latin West. To the Orthodox, confession and redemption were collective, and the endless liturgical plea 'O Lord, forgive me!' was gradually to lose its urgency and become the gentle talismanic password of today, like a hand outstretched against the Evil Eye.

The Russian need of *sobornost* seems to hark back to that old Slavic assembly, the *Mir*, which acted as the heart and conscience of a village. Its decisions, like those of Party conferences, had always to be unanimous. Any dissenter was a heretic, a threat. The collective was an end in itself, within which the individual lost—or attained—his meaning. To conceive of an allegiance beyond it required a leap of the imagination too immense for thought. 'The *Mir* cannot be judged,' they said. And to those who fell momentarily outside its pale, it contained absolute powers of forgiveness and redemption. The parallels with the Communist Party, as well as with the Church, are abundant.

Idly, in the middle of the liturgy, I followed a *babushka* who was carrying a sheaf of gladioli down a stairway at the back of the cathedral. The chanting above us faded away. I traversed a corridor and found myself outside the crypt. The woman had disappeared. Then, as I pushed through the doorway, a hideous, chthonic screaming exploded around me. It echoed and vibrated in the vaults like the howling of caged animals. The whole crypt was strewn with babies' garments, towels, dummies, diapers, toys. Such a wailing, screeching and whimpering seemed to herald a Herodian massacre rather than a Christian baptism. But I now saw that in the centre of the crypt a huge priest was remorselessly dunking babies in a silver tub. Mothers and grandmothers cooed and chirruped at their bellowing progeny, joggled and gurgled and jingled toys for their diversion. But the screaming raged like a fever. The infants were subjected to a pitiless triple immersion. 'Katya is baptised in the name of the Father, Amen. . . .' boomed the priest, and the baby's yells suddenly stopped as she vanished into the water then was lifted gleaming and bawling again into the light, only to be plunged implacably down 'in the name of the Son, Amen.' Once more she rose to swell the cacophony round her, her small eyes dilated in horror and her mouth blowing cloudy bubbles at either corner. Only the adults, clutching candles, looked pleased with her progress. But no sooner had the name of the Son roused her to a pitch of blubbering outrage than she was plummeted into the water and salvaged for the third time, reduced by the Holy Ghost to a whimpering, grey-white papoose. Fourteen infants were baptised in this pandemonium, and touched with oil on forehead, hands and feet, with six elder children who lifted long skirts and trousers coyly for their anointing. Then the parents and children together circumambulated the font—well-dressed and dowdy side by side, all beaming, all peaceful. The mass expulsion of original sin had shrivelled the babes-in-arms to a cyclorama of wet, distorted faces, eyes pinched with misery and mouths puckered in a stunned reverie.

Some baptisms are undertaken for reasons of sentiment and tradition rather than belief. But others are held in secret. Nobody knows how many Christians remain in Russia. In this empire of more than 260 million, perhaps thirty-five million are believers. But there are no true statistics. Bitterly persecuted in the twenties and thirties, and again by Kruschev, the Church is enjoying a quiet revival now, tolerated as a conservative moral force and as part of the immemorial personality of the Motherland.

The monotony of ordinary life may invest the contrasting liturgy with a magical allure—or render it brutally redundant. When I returned to the nave after the robust goings-on in the crypt, I stared with a renewed wonder at its *mise en scène*. It might have erupted into the present by a time-warp. Drifting in their immemorial sacrament, holding up crossed candles and golden fans, the long-haired and green-robed acolytes seemed as meaningless and effete as Byzantine angels. Despite the huge congregation, the nave spread half-empty. The place looked threatened and evanescent, the people so old. The chanting rose and fell with unbearable melancholy. Even the singing priest, his head thrown back for the Hymn of Heavenly Victory, intoned in the swallowed bass of a Chaliapin, as if his anthem sounded from the grave. Then the central gates of the iconostasis opened. Above them the holy dove spread its wings in an explosion of gold cloud and flame. And within, lifted high beyond the priest-crowded altar, the aged metropolitan of Leningrad leant like a wintry emperor on his pastoral stave and prayed in a tiny, faraway voice. His robes were of etiolated gold. He seemed almost faded away. It was as if the very epicentre of all this cathedral, of religion, and of God Himself, were a fluting whisper. Under the globular crown the silver-bearded face, framed in its white sanctuary, might have been speaking a mile or a millennium off.

For half an hour the people queued to receive communion by chalice and spoon, kissing the hands of the officiating priests. Then the metropolitan came shuffling down the aisle towards the exit, touching the foreheads of the women who surged forward for a blessing. I was almost crushed against him in the rush. Now, as they marched through us, the magisterial priests and ethereal acolytes turned to flesh and blood. They lost their numen and became what they were: portly peasants in fancy dress. The metropolitan himself was divested of majesty, and looked mundane as he fumbled past—a weak-faced old man. The theatre was over. It only remained for the old lady in her coffin to be committed to eternal life. Her friends kissed her on the brow—one weeping, comforted by a stately husband—and the lid was clamped over her.

Birth, marriage, death—there is no state ritual which can invest such moments with the same perspective as the Church does. Secular funerals are desultory affairs, and state-run weddings ring hollow: not because God is not there—that cannot be helped—but because a spurious effort is made to keep the trappings of religiosity where the promises of religion don't apply.

One day I added myself ashamedly to a group which was mounting the staircase of the 'wedding palace' on the Neva. Only little parties of relatives and friends attend these ceremonies, and this group perhaps numbered thirty in all. Tchaikovsky's Number One Piano Concerto sounded from behind a gilded screen as we ascended. Then we filed into a gallery, lining it on either side, and I took note of my adoptive relations. The same look of wooden uneasiness pervaded them all. They appeared pleasant but not very happy. Their gaze drifted incuriously over me. The men wore best suits in bland colours. Their hair was plastered down. Most of them fidgeted with a carnation or two, while the women, in short, styleless dresses, cradled bouquets of gladioli.

Then, from nowhere discernible, sounded the muffled blare of Mozart's Jupiter Symphony, the doors at the end of the gallery flew open, and in trudged a fat young couple—she in white, he in a lumpish brown suit. They looked wholesome and embarrassed, as if they were causing too much bother. The bride had a homely face, on which the lipstick and eye-shadow stood out like a betrayal. The next moment they were marching between our lines, which murmured and smiled, and we were crowding behind them into a chandeliered hall. In its centre the registry desk inevitably suggested an altar; but behind it, in place of an ordained priest, stood a swarthy, cross-eyed girl in dark green, who announced the couple's marriage with constant references to the Soviet Socialist Motherland, which sanctified their union. Seated on chairs behind them, their friends and relatives betrayed no pleasure, no tears, nothing at all. The couple were declared man and wife. But instead of the linked crowns and processional symbolism of the Orthodox rite, the Soviet national anthem played. Everybody stood to attention, except a deaf *babushka* who remained comfortably overflowing her chair. The couple signed the register among the strains of Rachmaninov, exchanged rings, and it was over.

I stared at the relatives as they lumbered together for their formal embraces, and hoped to be taken for a remote and unkissable Estonian cousin. The married couple accepted congratulations with dissociated smiles, and we proceeded back down the stairs in silence. I felt vaguely stricken. As we descended, I glanced back and saw another couple entering the gallery to the Jupiter Symphony. The affair had taken little more than ten minutes. The portentous music, palatial rooms and sacerdotal desk; the intense, worthy but inescapably unimportant clerk; the Soviet State presiding in place of God—all had thrown an inflated ceremonial around the precarious human promise of a bewildered man and woman. They suggested perspectives of eternity and moral absolutes which were forever gone. Something very simple and austere, I thought, would have been better, more fitting. But perhaps, if nobody had tried to recreate God under the chandeliers, I would have felt subtly cheated. There was no pleasing me.

The next evening, in a southern suburb of the city, I was flagged down for breaking one of the innumerable petty traffic laws which obsess the police. A gawkish young officer gave me a polite warning, then fell to discussing the speed and horsepower of my car. But after a minute somebody else emerged behind him: a thick-set man with crisp black hair, dressed in a black raincoat. He murmured something to the policeman, who backed away and vanished. Then he turned to me. Instead of speaking, he shouted. His questions detonated like pistol-shots. Where had I come from, where was I going to, where were my papers, why was I in this zone of Leningrad?

I did not have to ask what he was. I mumbled confused answers, resorting to worse Russian than I knew. In fact I was on my way to visit a known dissident.

Why was I not in the tourist part of the city? Where was I staying? Where was my *group*? I looked back at him numbly. His stare was a power-drill. I vaguely wondered in what degree such men were insensitive, cruel or patriotic; but I came to no conclusion. Then, after I had answered his questions, he smiled, walked backwards as if he were on a parade ground, and the next moment had merged with the crowd.

I gazed after him. The surface of Russian life had suddenly cracked open under my feet. Just as abruptly it had closed up again, but the ground no longer looked the same. I was disgusted to remember in the man's smile a trace of charm.

I drove through an abyss of empty streets on my way to the dissident, constantly checking that I was not followed. After I had entered his flat-block, I lingered under the well of the stairs like a thug in a low-grade movie; but nobody entered after me. I was thoroughly unnerved.

Volodya, like most dissidents, had been deprived of his job, and lived in one room of a shared flat. He was slight and high-strung—a shadow of a man, whose expression was so crestfallen that I could not imagine any strength in him. Yet he had been prominent in a disbanded human rights movement, he published underground literature, and had been harassed by the KGB for years in an unspectacular way. His room was crowded with seven or eight young men and girls, seated on cushions against the walls. A bloom of youth and hopefulness hung over them, permeating their conversation, glowing in their eyes. They were teachers, part-time artists and playwrights. Volodya, twenty years older than any, sat among them with his frail legs crossed in front of him. When he spoke, which was rarely, they listened to him intently. They held his intellect, his age and his sufferings in quiet awe, and when I compared his wrenched face to their clear ones, I was moved by the depth and cruelty of the divide which separated them.

They chattered with the sureness of undergraduates about underground art exhibitions and *samizdat*. I was sitting next to a would-be playwright who veered every few minutes between buoyancy and pessimism. He was trying to push his play through the multiple layers of censorship, and had already penetrated seven of them; but he reckoned he had several more to go. 'Of course the play's not openly critical of the system. I'd have to be a lunatic to try that. It's a kind of fable. Serious plays nowadays conceal themselves as something else—they masquerade as fairy stories or bits of harmless history. But by the time the censors have finished with them they're unrecognizable anyway.'

Volodya thrust a sheaf of bound papers into my hands. 'This is what I do.' It was a copy of the religio-cultural *samizdat* journal which he published. I fingered eagerly through it. It exuded the peculiar mana of all Russian underground literature—cobweb-thin foolscap pages of blurred carbon lines, worn and thumbed by numberless surreptitious hands. It was one of three such magazines in Leningrad, now in its twentieth edition, and contained poetry, religious and philosophical essays, and articles about non-conformist art. Elaborate diagrams accompanied a piece on aesthetics; a woman since fled to the West had written 'On the Existential and Religious Significance of Unofficial Culture.'

The labour of typing out innumerable copies must have been intense.

'Oh that's nothing,' Volodya said. 'We've typed out the whole of Solzhenitsyn's *Gulag Archipelago* with six carbons! One copy may go through thousands of hands. We can't even know how many—they get passed on anonymously.'

'We think we have a circulation of between three and five thousand,' said a voice beside me. I looked into a face of earnest dreaminess: a twenty-year-old girl. 'But we don't know. After the journal goes out we scarcely hear any more. There can't be any playback.' She added in a voice of hushed, childlike melodrama: 'We live in a phantom world.'

Yet when I turned to the back of the journal, the names and biographies of its contributors were boldly inscribed there, including Volodya's. I was amazed.

'Isn't that dangerous?'

'It's all dangerous,' Volodya said.

I gazed round the circle of callow men and soft-eyed girls, and thought of the KGB officer. They looked fearfully isolated. They lived in a garden of ideas, passions, possibilities still unfrustrated. They talked with all the brightness of their long, unknown futures. It was heady and irresponsible stuff, and reminded me of nights too long past when groups of students (I was one) in London perfected the world with the shake of an intellectual kaleidoscope. One man here was reading out some politically *risqué* poetry, another planning a dissident sculpture exhibition. The room vibrated with a half-adolescent excitement at the forbidden and the initiate. I felt afraid for them. Theirs was an energy which had tried for a better life in 1825, 1905, 1917; they were today's revolutionaries. But instead of dogma and ruthlessness, they wielded poetry. Sometimes, listening to them, I felt as if the policies of the Kremlin were no more than the wish-fulfilments of patriarchal old men trying to keep the world as they had known it. But it was impossible, I thought, that the KGB were ignorant of Volodya's journal and of its privately trumpeted contributors. And Volodya must know that they knew. Like the tsarist police before them, they preferred not to drive the whole apparatus of dissent underground, but to watch and control it. While the writers' refusal to conceal their names was a statement of guiltlessness. I assumed, also, that we were bugged.

'Have you seen these?' the girl asked. One by one she gave out specimens from a pile of hand-printed engravings. They were illicit samples from the studio of an artist in Lvov—pictures too avant-garde to hang. We passed them round like talismans from one to another. They were dense, abstract compositions, suggesting religious symbols. In the West, I thought, they would be judged pedantic. But here their honesty was exciting. The illicit had become equated with the good. The intensity with which the circle of faces scrutinized each engraving betrayed how starved they were of new ways of seeing, thinking, being, of any stimuli at all.

To the Soviet authorities it seems that the avant-garde book or picture wields a terrible disruptive power. And perhaps it does. The fear of an abstract painting, which may unlace the understanding to a world less simple than was apparent, is the fear that primacy may pass to the private, rather than the collective, vision. And there can be no return, once the journey has started, to tribal innocence.

True words or images in the Soviet Union are precious and powerful precisely because they are forbidden. 'A word of truth dropped into Russia,' wrote de Custine as long ago as 1839, 'is like a spark landing in a keg of gunpowder.' In such an atmosphere art becomes both more valuable and more dangerous. Small wonder, then, that canvases of Malevich and others have been lying unexhibited in the basements of museums for more than half a century. And when I visited Leningrad's Russian Museum, I was amazed to see in preparation an inaugural exhibition for Larionov, whose works have been familiar to the West since 1906.

In just such a way the dissidents themselves disturb the Kremlin not because of their numbers, which are tiny, but because they embody a truth. This truth accuses and makes guilty the whole system. It expresses what everybody in fact knows: that Communism is smaller than life. It dissolves the myth of the Soviet paradise. And for this it cannot be forgiven.

'What do you think of the engravings?' the girl asked, lifting the last of them off my knee. I said I thought them honest and interesting. Her eyes were shining. Even to me, the prints had taken on the excitement of contraband.

'Have you seen work like this in England?'

I remembered with irony the unheard clamour of writers and painters in the West, whose honesties were two a penny; meanwhile the Kremlin was turning art and thought here into the most precious commodity of all, had recognized its catalytic power and paid it the compliment of persecution.

But now the conversation was turning to criticism of Soviet life, and was rife with disillusion. Their pile of accusations went to join the pyramid already in my mind (almost everybody I met had added a stone or two): rampaging bribery, ingrained corruption and universal political hypocrisy. The self-accorded privileges of top Party members were a rankling sore—their numberless grades of private shops, the select schools, universities and bureaucratic posts into which they inveigled their children; their permits to travel abroad, their country *dachas*—even their yachts. In all this, my companions saw the mushrooming of a class system—both an upper hierarchy and a bourgeoisie in middle-level management—together with lethargy and growing materialism in their own generation, who did not talk of ideals any longer. The gerontocracy in the Kremlin created suffocating centralism and an inflexible fear of change. A rampant underground economy accounted for some twelve per cent of the average citizen's income (a Western statistic) and whole secret factories were turning out products in short supply. In Leningrad alone, said one man, there were more than twenty-six rouble-millionaires whose wealth derived from underground business.

On and on they talked, with a youthful cynicism which had already left rage or surprise behind it.

'Influence is more important than wealth,' Lucia said. 'Plenty of people have money, but they don't have access to anything worth buying.'

This remark seemed the sadder because we were walking up Nevsky Prospect, once the most fashionable street in Russia. 'The shops are utterly uninteresting,' she said. 'Anything of distinction vanishes the moment it appears—but it probably never appears.' As we went east, the three-mile boulevard unleashed itself before us in long, serene façades. The early palaces, banks and exclusive shops had sobered into offices and cinemas. Their upper storeys, with light mouldings or bold columns, plaster masks and friezes, dwindled below to neon signs, half-subterranean stores and a web of trolleybus cables. Every other vehicle was a ramshackle bus or van.

Lucia knew the Prospect by heart. 'I was brought up just a street away from here. Look how beautiful it is!' But she spoke of it with impending loss, which I did not understand. She pointed out the mansions as we went, calling them by their old names, half forgotten. Here Gogol lived, there Tchaikovsky died. In Number Thirty, Wagner and Berlioz had conducted, and Liszt played. A little way away, she said, Fabergé had his workshop. Nearby the Stroganov palace gazed at itself in the Moika canal—a green and white Narcissus. In the basement of the neighbouring Yusupov palace, Prince Felix had poisoned the atrocious Rasputin, who yet lived on until he was plunged under the ice of the Neva. Down one canal the barley-sugar spirals and jagged domes of a Muscovite-style church erupted like a curse. Little by little Lucia's talk divested the great street of its neon and trams and set the nineteenth century carriages trundling with their pearl-and-vermin aristocracy, summoned up the sartorial elegance and stately slowness of St Petersburg life—and the drab, almost unnoticed mass of the ancient poor too, moving in between, biding its time.

Opposite Kazan Cathedral (Museum of Atheism, tomb of Kutuzov) we plunged into an outlandish building topped by a glass tower and sculptured angels—once the office of the Singer sewing-machine company. It had been turned into Leningrad's largest bookshop. 'But there's nothing here worth reading,' Lucia said.

It was bemusing. Among the banks of scientific textbooks, war memoirs and indifferent novels, among all the snoring and paralyzed shelves of unsold Marx, Lenin and Brezhnev, I searched in vain for the Russian classics. Tolstoy, Pushkin, Dostoevsky, Chekhov, Yesenin—they were almost absent. Why? I never discovered for sure, but it was the same everywhere. Lucia said that the official reason was the paper shortage. But literally millions of unread political tracts are printed every day. In order to get rid of them and achieve their sales quota, shop staff may only part with a volume of Turgenev, for instance, in the compulsory company of four or five books on Marxism-Leninism and the Komsomol. I noticed a little shelf of works in English; they were dizzy bedfellows—Jack London (an old favourite), Scott Fitzgerald, Robert Penn Warren.

Lucia was looking round in despair. 'It's all so depressing.' When we came to a counter selling posters of the October Revolution and the Soviet Achievement, she said: 'Foreign friends of mine buy these to hang in their lavatories.' She started to laugh dangerously.

'Let's leave here.'

Then, as if ashamed, she began to praise her city. In the centuries-old rivalry between Leningrad and Moscow, she belonged heart and mind to Leningrad. 'Moscow's an eyesore, it can't compare. Even our metro's better than theirs. And we speak a purer Russian.' A ghostly Muscovite demurred inside me, but she silenced him with an imperious: 'We, after all, were built to rule.'

We wandered into a square dense with trees. On its far side the Pushkin Theatre—a *tour de force* of the architect Rossi—swam weightless in pale yellow and soft white, carved out of air or icing. Corinthian columns shaped its loggia in the sky, and high on its pediment a chariot of Apollo trampled.

'I pass this square every day to work,' Lucia said, 'and every day it fascinates me. That's the Kirov school on one side—the best ballet company in Russia [my ghostly Muscovite grumbled again.] The

Pushkin Theatre's gone downhill. We don't seem to have good young actors any more. But look what beauty!' Again her voice was full of anticipated loss, as if the building were passing away before her eyes. A faint flush had travelled along her cheekbones. 'I want to walk about this city all the time now, all day.'

Suddenly I realized that she meant to leave: not only Leningrad, but the Soviet Union. How she could achieve this, I had no idea; but beauty might be as potent a passport as money. She looked embarrassed and sad when I asked her, and only said: 'Yes, I'm leaving for the West. That's why it's strange to walk here now. It seems to grow lovelier as I look at it. It's like leaving a person. That makes it hard to bear.'

Her face all at once seemed depleted, older. She did not mention Anatoly. But I sensed that she was leaving him also. Anatoly was too old to begin afresh.

We started up the street from the little square. I did not ask her any more. Beyond the Anichkov Bridge, statued with horse-taming youths, the Nevsky Prospect grows young with a late nineteenth century gaucheness. Thunderous caryatids labour under unmanageable columns. Façades grow cluttered and inarticulate, mouldings coarse. So we remained in the square, inspecting its statue of Catherine the Great—a thirteen-foot bronze harridan cradling wreath and orb. Grouped about her statue's base, the bronze figures of her statesmen and lovers loll and strut and confabulate together so that we could almost smell their perfumed wigs and eavesdrop on their pompous and obscene chatter. The generous Orlovsky and cadaverous Suvorov, the bluestocking Princess Dashkova fondling a book, Derzhavin declaiming poetry (and nobody listening), the bear-like and sensual Potyomkin—they sat in her shadow, as they had in life.

It was not Catherine's humanity or liberalism, I imagine, which preserved her effigy from the anger of the Revolution. In nothing is the inconsistency of Soviet Communism greater than in the emperors it reveres or forgets. No monument remains, as far as I know, to the serf-emancipator Alexander II; yet the harsh and reactionary Nicholas I still rides his bronze charger inexplicably in St Isaac's Square. The tsars are forgiven, Russian-fashion, in proportion to their power, the power of the motherland emanating through them.

Stalin began the reinstatement. At the height of the Second World War, as Moscow verged on collapse, he invoked Russia's warrior-saints in the same breath as he did Lenin. After the battle of Stalingrad imperial-style guards regiments were instituted, military orders were named after the tsarist marshals Suvorov and Kutuzov, and officers' uniforms sprouted élitist epaulettes. Stalin's propagandists compared him unblushingly to Peter the Great and Ivan the Terrible, and the veneration of Peter—'the first Bolshevik'—has survived. The tsar's cottage and little summer palace are preserved as scrupulously as the houses where Lenin lived, and his simplicity of life is recalled in notices on the palace walls—quotations from his servants on his liking for porridge or kraut soup, and how nobody attended him at table. His statue by the French sculptor Falconet, which overlooks the Neva near the Admiralty he founded, is the site of patriotic pilgrimage. Now patinated green-grey, he canters a stallion of fiery glory up a 1500-ton stone plinth, whose steep ascent barely holds in the triumphal energies of horse and rider, and stretches out his arm towards the river. Professional photographers loiter to commemorate visiting groups, and bridal couples come to lay their bouquets at the statue's foot, which is always drenched in flowers.

Yet the man they honour was an imperial tyrant. He raised Leningrad on the bones of the workers, encouraged Capitalist entrepreneurs to spearhead Russia's drive into modernity, and tightened the grip of the land-owners over their helplessly enslaved peasants. All this has been ignored, of course, because the emperor reflects and embodies the nation's greatness.

The same may happen to buildings. The deconsecrated Cathedral of St Isaac, a begrimed hulk of marble and granite, pulls itself together under a golden dome, like a drab *babushka* in a flashy hat, and is still extolled by Russians for its immense proportions. And the colossal Winter Palace, seat of the emperors and theatre of the most extravagant court of its time, is the lodestar every day for thirty thousand proud and gaping visitors.

The palace was built by Bartolommeo Rastrelli for the luxury-loving empress Elizabeth between 1755 and 1762, and during another century it advanced north-eastward in the successive ranges of the Hermitage, until a stupendous barrage of buildings pushed for half a mile along the granite quays above the Neva. Russia can impose a curious genius on its foreign architects, and Rastrelli's baroque throbs with the native love for strong colours and for diversifying huge expanses with powerful ornament. Along its turquoise-coloured façades the columns gleam in brilliant, chalk-white tiers or cluster around gateways. Fantastical scrolls and mouldings tumble about the windows, whose pediments are crowned by leering cherubim, and stucco lion-masks with geriatric frowns and toothless mouths scowl and gape from the lunettes in a swirl of plaster manes. Even the sky is not left in peace, but is peopled by almost two hundred bronze gods and heroes, whose olympian gaze harries the rooftops. The whole effect is one of exuberant near-madness, an architectural incontinence which is yet so subtly ordered and impudently accomplished that it achieves an outrageous splendour.

To its south this mammoth confection flanks a stupendous square, embraced by the curving arms and plain majesty of Rossi's ministries. It is nearly empty. To drive here is to enter a stone and asphalt wilderness with only white lines in the tarmac to indicate direction. And in the square's centre towers another of those prodigies of Russian size, raised to commemorate Alexander I's victory over Napoleon. It is the tallest single stone ever cut, a monolithic column of pink-grey granite, 154 feet high to its crowning angel.

The same blinding statistics ramify meaninglessly about the Winter Palace—1500 rooms, 1786 doors, 1945 windows, 117 staircases. Although scoured by fire in 1837, the massed treasures of the Hermitage were saved by soldiers and firemen, and the interiors were soon restored in sumptuous classical taste. Yet inside, its sheer immensity comes as a shock. Long before I had traversed the vaulted and galleried halls of the ground floor, where the kitchens and services once spread, I was drowned in an ocean of variegated marble, my eyes aching and dazed with colour, drenched by ceilings which burst into a delicate glory of plasterwork or arched overhead in rococo vines and a blaze of armatures. Dragons and lions and a hundred mythological beasts stiffened among the foliage; cherubim kicked and squirmed; and the twin-headed Romanov eagle, talons sceptred and orbed, raked the void with his double glare.

After five hours I was washed up in stupefaction at the foot of the ceremonial stair. Circled by alabaster nymphs, its marble steps lifted in mountainous serenity towards painted ceilings where the ancient gods tumbled over Olympus. By now I was wandering in stunned anaesthesia. Around and above me, in room after room, there unfolded a panoply whose every square inch glittered with an insect's toil of gilded appliqué, the whirl and shriek of stucco griffins and thunder of gold-entangled lions. Raphael, Rembrandt, Leonardo, Rubens—their masterworks swam by me in a pageant of indigestible glory. I simply stared at the ceilings, the columns, the floors under my senselessly trudging feet. I wandered by fantastic torchères and caryatids sleepy with gold, and slithered over shining lakes of precious inlaid wood. All around me crowds of Russian tourists were tramping through the glamour of their repudiated past. Their mild, rustic faces, and the portraits of imperial courtiers, contemplated one another with mutual astonishment. On and on went the rooms, flowering into marble and porphyry stage-sets, reproducing themselves in ormolued mirrors, opening onto parquet pools of ebony, mahogany and amaranth, sinking under the drip and gush of crystal. In the Malachite Room, where vistas of the grey Neva and a troubled sky hung like pictures in the windows, the mantelpieces and columns were vivid with two tons of their green treasure, dug from the Urals. The great ballroom, scene of the innocent transvestite banquets of the empress Elizabeth, shone miraculous with 116 fluted pillars and pilasters and its mammoth chandeliers, blazoned with the arms of all the Russian provinces, filled the room with a ravishing incandescence, like frosted, aerial Christmas trees.

An old man of eighty-four attracted my attention in the Mikhailovsky gardens. He brandished a sabre-shaped walking-stick as he strode down the paths, his war medals dangled in ranks at his chest, and his features showed bellicose above a mist of white beard. He looked like God the Father peering over a cloud.

'I'm an Old Bolshevik,' he announced to me. 'One of the original Revolutionaries!'

A ghost from the twenties, he still exulted in the people's common ownership. He patted the tree trunks possessively as he marched by and frequently said 'This is *my* tree, and *this* is my tree.'

In 1907 he had become a revolutionary, and had been sent in chains to Siberia. But a fellow-prisoner, he said, had concealed a file in the lapel of his coat, and together they had cut through their manacles and fled back to Leningrad. Those were the days when Siberian exiles and prisoners—Trotsky, Stalin and Bakunin among them—escaped from Siberia with laughable ease and slipped over frontiers with the freedom of stray cats.

Then the old man had joined the Revolution and fought for three years against the Whites. He settled into a military stride as he spoke of it, and thrust out his beard like a torpedo, while all the time his gaze flashed and fulminated over the gardens. 'Get off the grass, comrade!' he bellowed. A young mother, seated on the sward beside her pram, looked up in bewilderment. 'Get off our motherland's grass!'

He embodied the intrusive precepts of early Communism, whose zealots were encouraged to scrutinize, shrive and denounce each other. He was the self-proclaimed guardian and persecutor of all about him, and he entered the 1980s with the anachronism of a mastodon. Farther on a girl was leaning in the fork of one of his precious trees. 'Keep away from there!' he roared. 'Can't you see you're stopping it grow? Get off!' She gaped at him, said nothing, did not move. He marched on unperturbed. He even anathematized a mousing cat. 'What are you looking for, comrade? Leave nature alone!' He did not seem to mind or notice that nobody obeyed him.

We rested under a clump of acacias. 'When I was a boy,' he said, 'I saw these trees planted.' He pointed to the largest of them, which bifurcated into a gnarled arm. 'That tree was no taller than a little lamp-post then. The garden was private, of course, but as a boy I often squeezed in over the railings. The tsar and tsaritsa used to walk here in the summer.' His voice dwindled from an alsatian growl to purring reminiscence. 'Once, while I was hiding in the shrubs, I saw them myself. . . . What were they like? It's hard to recall exactly. But she was a beautiful woman, I remember. She had her hand on his arm. And he seemed very large and handsome, and. . . .' But he never finished. The lurking commissar in him erupted again. 'What are you doing, comrade?' Beneath us, a man was raking weeds out of an ornamental pond. 'How can you weed a lake?'

The gardener looked up stoically. 'I'm at work.'

Work. The magic syllable.

Immediately, as if some benedictory hand had passed its grace across the old man's brow, his expression changed to a look of benign redress. 'Fine,' he murmured, 'work.' For him the word had the potency of 'revolution' or 'collective'. The mousing cat, too, had been at work, I thought, but had been unable to voice this watchword.

Before we parted he said: 'I'll give you my address. It's just a postal address, not the real one. That's secret. You see,' he repeated, 'I'm one of the Old Bolsheviks.'

I wondered then if he were not deranged. He scribbled out his address on the back of a newspaper, in enormous handwriting. It was only as he was leaving me that I realized from his age that the history he had given me was nonsense. The tsars did not send lone boys of eleven to Siberia.

'How old did you say you were?' I asked. For he looked timeless.

'I know what you're thinking,' he answered. His eyes twinkled at me collusively. 'You Estonians, you're a clever lot. You're thinking that I can't have been sent to Siberia aged eleven. But actually I'm *ninety-four*. . . .'—and he strode away through the trees.

One evening I went with Lucia to the Kirov Ballet. I had never seen a more ravishing auditorium—five tiers of gold, white and blue, and a blue-gold curtain about to lift on *Swan Lake*. But beneath it the audience, plumped out in its best clothes, was innocently styleless. Under banks of chandeliers and cupids lounging among gilded foliage, they sat in ill-fitting brown and grey suits or outlandish flowered dresses. The old imperial box was stuffed with portly municipal dignitaries and their wives. They cheered tremendously.

The Kirov was once to the Bolshoi what Leningrad is to Moscow, and the company would dance with a classical line and restrained brilliance which could make the Bolshoi's vigour seem crude. But tonight this no longer seemed so, and a new flamboyance was seeping through both company and audience. Here was a chubby-looking ballerina whose unexpected dash produced volleys of clapping from all over the house. A claque in the gallery was cheering on the male principal with obtrusive shouting, and feats of technique were applauded in mid-leap, as Italian audiences greet High Cs.

'It's not a proper Leningrad audience,' Lucia insisted angrily. 'Some of them aren't even wearing ties.'

But performers and spectators were one. A love of the dance infected them all. This, I remembered, was the nursery of Pavlova, Karsavina, Nijinsky, Ulanova, Nureyev, Makarova. Beneath the classical discipline an ancient Russian fire was breathing up and spilling into the audience, some of whom sprang to their feet at the end of the Black Swan's thirty-two *fouettés*, and drowned the music in cheers.

But in the intervals, suddenly sedate, they ambulated anti-clockwise arm in arm along the carpet of the upper vestibule. Now that the lights were up, their faces had returned to vacancy. One could not have guessed that five minutes earlier, released by the darkness into that wordless ritual of grace and strength, they had left behind all constraints and emptied their souls.

I visited Pushkin's home in the city's heart—a modest, first-storey apartment where the poet was brought back mortally wounded in January 1837, after fighting a duel against a French emigré with whom his wife was probably in love. He took a day and two nights to die, while gangrene spread in his wound. Then for two days the common people of St Petersburg flooded through the house in spontaneous tribute.

The place is still a shrine. Its guides speak in tones of hushed melancholy. His desk is scattered with papers as he left it; the waistcoat and gloves in which he duelled are devoutly preserved; the couch where he died remains.

Pushkin's protean output embraced almost every literary form, and he created the very language of modern Russian poetry. It was he, too, who sensed some phantasmagoric strain in Leningrad. In *The Bronze Horseman* he conceived of Peter the Great's statue waking to life and pursuing men through moonlit streets. The very size of Leningrad's buildings and the resonant spaces between them, the long parks and only distantly contained squares, seem still to invite this nightmare. Now Pushkin has become national property. The number of his statues is exceeded only by those of Lenin. In every town through which he travelled a monument commemorates him. His liberal views were suspect in his day—he attacked serfdom—and many of his works were circulated in *samizdat*. So Communism has easily enrolled him as a rebel and posthumous 'man of the people'. His dissipations (like those of Yesenin) are minimized by Soviet critics, and his bawdier writings are suppressed altogether. For no nation persecutes and honours its writers as the Russians do. They go on hounding and recreating them long after their deaths, and enclose them at last in a proud and myopic love.

In Dostoevsky's apartment in a poorer quarter of the city, where the great novelist lived for two years until his death in 1881, the reshaping of the past continues. Much is made of his fake execution for alleged political intrigue against the tsars—he was reprieved as he faced the firing-squad—and of his exile to Siberia. But his deep religious and monarchical traditionalism is clouded over.

His home has been tenderly reconstituted from photographs, relics and memories. Before arriving, I had found it hard to envisage that tormented prophet living anywhere at all. But here were the books which he had read to his children, his tobacco box, his icon, a love-note from his daughter. And here the weak and faded-looking epileptic, working at night under the stimulus of countless cups of bitter tea, completed *The Brothers Karamazov*: an integration, perhaps, of his own divided soul.

Lost in the suburbs, I approached a building site where a gang of labourers was shovelling rubble into a cart, and tapped one of them on the shoulder to ask the way. Under its dented helmet the face which turned to mine was framed by long earrings and dashed with lipstick. She was a delicate blonde. The others turned too, chattering in soprano voices.

It was their slenderness, I suppose, which surprised me, since I had long grown used to those sad, androgynous-looking women who sweep the streets and mend the roads. Equality of the sexes is Marxist dogma. But on the building site in front of me, typically, the foreman and the crane-operator were men, and the labourers women.

I must have looked surprised at the blonde builder, because she was grinning at me. When I asked her why she undertook such work, she frowned and pulled off her helmet, releasing a torrent of hair. Momentarily I expected her to reiterate some Party slogan about building the Motherland.

But she said: 'Why? Because it's so damn boring staying at home, that's why. What else would I do?'

I drove out with Lucia to the Yekaterinsky Palace, whose gold and azure body stretches above its parklands for a thousand feet. Lucia wielded unashamed *blat*. At her touch doorkeepers and museum directors unbent, and we entered parts of the palace usually unseen. It was nearly gutted during the war, but was being restored with the finest and most accurate materials. No other nation on earth has spent so much care and expertise in preserving its aristocratic heritage as Russia has. We walked through an enfilade of dazzling rooms. Almost everything we looked at was new, but the illusion was perfect, so scrupulous, so rich and so sensitive was their resurrection.

But in the nearby palace of Pavlovsk, the baroque funfair of the mid-eighteenth century grinds to a decorous halt. The Yekaterinsky Palace flaunts its charms to the sky, but Pavlovsk is a gentleman (a proper little *dacha*, said Lucia delightedly). It hangs back in the English informality of its gardens. Here, among temples and pavilions and a river cultured into canals and lakes, the emperor Paul held tedious court with his parsimonious wife—and Lucia and I were trapped by a thunderstorm. Slowly at first, then heavier, the rain came filtering through the thick weft of oak leaves above us, plastered our hair and dribbled down our cheeks. Finally it settled into a long, disconsolate roar. It hit us in huge drops out of the trees and seemed to fall on unprotected skin.

Lucia, in a blouse already drenched, was smiling all over her face. 'It's nothing,' she said, 'it's fun.' And when the tempest was at its height, with her hair flattened and mascara bleeding comically down her cheeks, she shouted like a schoolgirl: 'Race you to the car!'

We might as well have swum. The car was parked a mile away. Lucia's St Petersburg sophistication had dissolved with her mascara. Now, her hair flying lank against her Tartar cheekbones, she appeared to be running out of some other century altogether, and to be as rustic and obstinate as all the rest of her long-enduring countrywomen. I could see why Anatoly loved her.

Sergei lived somewhere in the northern suburbs. I had been given his address by a friend in Moscow, with the warning that he was 'a bit wild'.

But I despaired of finding him. For miles northward the apartment blocks barged and elbowed one another along near-carless streets. They clustered together with the aridity of mathematical symbols transferred raw from the drawing-board to earth, and their broilerized occupants walked tiny in the wilderness beneath. Some blocks divided into three or four hundred flats each; but when I approached them, their magisterial ranks shifted and separated, and the land between seemed huge and derelict. Wherever building was newly finished, stagnant pools collected, and a wasteland of twisted metal and concrete became the playground of boys. A current Soviet television programme, I remembered, ridiculed the sameness of these dormitory towns by having its Leningrader hero visit Moscow, but absent-mindedly assume himself to be at home; so similar is the environment that he finds what he imagines is his street, his block, his apartment—and even his key fits.

Somewhere in this planetary landscape Sergei lived. I found the street by chance. It was straddled by a mammoth portrait of Lenin, superscribed 'Lenin's Precepts are True'. Enormous, half-empty shops sprawled alongside. There were no queues, because there was almost nothing to queue for. A few women were walking around in pairs with their babies in their arms.

I hesitated before Sergei's flat, wondering what a Russian was like 'a bit wild'. Leningrad has more than its share of eccentrics and down-and-outs. Its inner streets are haunted by loitering drunks, whose flushed faces and paled eyes would occasionally gape through my car windows yelling for dollars. I had briefly met a surly messiah who went about swathed in an orange prayer-shawl, his head banded in gold, with a broken guitar on his back. In Chelsea or Greenwich Village he might have passed unnoticed, but here such dress was like a manifesto.

I rang the bell and Sergei's head popped out, deprived of its body by the angle of the door. He looked far younger than his thirty-three years. A vertical gush of black hair unfurled above his head, whose eyes bulged with excitement.

'You've come from Viktor? Did he tell you the news?' Then he rammed a theatrical finger against his lips. 'But *shshshsh*—my wife doesn't like it. *Shshsh.*'

I had no idea what he was talking about. We sat in his kitchen downing vodka and salami, while his red-haired wife watched me with intent green eyes. She seemed nervous and dispirited.

'She's crazy about the apartment,' said Sergei, talking as if she wasn't there. 'It's her dream. Before this we occupied a single room. But now we even have *running hot water.*' His head trembled with delight and for instants afterwards his strange hair went on shaking independently above it. 'I'll show you round. It's a real palace here.'

They seemed to have more room than they could fill. In Leningrad, which is so overcrowded that a resident's permit is priceless, this was extraordinary. In one room his two doe-eyed daughters were sitting on a couch watching television. They smiled at me shyly, and settled their frocks round their knees. In another a mongrel bitch lay twined among her fourteen puppies. The paper-thin walls mingled the girls' giggling and the puppies' squeals.

Sergei's delight at his new flat rebuked my depression with these suburbs. For such rootless feats of buildings, for all their Euclidian blankness, are an impressive embodiment of the national will. Thirty years ago scarcely an urban family occupied a flat of its own. People lived crammed together, sometimes two or three families to a room, separated only by a line of washing, a barrage of tawdry furniture, or nothing at all. Kitchens and bathrooms were shared, or did not exist. Against this poverty, for the past quarter century, the government has launched a titanic rehousing campaign. Every year between two and three million new apartments have been built. They are aesthetically null, and poorly constructed; almost before they are up, the bricks drop off, the concrete cracks, the paint flakes away. But they have transformed their people's lives.

'Didn't Viktor tell you?' whispered Sergei, as soon as his wife was out of the kitchen. 'I'm leaving in the autumn, getting out of here. First to Finland, then to Germany.' All the time he was speaking, his face ignited and dimmed in a chiaroscuro of joy and anxiety. It looked trusting and foolish. 'I want to join a pop group.'

'What pop group?'

'A Christian pop group. I don't know where or how. But God will show me. Yes! I want to serve my God!' His hair danced a fandango. 'I love my country, but I can't serve Christ here. It's all too . . . too difficult. But over there, in Sweden or in London perhaps. . . .' He clasped my arm. Siren cities and countries were unwrapping behind his eyes. 'Maybe New York!'

'It can't be easy.'

'God will show me! I love my God!' I thought he must have fallen in with some clandestine evangelical group. He was shaking with a colossal, unworldly optimism, and chewing salami like a horse.

'How will you go?'

'I'll escape,' he said. The anxiety crawled back across his features. 'I'm going with a friend, in September when the sea is warm. We're swimming underwater, with aqualungs, across the Gulf of Finland.'

'That's impossible,' I said, not knowing.

'We've worked it out. It's not easy, but it's possible. God will be with us.'

'God won't help you if you're impatient,' I said, not knowing this either. 'How often have you dived?'

'I've never done it before.'

I stared at him. His face was bright, laughing, filled with the terrible simplicity of his heart. Somewhere in the pages of Dostoevsky, I must have met him before. 'And your friend?'

'He's a good lad.' He poured out the last of the vodka in celebration. 'When I get to Helsinki, I'll join a group. I don't want any money. I just want to sing for my Christ, I just want. . . .'

His wife walked back into the kitchen and sat beside us in silence. Her green eyes fixed me with resentful understanding. She must have known exactly what was up. Sergei seemed all but mad. I imagined her wondering how soon she would be widowed, and her children orphans.

Sergei looked out of the window. 'Where's your car?'

'I parked it some way off,' I said. 'I thought that was better.'

'No, it's better my neighbours see it,' he said. 'Then they'll know I have important friends, foreigners. Bring it round here, and give the girls a ride.'

For half an hour I drove them about the barren streets with their father. Dusk was falling. The white arithmetic of the suburbs added its spectral lunacy to ours. The little girls sat on my mattress, their four dilated eyes shining disembodied in the twilight.

'Isn't it a beautiful car?' Sergei asked them. It was caked in mud.

'Beautiful,' they echoed.

'Sergei,' I murmured a minute later, 'what about *them*?'

'I'll come back,' he muttered. 'My country will forgive me, when it understands I really love it.'

'It may not forgive you.'

I brought them back to their flat-block. It overbore the night sky with a hundred curtained cubes and rectangles of light. Sergei's tragic-faced wife herded her daughters back into their hall. I could only say goodbye to them by telling myself that all his plans were fantasy, a harmless stratagem to appease his day-to-day frustration by the magic of the unachievable.

But I never knew.

On my last evening Lucia, Anatoly and I went to the little Maly Theatre. It is decorated in orange, white and gold: a lustrous jewel box. Lucia wore a dress sent by friends from England, and the gaze of surrounding women devoured her. She quietly enjoyed this.

We witnessed a Sunday programme of sentimental songs and 'cello solos. Then a chubby, middle-aged man stepped forward and recited poetry with that priestly intonation which is reserved for Pushkin, abstract political pronouncements, television obituaries and the like. A Western audience would be convulsed by laughter; but the lake of Russian faces was ruffled only by a tremor of ravaged soulfulness. A long, reverberating salvo of romance, truth and meaning poured from the orator's mouth. I felt deeply embarrassed for Lucia, on whose insistence we had come here. For a time I dared not look at her. I could not guess whether she was holding back a tumult of laughter or cynicism. But when I finally glanced at her face, she did not even notice.

A stream of mascara and tears was trickling down her cheeks.

Hours later we hovered in the well of the courtyard saying goodbye. 'You're going to Estonia?' Anatoly asked. 'Well, I wouldn't speak Russian there, if I were you. Try a bit of German. The Estonians hate us—we conquered them.'

Lucia said plaintively: 'Give us your address—your address in England.'

I wrote it down. Looking at her pensive face, I wondered how much greater were her chances of leaving Russia than those of Sergei.

'Write us a postcard,' Anatoly said.

'Yes, of course.' Then I realized that I didn't even know their surname. They had been introduced simply as Lucia and Anatoly.

'Anatoly's name is Barinov,' she said. 'I'm Lucia Krukovskaya.'

So they were not married.

We hugged Russian-fashion, and from far down the street I saw them still waving, silhouetted in a lake of lamplight. For a few days their valedictory shapes had incarnated Leningrad for me—its Western beauty and native generosity, its grace and sadness.

One of the blessings of bureaucracy is its aptitude for self-defeat. I returned to my camp to find that the authorities had bungled my papers and had assigned me to a site which did not exist. So I became an unperson. Free. With this airy status I camped in peace by the Baltic Sea, listening to the melancholy fall of waves and the cries of birds I didn't know.

Twenty miles to the west the most sumptuous summer palace of the tsars, Petrodvorets, browses on the southern shores of the Gulf of Finland. It was my last glimpse of Leningrad. Begun in the reign of Peter the Great, enlarged in that of the empress Elizabeth, it straddles a stairway of stupendous fountains whose waters glide away beneath it into the Baltic Sea. This Grand Cascade was conceived by Peter himself as the rival of Versailles and as a commemoration of his victory over the Swedes at the battle of Poltava in 1709.

The whole hillside has become a dizzying *coup de théâtre*. Beneath the hovering symmetry of the palace, the double stairway drops in giant, glistening steps among a hubbub of gilded gods and goddesses who blaze and shimmer between leaping and corkscrewing fountains. Never was there such a hill-full of dribbling and spuming beasts and deities. Among the celebratory clamour and cross-fire of the water they dance and lounge and wrestle on their pedestals, or fondle one another in grottoes under the main terrace. Satyrs clash cymbals and wave grapes; Venuses hesitate; urns and vases crowd whatever space is left by the water—water tortured into arcs and columns, flung against gravity, spun to muslin.

For a moment of planned peace, this *feu de joie* succumbs onto a wider platform. Then the tumult begins again as sculptured serpents, throttled in the fists of giants, cough their poisoned streams into the wind. Momentarily the torrent dives underground or gurgles beneath the knees of reclining river gods to slither down fountain walls of greenish ferns. But far beneath, in the grand basin where all this contorted and flung spray at last collects, a monstrous gold Samson tears the jaws of a domesticated-looking lion, from whose stricken mouth a sixty-two-foot jet of water roars skyward. Gilded fish flounder and spout around his feet. Nereids blow their watery conches. Dolphins spurt. Frogs gurgitate. Everything is puffing and spewing, until at last, quiet at the foot of the hill, the water steals through a fountained corridor to the sea, where hydrofoils ply along the wooded slopes of the Gulf of Finland.

All down this cascade, during those spirited *fêtes champêtres* attended by peasants and nobles, tens of thousands of lamps once glowed with an unearthly charm beneath the fountain waters; while far away, terminating the vista, an imitation sun sixty feet in diameter seemed to be setting over the Baltic. The whole aqueous pageant belongs less to a garden than to a victory parade. It lacks the serene majesty of Versailles on which it was modelled. Something, in fact, is wrong. The place reeks of bombast, and perhaps of insecurity. It is an early example of Russian gigantism. Through the mask of Hellenism and Louis XIV, a barbarian face is leering.

'What do you think of Petrodvorets?' asked a genial passer-by while I was strolling in the grounds. 'Is there anything like this in America?'

There isn't. The 300-acre gardens have become the most massive of all Parks of Rest and Culture. They bristle with the villas and pavilions of Peter the Great, with more cascades, ingenious water-jokes, fake trees. Huge fountains rustle and slop in formal gardens. The summer crowds follow paths to souvenir kiosks, outdoor theatres, restaurants, beaches.

But they generally return in the end to where the central terrace drops in trembling life towards the sea, and the bullying figure of Samson—the lion symbolizes defeated Sweden—releases its jet of national glory to the sky.

5. On The Baltic

IN EARLY SEPTEMBER I drove west from Leningrad towards those troubled Baltic states—Estonia, Latvia, Lithuania—whose tragedy has been their tiny size, squeezed as they are between the twin bludgeons of Germany and Russia. The clouds which had been butting along the skyline all morning loosened and grew dark towards noon. At Narva, whose castles confront each other half-ruined over the fast-flowing Narova river, I crossed the boundary into the Soviet republic of Estonia, while to the north the Baltic Sea showed shipless and sombre in the rain.

I picked up a hitch-hiking student: a haggard Estonian. He lifted his booted feet gingerly onto the mattress which replaced my passenger-seat, and ran nervous fingers through a thicket of dripping blond hair. Such moments were perfect for honesty. Alone in a British car, met by chance and not even knowing one another's names, we talked without fear. He was reading archaeology at Estonia's Tartu University. Every student, he said—almost every Estonian—loathed the Russians. Official protestations of brotherhood with the Soviet Union were a degrading farce. The trouble was that the population growth of the Estonians and Latvians was virtually zero, while the Russians were pouring into their cities to take up jobs in industry. In the Estonian capital of Tallinn (we were already in sight of it) the Russians almost outnumbered the natives; in the Latvian capital of Riga they already did. The republics had the highest standard of living in the Soviet Union, he said, but their people were headed for extinction.

He clasped my shoulder with a fierce intimacy before parting. Little Estonia was lovelier than all Russia, he said. Had I liked Leningrad—that cold classicism? Well, Tallinn was more beautiful, more human. He said an Estonian goodbye—*Hääd aega* (it sounded defiantly Scandinavian)—and walked away through the thinning rain.

No wonder nationalism is the Kremlin's nightmare. The Baltic population may be stable, but that of the Moslem republics is increasing at five times the Russian average and within twenty years may have swollen to a third of the young populace. National consciousness has been fostered, not dimmed, by evolving education, and now matches Russian patriotism with thwarted feelings all around it. Within a few years the ethnic Russians—already only fifty-two per cent of the total populace—will be a minority in their own empire. Moscow may conceive the federal states as in transition towards a society of *Homo Sovieticus*—and Russians occupy powerful, quasi-independent positions in the Party branches of every republic—but the republics themselves show every sign of wanting to freeze or elevate their status into greater autonomy.

In the campsite at Tallinn I found many Estonians from Sweden or Finland, where they or their parents had fled in 1944 before the fleeting independence of the Baltic states was strangled by Stalin. They returned to Estonia on holiday now. Their big cars gleamed among the camping huts; their transistors roared; their wives and children were bright in Scandinavian cottons. Released from the restrictive Finnish drinking laws, they celebrated into the night in a long, free uproar, while the Soviet Estonians sat dourly round their Primus stoves, frying lumps of fish and boiling semolina.

Meanwhile the Russians themselves, picnicking in their spartan tents, listened to the expatriates' jubilation with faint distaste or bemusement. This Soviet middle class was repeated through all the campsites where I stayed. They were technicians, engineers, minor civil servants, perhaps earning three hundred roubles (some 380 dollars) a month. They drove their family cars with the cautious pride of new owners. Their pale eyes watched me with reserve: an instinctive defensiveness in public places. They seemed stoically incurious.

As for the Estonians, some were of Scandinavian height, and statuesque. They spoke in a vowel-filled tongue close to Finnish, and the television aerials which covered the city rooftops were not receiving Moscow, but Western-orientated programmes from Helsinki fifty miles over the water. Tallinn's great semicircular bay, where ships idled on a grey calm, reminded me of their age-old love for the communicating sea.

Tallinn itself is redolent of those centuries of twilit confusion—history spent in the shadow of others—which shuffled the Baltic states between German merchants, Swedish kings and the rising might of Russia. The old town descends from castled heights in jumbled lanes and turrets to the sea. The pastel façades of its houses lean and overlap under pitched roofs and high-pointed gables. Iron gates swing onto courtyards of yawning emptiness. The town seems still to belong to

[108]

those three centuries before 1561 when it was fat with Hanseatic burghers and dominated by the Teutonic Knights—a city not built for show, but for expedience, trade and creature comforts. A bourgeois modesty pervades it. It is more crowded and intimate than its Russian counterparts, sweeter, more proportional, yet a little sombre. The larger buildings do not spread in the Russian way, but rise suddenly, as if by accident, round the corners of winding streets. Gothic replaces Byzantine. Collegiate churches and guildhalls nudge together under Lutheran steeples and spires, and the skyline blossoms into a sudden delicacy of weather-vanes—iron or copper banners flying in the wind, crowned by mermaids and dragons.

Nothing seems to belong to the native Estonians. The German walls climb in broken ramparts to an ancient Danish citadel. The cathedral aisles drip with the hatchments of Baltic barons long since gone, and the grave-slabs of German guilds—butchers, cobblers, cordwainers—crowd its nave, with the tombs of Swedish marshals and a Russian admiral. Only the limestone hill where all this stands is attributed to the colossal and mythic progenitress of the Estonian people. It is not a hill at all, they say, but the grave-mound of the folk-hero Kalev, piled up by his mother, whose tears formed the lake beyond. A statue of this formidable ancestress, swathed in a decolleté bear's skin, was unveiled in the years of Estonia's incompetent but treasured independence between 1919 and 1940, and still presides over a park frequented by lovers and drunks.

I followed alleys filled with idiosyncracy: wrought-iron lamp-brackets, a tremulous seventeenth century clock, lintels sculptured with the crests of Hanseatic cities—Novgorod, Bruges, London. Sometimes the ramparts grew strong with turrets or split into gutted gate-towers splashed by creepers. A few Russian tourists were about, and Estonian sailors walking in pairs. Once, from behind high walls, I heard the Tyrolean lilt of an accordion. Then the battlements became grey and troubled, and shouldered their path through lanes dank and almost unlived-in. Cobbled alleys roughened and swelled underfoot, and once the way darkened to a cul-de-sac where tombstones were clamped to fetid walls, blazoned with extinguished arms. From a Dominican monastery, whose entrance was superscribed 'Here truly is the house of God and the Gate of Heaven', the chanting rose reedy and hesitant from an ageing congregation.

I sat down on a bench. An Estonian docker with the bleared eyes of the perpetually drunk sank beside me and asked so candidly for drink money that I gave him twenty kopeks. He kissed my cheeks and marched away. Even in summer a leftover feeling of wartime brooded over the town. The interiors of offices and banks were austere and wan-lit. The restaurant where I lunched was the same. Sad-faced waitresses with plaited Rhine-maiden hair were serving sausages to tourists instead of gold to the Nibelungen, and an elderly violinist was persecuting the Russian holidaymakers with German folk-tunes. I settled to a dish of macaroni and smetana, and tried to talk to the swarthy Estonian opposite. He grunted that he didn't speak Russian, and kept his harsh eyes fixed on his meal, as if it might escape.

But the feeling of poverty is half an illusion. Life here is better than almost anywhere else in the Soviet Union. The people are brighter dressed, better paid. They enjoy cultural freedoms unknown to Moscow. Abstract art has made a shy beginning; the bookshops, I noticed, stocked Proust, Evelyn Waugh, P. G. Wodehouse, Jack Kerouac.

In the old market square I saw a man with *To the Lighthouse* sticking out of one pocket, and made it an excuse for conversation. Jaan turned out to be a chemist and a Methodist. Behind his thin-rimmed spectacles the eyes shone heavy and slow, and the waxy pallor of his face, swept by black locks, lent him a starved, Bohemian look. He seemed older than his thirty-one years—his gangling body was stooped—but when he spoke about what mattered to him his voice became urgent, even harsh, and its stammer made him angry. He talked to me freely. Either my nationality or my evanescence incurred his trust.

The familiar refrain of Russian immigration came up. The development of Baltic industry—heavy engineering, chemicals, oil shale—had created jobs which the native people were too few to fill, he said. So the Russians came. He spoke of them as an Englishman might speak of the Irish. They lived in great apartment blocks, dirtily, like pigs. They had money enough, but spent it on drink. That was the problem with his own saddened people too, he said. Many Estonians and Russians drank away half their salaries. 'They drink because they're bored—they've nothing else to think about. They've nowhere to go, nothing to do. When they remember the emptiness of their lives, they drink.'

As we drove to his home, the Russian districts fell behind us in sterile flat-blocks, and we entered a pure Estonian quarter: stucco or wooden houses coddled in their gardens. Jaan lived with his wife and infant son on the upper floor of his parents' home—a cottage in a garden going to wild under the pines. Gooseberry bushes and tiger lilies grew together in weird propinquity, and a buxom dog lived in an upturned crate among the flowers.

Jaan's wife was like a Nordic angel: blue eyes, china skin. Their baby son, who was fairer still, took his first step in my honour, before falling in a rubbery heap. She apologised for their three rooms, floored with worn linoleum and set with roughly-carpentered furniture. Jaan and she were waiting for a house of their own, she explained; they were on the lists.

'And we'll have to wait a long time,' he said. 'That's what can happen to Methodists here. It's unspectacular, this persecution, but it's everywhere. You may wait longer for a house, a car, a new job, anything. Our pastors are the worst hit. They're less likely to be arrested on some trumped-up charge—they're too conspicuous—but they may be harassed for years.' His voice started to stammer. 'At university I was threatened with expulsion five times because of my faith, but I survived. I had a Christian friend who said he'd keep God in his heart and conform officially to Communist ritual—but he took to drink. The outward signs, you see, are important. I know a girl who was posted to a distant village as schoolmistress. She couldn't go to church there without being noticed, so she had to choose between her faith and her profession—and she chose her profession.' Suddenly he looked bitter. 'That's how they take our souls.'

He and his wife seemed to live in Calvinist purity. They didn't drink, they didn't smoke. They didn't even do things a little *na levo*, as the Russians say.

'Everybody cheats here,' Jaan said. 'If you want to sell your car, for instance, you do it automatically on the black market. You take out a receipt at the official rate—three thousand roubles, perhaps—then you sell for eight thousand, cars are so scarce. But how can a Christian do things like that?' He leant forward and took his wife's hand in her lap. 'We can't. So of course we're poor.' But they were both smiling, as if this were an irrelevance. 'My wedding suit cost me three months' salary. That was without my tie and shoes.'

We ate a frugal meal together, Jaan saying grace. The walls of the kitchen were hung with posters of cities and landscapes which they would never see: Milan, the Dordogne, Africa. A calendar read: 'Come to Cornwall for the International Church Youth Conference.'

Methodism, Jaan said, had survived in the Soviet Union only in Estonia. 'In Leningrad, in Moscow, in Latvia, we were wiped out. Only here we were strong and lasted. In Tallinn we often have a Sunday congregation of seven hundred, so that two hundred have to stand. Sometimes I look round them and marvel how they're either young or very old. That middle generation—the Stalin generation—isn't there. But I know many who are secret Christians—professional people, mostly. They take communion in their homes. That happens here. . . .'

Next morning, when I peered into the Methodist headquarters near the market square, I found only a tiny old pastor who lived in the flat upstairs. His splayed feet were clothed in splitting slippers, and a gold watch-chain dribbled from his trouser pocket as if in memory of some happier time. He showed me the meeting-room with its few chairs and piano. So I was from England? He could remember Portsmouth, Hull. . . .

A typical Estonian, I thought, he knows the seaports. He began to reminisce in a mishmash of German and English. But it was hard truly to envisage the past of a man of his age (he was almost ninety) and nationality. When the Latvians and Estonians fought off the Russians in 1918–19 and took their independence, he was already a serving sailor. And by the end of the Second World War—through Stalin's 1940 deportations and his execution of over sixty thousand Estonians, through the Jewish holocaust of the Nazis' return and the mass internal exiles of the Russian revenge—he was far into middle age. What had he not seen?

But it was not these things which floated in the old man's mind. 'My memory, I'm so old now. . . .' His eyes puckered with the uncertainty of thinking. He hunted for words. He remembered going to sea at the age of sixteen, when Tsar Nicholas II was still young on his throne. He had worked on a clipper carrying timber from Riga to Yarmouth. 'And from Yarmouth I walked to Hull. I had no money, you see. But what's that to a young man?' He massaged his head as if to warm up memories, pictures. A glaze of white hair trickled in his fingers. 'From Hull I worked on steamers as a deck-hand or stoker. In the winter I found jobs in the boiler-room away from the cold. In the summer I got posts on deck away from the heat.' He twinkled fitfully with the memory of his cleverness. Then, five days out from Oslo, his ship had caught fire. A burnt finger of his right hand was amputated in an Oslo hospital. He held up the stub where it should have been; the skin, after seventy years, was discoloured, almost translucent.

'But that was my way to God,' he said. 'My nurse in the hospital was a girl of eighteen, a Methodist, and she converted me.' He laughed again—at himself, I think. He was remembering. 'For two years I studied in the Frankfurt seminary, then returned to Estonia as pastor of a flock of fifty in Tapa. That was my first congregation. . . .'

We walked in his garden: marguerites, roses and hostas gathered round a reedy pond. His florid face kept turning to mine. 'I think you're an educated man. I wish I had been. I used to love geography, even though I had no time to read.' He took a pair of spectacles from his pocket as if in preparation for something, and straightened his waistcoat. 'But when you sail, you know, you begin to feel the shape and size of the world. It's a way of study.'

But the brightness had faded out of him. Things had not been easy, he said. During the Second World War their chapel in Tallinn was destroyed; so were their offices, but they had built them up again with their own hands. Now they shared a church with the Seventh Day Adventists—a rather extreme lot, he thought. But Christians must share. . . .

He was thankful for my visit, he said. He felt stronger for it, comforted. Perhaps God had sent me. Before we parted he clasped my fingers in his stunted hand. 'How old are you?'

'Forty-one.'

'Well, I'm an old man now.' He was not looking at me. 'You're young and I'm old, so we won't meet again.' Suddenly he was shaking. His round eyes winced, and I saw tears shining under the rim of his spectacles. 'We shan't meet again, not here.' He pointed up the stair. 'We'll meet up there.' For a moment I thought he was indicating his apartment. But he meant heaven.

I stood confused in the doorway, helpless before his loneliness. To him, I sensed, I came like an ambassador from a great believing world—the Christian West—which for years he had not seen.

'We have God,' he said hoarsely, 'we have God.'

Then I felt his farness, the shadow of world politics between us, and the still darker passage of time. He seemed isolated in his trust and ignorance. I took his old face in my hands, and kissed him.

He stumbled up the stairs, the tears falling onto his coat, and I into the market square.

Evening. Close to my campsite lay the city's largest graveyard—a pine-scented valley of the dead, shimmering with flowers. Half the modern graves showed Christian symbols. Their lit candles glowed among the wreaths. Many were set with little benches; even today some families eat meals at the tombs of the deceased—a survival from the pagan feasts of the dead.

In this state cemetery all faiths lay together. I even saw the sculptured menorah of a Jew. Other graves showed the Communist star or the atheist flame (the flames of Hell, joke Christians). I vaguely wondered what an atheist funeral was like. 'They read poems,' Jaan had said, 'and sing songs about Nature and the birds carolling in the trees. It's grotesque.' But their inscriptions were simple and honest. 'Remembrance of you remains'. They faced grief unsupported, in the hope only that a person's memory outshine the dissolution of death.

Two days later I flew to Riga, the capital of Latvia. In the seat on my left sat the leader of a Dutch poultry-farming delegation, on my right snored an army officer. Beneath our cruising Tupolev, the Estonian flatlands smoothed into rectangles of yellowing wheat, pastureland scattered with piebald cattle, forests cut by rides. A land of pig-breeding, potatoes, grain, flax. Latvia, too. I stared down on a white symmetry of collective farms, and on those unpaved roads which foreigners never travel. German agricultural traditions (said the Dutchman) turned these lands into the most efficiently farmed in the Soviet Union.

Cups of mineral water were distributed in mid-flight. Everybody drank, then relapsed into *Pravda*, *Soviet Sport* or sleep. Twenty minutes from Riga the army officer's mineral water awoke him with a burp, and we fell into lustreless conversation. The moment I enquired about the army, he retreated into his carapace like a turtle, only poking out his head to inspect me with little reptile eyes and agree with whatever I said.

Did the army give him much spare time, I asked?

'We have spare time.'

'Much?'

'Some.'

Did he find it an interesting life?

'It has interest.' And so on.

I touched the insignia on his shoulder. 'What rank is that?'

Half a minute passed—thirty seconds of knotted brows and pursed lips—before this momentous secret could be declassified.

'Major.'

We were flying over loose-knit villages now, then circled above the sea and came in low where the watershed of the Daugava river pushed fat, sleepy fingers into the mist.

Two hours later, from the twenty-third storey of Riga's newest hotel, I stared out into a blanket of rain. The hotel itself conformed miserably to expectation. It was huge, charmless, exhibitionist. Latvians joke that these tourist ghettoes are made of sixty per cent glass, thirty per cent ferro-concrete and ten per cent microphones. All their minor fittings, all those things by which a civilization may be gauged by archaeologists after it has gone, were wretchedly poor. When I turned on the light-switch the electricity made a scuttling like rats along the curtain-rails, then died. The furniture was of black-varnished pine; the curtains chiffon-thin. The lukewarm water which trickled from the shower was augmented by surreptitious leaks in other places, and the rain had enfiladed the double-glazed windows to stream down the frames. I noticed these things only with muted astonishment. I didn't care; and nor, very much, do the Russians. They are used to discomfort. Such hotels belonged merely to the ghost-landscape of Soviet appearances: architectural status-symbols, metaphors for civilisation.

The hotel was predictably supervised. To the average citizen of Riga it was *terra incognita*. Nobody who did not have a permit could pass its doormen. Huge and wakeful at her desk on each landing, the *dezhurnaya* held autocratic sway. With her sleepless stint of twenty-four hours on watch (followed by three days off) such a guardian seemed to incarnate the Russian mania for supervision. She was generally middle-aged or old, and always poor. Very likely her young womanhood had been engulfed by the Second World War, leaving her husbandless. She was only outwardly formidable. A joke or a kindness would split her granite face into a motherly smile. She would grow sentimental and indulgent, produce extra bulbs and blankets, offer to wash clothes. My youngest *dezhurnaya* in Riga had been to Cuba three years before (but avoided telling me why) and had been inspired to paint by the mammoth flowers and the tropical sun. When she spoke of those swarming West Indian towns, the brilliant sugar-cane and tobacco fields, she shook her head in disbelief that she had ever been there. Later I met other Russians whose cultural insulation had been shattered by the sensual or intellectual shock of a new country. They never returned quite the same.

Darkness replaced the vanishing rain, and all I had glimpsed of Riga was a watery silhouette shimmering in the rectangle of my hotel window. I went downstairs in the hope of supper. But of the hotel's three restaurants, one was closed for repair, one had the day off, and the door of the third displayed a notice refusing entry to anybody not wearing a suit and tie. Such things no longer surprised me. Suitless, tieless and not a group, I wandered into the city.

But it was nine o'clock and the whole place a wilderness. The street-lamps shed pools of dimness over empty pavements. Even the main road showed little but blacked-out windows. Wherever a notice proclaimed 'Restaurant', stout concierges or imperturbable porters

[115]

closed the doors against all enquiry. A few young couples were walking the streets on the same desultory search as I. When we saw a restaurant we squashed our starved and accusing faces against the glass doors and made ignored signs to the guardians inside.

But in all the capital of Latvia, it seemed, no eating-place was open to ordinary people. We were refused entry for no reason we knew. Simply there was no incentive to let us in. Nothing belonged to anybody; and the bourgeois balance of supply-and-demand did not exist.

I went back to my hotel and tried to penetrate its night-club.

'You need a ticket,' I was told.

'I'll buy one.'

'There aren't any.'

'But the club's almost empty,' I said.

'But there are no tickets.'

So I gave up this *Through the Looking-glass* enterprise, and went upstairs to bed. The rat-scuttling electricity still didn't work, and I jotted down the events of my evening—precisely because they were so ordinary—by the glow of the state advertisement sprawled across the opposite roof: 'The ideas of Lenin. . . .'

Morning transformed the city. From the glass eyrie of my bedroom I gazed on a rumpled panorama of roofs which interlocked in salients of silver-black tiles and rusted tin. The whole skyline bristled with the multi-headed chimneys, spires, crosses, aerials, domes, flags of an apparently streetless city, vanishing northward where the island-studded Daugava eased in a sombre estuary out to sea.

If Tallinn has a portly, well-to-do relative, it is Riga. It still has the solid, stately look of an old banking centre. Handsome nineteenth century buildings spread along a tree-lined canal—the moat to ramparts now vanished—and the town beyond jostles with churches, guildhalls and mediaeval warehouses. Here and there rise the steep-pitched roofs and gabled fronts of merchants' mansions—sixteenth or seventeenth century, going to seed. The churches loom in unlovely hulks of brick and sooty tiles: battered mongrels whose Gothic bodies are crowned with baroque spires. But all look deeply German. Common sense and bourgeois self-interest are in the air. The Russian enormousness is not here. Wagner was resident conductor at the opera house before fleeing his creditors in 1839, and Schumann gave piano concerts and wrote home that the citizens knew nothing about music and only talked about food.

Riga shares Tallinn's history too—the same reduction of its native peoples to serfdom by Christianising Germans; the same dim and confused clashings of Teutonic Knights, Hanseatic burghers and fighting bishops. Latvia was always surrounded by giants. But it grew rich in merchandise. Even its Knights (whose castle is still here) dealt 'in every trade unbecoming to knighthood,' wailed the competing merchants, 'selling fruit, cabbages, radishes, onions. . . .' The city reeks of commerce still. And there followed the same tormenting as all the Baltic suffered: Sweden, Poland and Russia countermarching over its frontiers, with a moment's blaze of independence between the World Wars. Its Germanized people saved themselves by hard work. Even today Latvia is not only a land of heavy engineering, like Estonia, but produces the Soviet Union's finest consumer goods. Riga is well-known for its radios, refrigerators, washing machines and clothes. Russian workers flood its industries. Its people were better dressed than any I saw elsewhere (jeans suits were the rage) and seemed to fill the old streets with something like security.

But even here Russian-style queues—a hundred and fifty people lined up for fatty bacon, seventy-five for ice cream—twined through the cobbled lanes, where I took to wandering at random; and when I visited the Church of the Nativity, I found it turned into a planetarium ('Mars—planet of riddles' was showing at twelve o'clock).

I saw a group of gypsies reading palms. They wove among the crowds with loose strides in a shocking flare of scarves and pavement-sweeping dresses: handsome, satanic women clutching olive-skinned babies. Nobody could tell me where they came from. Moldavia, said one man; Georgia, thought another. In any case, it was agreed, they were beyond control. I followed their progress with amazement along the streets. They walked like scandalous royalty, anarchic and free. People averted their eyes.

During my second day in Riga I encountered an independence more bitter and sophisticated than theirs. I met Edvigs on a street corner by a machine which produced watery apple juice for three kopeks. He was thirty years old, heavy, balding, casually dressed. The machine ingested our money but gave back no apple juice. Edvigs kicked it on one side, I thumped it on the other. Then we began to laugh. He enquired my nationality, and I his. He was Latvian.

In 1919, he reminded me, the British had helped Latvia to its brief independence. His gaze snaked over my clothes to confirm my foreignness, before he landed a farewell kick on the machine. 'I bet it's Russian.'

Everything about Edvigs asserted a bruised independence. He looked like a bulldog running to fat. But he was nervous at being seen with me. His job—he was an interpreter—rendered him vulnerable. We ate in a restaurant frequented by middle-class Latvians, and spent the afternoon at the Mezoparks cemeteries far on the city's outskirts, where the graves of the war dead stretch in desolating avenues. For two years until 1917 the Latvians fought the Germans to a standstill along the Daugava, and thousands of their fallen are buried here, together with men who fended off the Bolsheviks in 1919. Nearby, the city's later graveyards flood beneath the birch trees in white wooden crosses, black headstones, weeping angels and little benches where nobody was sitting. As we neared the memorial to Rainis, Latvia's national poet, the crosses gave way to the tombstones of Party dignitaries, inscribed with due titles and inset with photographic portraits—prestigious faces above medal-spattered chests. I wondered again what an atheist funeral could be like.

'You hire professional speakers,' Edvigs said with disgust. 'They charge per speech. It's fantastically well paid. They get two or three hundred roubles a day if they cram in six orations.' He burst into sour laughter. 'That's something I should have done! They earn ten times what I do! They're given a lot of data about the deceased, of course. But they muddle all the dead up. It's horrific. They start talking about *he* instead of *she* and confer decorations and children on people who never had any. I've heard some speeches like I can't describe to you. And the priests are just as bad.'

His face was scrunched into a pugnacious knot, and a continuous, characteristic gesture—an outward twist of his palms and splayed fingers—scattered these spoken horrors into the surrounding air. 'I'm in the wrong trade! Christ! At university I studied foreign literature. But what the hell's the use of that? It's not even safe to write a critical defence of some dead author—before you've finished the whole fashion's changed. Steinbeck, for instance, used to be popular here. Then he wrote in favour of the Vietnam war, and vanished overnight.' A jerk of his palms polluted the air with these absurdities. 'And now Somerset Maugham's come up. Why? God knows, he was such a bourgeois.'

It was the professions and the arts which appealed to Edvigs. They had remained in the hands of conservative, middle-aged Latvians, he said, who jealously excluded the Russians from their field. But a deep divide opened between his own age group and theirs. 'That middle generation, and the old, are always talking about the country—Latvia—

what's good or bad for it. They're still idealistic. They loathe the Russians. They're for ever discussing freedom. And they've been through Hell. My parents, for instance, were shaped by the war and the Stalin years—the fight for material things. But those battles have been won now. Nobody dies on the streets here any more.' He sounded hard, weary. 'I can't remember the war or even Stalin. None of us young can. We're tired of all that. We want to be free, of course, but we're philosophical. It's only our parents who talk about quick miracles.' Another flicker of his hands dismissed such things. 'My whole generation is cynical about politics.'

'That's how you'll be absorbed,' I said cruelly. Young Latvians intermarry with the Russians now.

Edvigs gave his sour laugh, and didn't answer. All the time we were talking the massed graves of his countrymen flowed past us in a dumb, accusing undergrowth. When we passed the tomb of the poet Rainis, Edvigs was touched by a fleeting, bitter nationalism. 'This man would have been a Goethe or a Shakespeare if he'd been born anywhere else. But he wrote in Latvian . . . and who reads that? Poetry, politics, religion—we've lost them all. Latvia's like anywhere else now. We young ones look for something to replace it all. But what do you do? Drink, sex . . . ? You face a vacuum.'

Around us, under dappled avenues of lime trees, the crosses thickened again where Christians and atheists lay side by side in an unplanned communism of death. Some of the dead, even here, were bolstered by photographs and titles, but most were buried only with the compassion of memory—loving fathers, cherished wives. Tombstones, Edvigs said, ensured that our hypocrisy continued to the end in professed love, professed faith. Yet these graves were the most tenderly kept, the most personal, that I had ever seen, separated by tall hedges and nurtured flower-beds, and each with more space in death than a city apartment might give in life.

'Resurrection, heaven . . . I'd like to believe in all that,' he said. 'My parents are church-going Lutherans, but I'm an atheist. For years I didn't even see the necessity for this God of theirs.' His voice lowered, although nobody was near. 'Then my father got into trouble. He was in charge of a Young Pioneer camp, and he could have been sentenced to eight years for embezzling Party funds. He was too trusting of people round him. Even though he was acquitted, his career was ruined. You know how it is: a man has a coat stolen off him and five years later nobody can remember if he was the thief or the victim—he just goes on smelling rotten. Well, it was after this that I began to change. I found myself walking round the streets thinking: what else, what else? I realized then that my parents weren't religious at all. They just went to church out of habit.'

We had slowed to a standstill. Two women were embracing over a nearby grave, clutching at each other, weeping. They were Russians. The older was wailing in half-pagan grief.

Edvigs turned away. 'I think ninety per cent of my friends feel as I do,' he said. 'They're religious at heart . . . But there's no God left.'

Between the World Wars there was a place commemorated in this cemetery where the bodies of Latvian civilians, executed by Bolsheviks in 1919, were thrown into a pit. It used to be marked simply by a crucifix nailed to the trunk of a pine tree, and inscribed astonishingly 'Father, forgive them'. It has, of course, gone.

Edvigs had not even heard of it. This history, too, belonged to his parents. And in a way, he said, he envied them. Such memories were a kind of freedom, whereas his generation had been brought up from infancy in a world of fallacy and intrusion.

'You're always treated like a child. There's nothing but bureaucracy, dogma, interference! It's all so stupid. They even ask you questions if you're still unmarried at my age. Not officially, of course, but things are insinuated. They want to know what's wrong with you.' The bulldog jowls quivered. 'But not being married could be precisely a man's most vulnerable point—some real grief—impotence, homosexuality. And this interference starts from the moment you're born. If you do badly at primary school your parents and schoolmaster get together and say: "What's wrong with you, little Edvigs, why don't you want to work?" They set up a commission. You're considered abnormal. And it's like that all the way through. You're made to feel you're letting down society, the system, the country. God!' he blazed incongruously, 'Who *is* the country, the system? The country is *me* too! Let me breathe!'

My last evening in Riga was spent at a concert in the city's cathedral, whose towering Romanesque nave, lined with the tombs and memorials of Teutonic bishops, sent up a heady cloud of Germanism. More than two thousand people—plain-dressed Latvians mostly, with blunt working faces—listened to Bach preludes with a reverent intentness. The cathedral's organ is the fourth largest in the world—6,768 pipes of different woods and metal alloys, ranging in length from ten meters to a few millimetres. It touched the darkening air with a fathomless hush, and rolled its *fortissimi* effortlessly down the aisles.

As the light faded in the stained-glass windows, the carved and painted coats-of-arms of German barons glimmered out of the walls and pillars where they hung—stupendous Gothic armatures drowned in Renaissance detail. Above each scutcheoned shield, notched for its jousting-lance and blazoned with turrets and crowns, lodged a helmet mantled in fountains of strawberry-leaves and ribbonry; while on either side wyverns and lions and stallions—rampant, couchant, winged, maned, horned—grappled with swords and banners or made way for officious-looking Prussian cupids. As twilight filled the aisles, and the choir launched on Mozart's *Requiem*, this defunct heraldry only brooded huger on the walls, as if its dispersed owners—worshippers of soldier-saints and a martial variant of the Virgin Mary—might yet return to fight the Swedes or bully Hanseatic cities. But the coats-of-arms betray them. In these, the sober arsenal of the early knights—a grim Westphalian nobility of liege-lords and landmeisters—have frothed and fattened into the snobbish paraphernalia of an emasculated sixteenth century chivalry. For by the time these hatchments flowered into their final quarterings and marshallings, and the last lozenges and roundels were in place, the Teutonic Knights had declined into a ceremonial and near-powerless court, vassals of Poland.

Yet their influence lived on. Their surviving aristocracy was not disenfranchized until the land reforms of Latvian independence between the World Wars. And their culture continued obliquely all about me in the solemn Lutheran faces which drank in the pathos of Mozart's *Lacrimosa* and the exultant bonfire of the *Sanctus*.

Orchestra and choir together were concealed beneath the organ case, a harvest of grey-gold sheafs hung up in the gloom, and their music filled the nave with unearthly fervour. I was disproportionately moved by it. The soloists, I could tell, were poor. But for the moment they seemed to offer some international sacrament, a force of healing.

'Hopeless,' murmured the girl beside me, as the *Agnus Dei* lifted to its end. She had been shaking her head in the interval and complaining about the vocal standard. 'I could sing the contralto better myself.'

She seemed to mean it. I looked into a face of Latvian freshness. She'd longed to be a singer, she said—she had even trained with Arkhipova in Moscow—but her tuition had been ended by two operations. We left the cathedral together and walked back through the lanes. She was staying in the same hotel as me, she said. This was strange. I wondered vaguely if she were attached to the KGB, then mislaid the thought. She gave out an almost infantile frankness. She prattled about music and Western cosmetics, and brushed her body against mine as we walked. She seemed a living illustration of that tender, incontinent quality—the Russians untranslatably call it *umileniye*—that belongs to a world in which nothing intrudes between a feeling and its expression.

We sat beside the moat under the trees. Before her vocal training could be finished, she said, she had been in hospital for almost a year. When she returned to singing, both her will and her strength had gone. But she was smiling without self-pity. She was like a child listening to her own story. She said: 'I'd like to sing for you some time. When are you leaving?'

'Tomorrow.'

'Tomorrow!' With the same delight as she had begun talking to me, her expression clouded and she lowered her head. 'But I've only just got to know you!'

For a few minutes, while we discussed other things, her gaze hunted about the black trees and the star-filled moat. Then, warmed by new thoughts, she began to talk of her past again, staring at me through her strange, pale eyes and pressing her thigh against mine. Her hair brushed my neck. Although her father was dead, she said, her family was rich—yes, there were many rich Latvian families—and she didn't have to work. At the age of twenty-two she'd adopted a baby boy whose parents were dead (was he in fact, I wondered, her own?) and the child had become everything to her, and she to him: mother, father, sister. Did I like children, she wondered? And soon she was asking me about my own life with the same rather haunting frankness. What did I do? Why was I alone?

Most of her questions seemed unanswerable. Looking into her open face with its commonplace shine of teeth through parted lips and the yeasty candour of her eyes, I felt unforgivably complex. When I said that I loved a woman in England, the brightness drained from her. We fell foolishly silent. I remembered a British student at Moscow University who had received eleven proposals from girls to whom the West seemed a Mecca of youthful emancipation. It wasn't a Mecca which I felt I suggested. When the girl stared at me, I had no idea what she saw. In the darkness, I suppose, I looked young enough, and seemed gentle, and was listening.

But the next moment she had recovered and was laughing and whispering rude things about the Russians in my ear. We walked slowly back to our separate rooms. She squeezed her fingers between mine. Even her brazenness did not seem to be that at all, but the lonely need of an orphan.

6. Toward Caucasus

A FEW MILES south-west of Moscow the village of Peredelkino is scattered among woods and ponds. It was created as a colony for writers in the thirties, and its trees are interspersed with wooden dachas in orchards and wild gardens. Over its steep hillside an overgrown cemetery climbs in dense throngs of headstones and iron-grilled mounds, threaded by paths.

I stopped here one evening on my way south and sought out the grave of Pasternak. A simple plinth on the lip of the slope, it was crowded by jars of phlox and daisies, and strewn with berried twigs.

Beyond, across a ploughed field, the dacha where he lived for twenty-five years until his death in 1960 stood in silence. It looked private, deathly still. It was here, while almost all his great contemporaries were swallowed up by labour-camps or suicide, that Pasternak—on Stalin's inexplicable whim—survived. Through 1957, when *Doctor Zhivago* was being scrutinized by Soviet officials and published with uproar in Italy, his time was spent in the secluded house, ordered by a formidable, sad and half-estranged second wife. Here too he received news of his Nobel Prize award, and marched out to think in the rain-filled woods, where hours later a bevy of foreign newspaper correspondents found him still walking. Already the monolithic Party machine was moving against him.

I stared along an overgrown drive. Only since entering Russia had I understood the dead weight of patriotism in this persecuted land—truth is only a troubling spectre in the balance against it—and how a single book or poem can threaten the fantasy of Party infallibility. That *Doctor Zhivago* could be castigated as it was, is both a measure of profound insecurity and of the strength of Pasternak's commitment to something else. 'The Russian poet,' wrote Maxim Gorky, 'is an indescribably lonely, tragically lonely figure.'

As I walked up the dacha's drive (I had an introduction to Pasternak's eldest son) the place already seemed a cenotaph. The house showed no lights. Even the birches were still. Nearby a path wound among twisted tree-roots to a plank bridge over a little lake, where once lived the woman Pasternak loved, the prototype of *Doctor Zhivago*'s heroine, Lara.

Zhenya Pasternak looked startlingly like his father. He lived in a cottage beside the larger house, with his wife and daughter. A dust of grey hair was thinning from his brows, yet he seemed young. His face held the gaunt, Pasternak distinction, touched by a kind of harrowed sweetness. The same indrawn cheeks and jowls separated the forehead from the full-lipped mouth, as if dividing continents. He had spent his early life as a technical engineer, he said—his father had warned him that the arts were dangerous—but now he devoted himself to collecting his father's letters, and to publishing his works when he could.

We sat in his kitchen. A clock cuckooed on one wall; a samovar gleamed on top of a cupboard. Our conversation ranged over poetry, archaeology, friends in England. He was gently learned. He scented my interest in the Middle East and discussed the site of Ebla and the origins of the alphabet, speaking in a soft drawl. Usually his gaze would be fixed on a point somewhere along the table's edge. Then his tall forehead would appear dissociated from the rest of his face, its brown eyebrows stuck there independently, until he would suddenly look up and his expression coalesce again around hazel-grey eyes.

We ate a simple supper, and went on talking between spoonfuls of unboiled jam—a Russian speciality—and cups of tea. His family joined us. His open-faced wife seemed half his age; his daughter had inherited the Pasternak physiognomy, and promised to be beautiful. But eventually our talk would always return to his father, to his poetry, and to his translations of Shakespeare which had been his only true way of utterance during the purges of the thirties. It was in the European tradition, Zhenya said, that Russia's true civilization had always lain. To the east loomed Asia, the Mongol memory, barbarism. To the west sprang the fount of humanity, the world in which he placed 'Pasternak' as he called him (never 'my father'), and looked to the future.

We wandered up his drive in the darkening evening. His wife's voice sounded softly through a bedroom window, reading Pushkin's fairy tales to their daughter. Beyond the gate the hill where his father was buried had blurred into dusk. ('Hundreds of people go there—the grave's covered in flowers even in the worst weather.') Beside us, in the big house, lights were glowing behind drawn curtains. 'My brother's widow lives there now,' Zhenya said. 'The house has stayed with our family, rented to us by the Writers' Union. It's a strange situation. It's as if they're waiting for the time when Pasternak will be reinstated. Then, I believe, the house will become a museum in his memory.'

So Boris Pasternak remains in a limbo somewhere between canonization and disgrace. Soon, for the first time, the journal *Novy mir* was to publish an article purely in his praise, without reference to his 'mistakes'—an early sign that he will eventually be rehabilitated through the perverse patriotism by which Russia embraces its choicest men after the embarrassment of their living truth is safely gone.

When I turned south next day, my road was scattered with the memories of writers—Turgenev, Tolstoy, Lermontov—who belonged to the European family of which Zhenya had spoken. The artist in Russia becomes either saint or sacrifice. Above all the writer, inhabiting his private nexus of ideas and freedoms, receives the accolade of persecution. Even the long-dead have had to be redefined, and the nineteenth century giants drummed into line as prophetic Marxists.

'My belief in a future justice is unshakable'—the words are not Lenin's but Tchaikovsky's, lifted out of context and inscribed beneath the composer's bust in his house at Klin. Soviet visitors pass this absurdity without a smile, barely noticing that their beloved composer—in fact a fervent monarchist—has been shepherded into the ideological fold. Neither his morbid neurosis, nor his homosexuality, are ever mentioned.

But when I stopped in the car-park before Tolstoy's home of Yasnaya Polyana, more than a hundred miles south of Moscow, the seething crowds reminded me of that Russian passion for literature which can fill a Moscow sports stadium before a poetry reading. The house stood in a country of smooth valleys. Beyond its gate-towers, which had filled the low-born Chekhov with such panic that he turned back from visiting Tolstoy, it rose from its trees in two long storeys skirted by verandahs and balconies—a rambling, habitable mansion of brick and wood. I walked between small lakes shining among willows, and up through copses and orchards. At the entrance families were posing before cameras. They looked solemn and proud, as if a photograph bestowed on them the numen of the place. Inside, we covered our shoes with huge, obligatory slippers, as in a mosque, and shuffled platypus-like over the wooden floors.

Tolstoy spent seventy of his eighty-two years here. The place was his fatherland, he said, his quintessential Russia. The wooden wing in which he was born was dismantled long ago; he sold it off while serving in the Crimean War, and lost the proceeds during two days' gambling in a God-forsaken artillery battery near Sebastopol. But the house and the wandering parklands are redolent of the childhood of his *Recollections*, and of the impoverished relations who wove an eccentric family around the high-strung child. Despotic, motherly or half-mad aunts and housekeepers, smelling of resin and urine, mingled in his remembrance with serfs gossiping around the stoves or snoringly asleep in out-of-the-way rooms, with monks, pilgrims and distant cousins who came and went—or stayed for ever. His parents both died in his childhood, leaving themselves perfect in his imagination—his father debonair, genial; his mother (who died before he was two) a powerful and idealized silhouette, ever-loving. But in her place intruded the memory of a fantastical grandmother. Seated in a high-sprung yellow cabriolet harnessed to two serfs, she would ride among hazel trees ordering the footmen to bend the choicest boughs for her picking; and at night, when one of the children shared her bedroom, she lay propped among pillows before her guttering icon-lamp, while a blind servant droned stories to her, until she merged into the dreams of the infant Tolstoy as a parchment-yellow queen on a throne of snow.

In half the rooms of the house tourist guides now declaim in reverential parrot. It is filled with the artefacts of Tolstoy's maturity and old age: the painted table at which his wife transcribed the endlessly-corrected manuscripts of *Anna Karenina* from his near-illegible handwriting; the low chair and table where he wrote, his myopic gaze hugging the page; his iron bed; his books—some in ancient Greek, Hebrew, Tartar, Arabic—covered with crayon notes; the thick walls and double doors of the vaulted chamber where he started *War and Peace*.

Gawping, expectant, we trudged from library to bedroom to study, as if they must yield up some essence of the titan who inhabited them. But they were all but immaterial to him. Ghosts. He grew to hate their luxury, the place itself, his hysterical wife—all but the trees, the memories. A bee-like murmur of sympathy arose from the visitors at the sight of the coarse blouse and floppy hat which he had worn in emulation of his peasants. More than any serf, he wanted to be a man of the people; until at last, in old age, feeling his life a welter of domestic failure and moral dissimilitude, existing at hopeless odds with his own philosophy, he fled his house altogether one night, and died of pneumonia in the stationmaster's cottage of a tiny village.

Such things have endeared him to contemporary ideology—despite his pacifism, despite his religiosity. But even his personal and changing creeds withered in his own mental furnace, and one leaves these rooms—their generous spaces, their workmanlike cane and mahogany furniture—with the sense of a man too exacting for any stillness of belief.

Everything he loved or mentioned has been preserved. The huge, three-pronged trunk of his favourite oak tree still writhes, dead and smooth now, from the garden's earth; and the school which he opened for peasant children in 1859—offering a profoundly un-Soviet individualist education—is a hushed museum. The woodland paths which he walked are still cut. I sat on his favourite bench. And he was buried as he wanted, without consecration, in a glade of his woods.

I followed a wedding party down the long forest path to the grave. It is a well-trodden way. Brides come to place their bouquets here, as they do on war memorials, looking for the god they have lost. And Tolstoy's spiritual stature—even his beard-lapped and Pantocratic face—are as close an earthly substitute for God the Father as they may find. 'Let no ceremonies be performed in putting my body into the earth,' he had asked. 'Just a wooden coffin and whoever wishes may carry it or cart it to Zakaz, opposite the ravine at the place of the "green stick".' More than three quarters of a century before, while he was still a small boy, he and his brothers had indulged a childhood fancy that there was hidden in this ravine a stick on which was inscribed the secret of lost happiness.

So he is buried under a grass mound in the woods. There is nothing more: no stone, no word. Someone had laid gladioli there, and a few oak and ash leaves were drifting over the grave. The bride looked embarrassed in the silent clearing, then placed her bouquet hesitantly against the mound. If there was a feeling of incompleteness, the party around her did not show it, but only lingered a moment, as if something might happen, while the yellow leaves went on falling in the glen.

It was almost dusk when I reached Spasskoye-Lutovinovo, the home of Turgenev. By contrast to Tolstoy's house, it looked half deserted. The mansion where he lived had been swept away by fire, like so many of these wooden palaces, but one wing restored as he had known it. A caretaker found me peering through the curtained windows, and let me in out of hours. Much of the furniture had survived, elegant in rosewood and birch, and she pointed out each piece to me until what had started as a favour became a pleasure, then a passion. Here was the English grandfather clock mentioned in *The Brigadier*, she said; there was the author's shotgun—had I read *Sketches from a Hunter's Album*? On one wall hung the drawing of a strange, gnomic child: Ivan Turgenev, aged six. The body was that of an infant, whose feet could not touch the floor from the chair in which he sat, but the face was shockingly old. From its preternaturally big head the eyes stared out with a depthless watchfulness. They looked ancient as time. In fact it was not an infant who sat there at all, but a premonition of adult suffering.

Of his father, who had married for money and was often away, the boy remembered only aloofness. But his mother was a hideous, black-eyed barbarian whose own atrocious upbringing was visited on her children and servants. She dealt out punishment and favour with the stark capriciousness of the unloved. She smothered Ivan with a perverted possessiveness, alternately pampered and flogged him. Five thousand serfs groaned under her yoke. She ruled them in grotesque etiquette and rusticity. Once she even pretended to die, so that she could punish whichever looked pleased.

The boy fled to the parklands of the estate, which are magnificent still. The trees rise in their lordly hundreds. Huge, wind-pushed birches lean and stagger together, and giant lime trees draw their avenues across the woods. The fragrance of these trees, the noise of their orioles and siskins and nightingales, the violets and the broken circles of sunlight shed on the black earth, fill Turgenev's novels with their sound and scent. The boy lay beneath them mesmerized by insects, birdsong; but it was under these trees, too, that the unequal duel between an adder and a toad first made him doubt the goodness of heaven.

At the park's end the avenues merge into woods around a sunken lake. Here, where the melancholy child fed the fish by hand, nothing has changed. In the deepening twilight the pool lay stagnant and sinister. Its whole surface was glazed with a thick weed which creaked weirdly in the silence, and was broken only by concentric circles motionless in its centre, as if something important had risen or been dropped there centuries ago.

Although he spent much of his life in western Europe, following the woman he loved—the singer Pauline Viardot, dark and exotically ugly as his mother—Turgenev returned again and again to Spasskoye. He was exiled here in 1852 after composing a too-complimentary obituary on Gogol, and eked out his time in writing, shooting game and flirting with serf girls. By now his mother was dead, and the place filled with a half-bitter nostalgia. The remembered servants had wizened. Soon before his death he returned to a mismanaged estate—its garden grown silent, rooks cawing, ivy crawling over the verandahs. Even now he entertained passing affections—an aristocratic widow, and a young actress for whom he built a bathing-hut by the edge of the dark,

Excaliburish lake; but his love remained a thing of distance and oblique sensuality, a fantasy, an endless goodbye.

Many of his contemporaries never forgave Turgenev for his expatriate life; it was like a personal affront. He is the most Western of the great Russian novelists, and for the Marxist he should be—but is not—an unacceptable hero. Communism's socialist realism, like most religious art, celebrates a revealed truth. It precludes the shifting awareness, that sense of the unrealizable, which haunt the pages of Turgenev. His people can exemplify nothing so evanescent as a certainty. He is the poet of the spirit's strangeness.

I was only forty miles from the campsite at Oryol, 'the writer's capital'. In the night, as I drove, the eventless fields and forests of this region needed no imagining. My head was full of remembered literature—of the gaping hours and blank distances around those nineteenth century landowners isolated far from Moscow and one another in a frittering, autumnal boredom. Through the pages of Chekhov and Goncharov and Turgenev they flourish and dissipate unconfined by work or purpose. The hours yawn. Rooted in that ampler, Russian destiny which enfolds and eventually obliterates them, they are, in their way, profoundly collective. Even the wayward peasants and petty bureaucrats of Gogol, so miserably unsuited to factories but obsessed by material things—overcoats, boots, cabbages, anything—are perfectly recognizable queueing outside Oryol's shops.

Next morning, while I wandered round the little writers' museum, it was almost painful to witness how piously each artist was enshrined. Bunin, Andreyev, Fet, Leskov—the leaves from their manuscripts were preserved in glass like bible parchment, their desks and inkwells and paper-weights exhibited in perfect working order like reliquaries which could yet hold nothing. As I shuffled from one to the next—I had slept badly and was feeling depressed—I had a fantasy that these literary artefacts were flotsam from an individualistic past which had forever been lost, and that Russia had regressed to a conformity worse than mediaeval.

When I sidled into conversation with a student, the only other person in the museum, I must have voiced my depression crudely, because a fleeting hurt crossed his face.

'How can you imagine we all think what we're told to think in this country?' He stuffed his hands into the pockets of his frayed bomber-jacket and fixed me with the type of wide-spread Russian eyes which I had grown to trust. 'The government may try to make us think their way, but I don't know a soul who does. Not a soul! Everybody I know has ideas of his own—even the most bone-headed farmer.' Of course people were affected by Party propaganda, he said, but they were independent of it too. The system was simply a feature of life. People used it or ignored it or evaded it. They didn't love or fight it. The private values of *Doctor Zhivago*, which had agonized the Soviet authorities in 1958, were second nature to his generation. He was engaged instead with writers who had found their voice in the Kruschev era and had weathered the retrenchment of the late sixties and seventies—Yevtushenko, Voznesensky, Aksyonov. (But Moscow intellectuals had long been saying Yevtushenko was a Party hack.)

We stopped before a table displaying novels by modern authors, names unknown to me. Their covers blazed with heroism: industry, war. The student's gaze drifted over them with an indifference too total even for contempt.

'That's all pulp,' he said. 'Fairy stories! You can tell they don't mean a word of it. Sometimes I read them like I read science fiction, if I can't lay my hands on anything better. But normally I wouldn't even bother to open them. After a while you develop an instinct just by glancing at the covers.'

Not that these authors were charlatans, he said, merely they were servants of the state. If they perverted truth, it was in the cause of communal morality. They were simply small, superfluous. The gap between their written beliefs and their actual experience had become fatally wide. The student waved them away. 'You don't have that in the West.'

No, I said, we had our own printed effluent: not corporate myths, but personal ones—romance, porn. The difference was that in the West our rulers didn't suppress excellence.

A shadow of insult crossed his face again. 'Our government may fear it but they can't suppress it. Not always. Not all of it. He delved deeper into his pockets and pulled out a book wrapped in layers of brown paper. He'd managed to buy it for twenty pounds, more than thirty times the published price. 'Listen.'

It fell open in his hands. He began to declaim. And the extraordinary thing was that a student in provincial Oryol, who had been surrounded by propaganda from birth, had instinctively sensed its unreality and grown passionate instead about the most bitter poems of Voznesensky.

'As in delirium, everything falls apart
People disconnect . . .

'That's what I admire! A man who can get such power in a handful of words! That's what I love about the Japanese poets too. Have you read Issa? Basho? . . . What do you think of Verlaine? . . .'

While we thrust through the last rooms of the museum, followed by the sombre gaze of writers' photographs, their wives, mistresses, children, the names of his cultural heroes evolved into an outlandish archipelago: Kurt Vonnegut, Tarkovsky, The Rolling Stones, Stendhal, Matsuo Basho, Iris Murdoch. He'd recently given fifteen roubles for a paperback of Murdoch's *The Black Prince*.

'Most foreign novels you just can't buy. A bookseller will charge anything for one in Russian translation. People want them just because it's the vogue.' He folded up Voznesensky's poetry carefully—its pages were falling out, unhinged by constant use—and tucked it back in his pocket. 'But sometimes you hear of secret places where books are exchanged on the black market. Usually in parks. Luckily the police are pretty uneducated, you know, so they don't get to hear about it. I got Vonnegut's *Slaughterhouse Five* that way—and only *eight roubles*.'

He was (he said) typical of his generation at university. To them, Revolutionary history was boring. His father, a cab driver, had instilled in him a love of the Russian classics. The Revolution could no more cut the flow of that tradition than a knife could cut a river, he said. In Oryol it was hard to find the works of Mandelshtam, let alone of Solzhenitsyn. But reading Tolstoy was a restitution.

The road lifted and fell in great calm sighs, flowing between fields of maize and birch forest. Here and there a line of willows traced the idling of a river, and hundreds of black and white cattle drifted nomadically over the pastures. The highway, the main artery to the south, was no more than a stubbly, two-lane scrawl. I was still a thousand miles north of the Caucasus. For two days I drove in a clanking file of lorries, and ate at roadside canteens where truck-drivers talked gloomily about football or prices, drank their watery beer and downed bowls of noodles, sausage and cabbage soup. Imperceptibly we passed from the headwaters of one river-family to those of another. At first the westernmost tributary of the Oka wound among islets; then branches of the Dnieper appeared—marsh-filled coils of water, lazy with fishermen and canoes. Sometimes the road would lift to show a vista of rain-soaked woods or farmlands, but the trees had grown bright and deciduous in windbreaks of oak and acacia.

Something else was changing too. The stifling waves of authority which rippled out from Moscow had begun to subside, the formal grip of the police easing. The distances elongated between check-points. Roadside markets appeared: gatherings of *babushkas* who bargained stoutly with passing motorists over baskets of apples and potatoes. These sparks of enterprise warmed me. Nowadays I was comforted, rather than disappointed, by the shortcomings of Communism. I had undergone an obscure change of heart. I belonged too deeply to the world of private love and choice which Communism sought to supersede. The danger was that like a Soviet visitor to the West disgusted by things alien to his society—unemployment, organized crime, pornography—my observation might be held too compulsively by the shortcomings which consoled me.

But now I was driving through a region which thirty-five years before had lain derelict. Oryol, Kursk, Belgorod, Kharkov—they had risen up from devastated cores. South of Kharkov I struck the *chernozem*— the darkly glittering earth which spreads from the Ukraine into Siberia for more than three thousand miles. This is the steppeland soil whose horse-high grasslands nourished the Tartars westward; and the millennial decay of these same grasses created the rich black humus which today bears the great Soviet cornlands. It was patterned over the shallow valleys as if scorched there. I hid my car among trees and wandered along its fields. Around my feet the no-man's-land of sedge and cornflowers sent up a whirr and chirrup of insects. The earth crumbled through my fingers; the land was flooded in sunlight. I was in the south at last.

I plunged into a mammoth field of sunflowers. Their spatular leaves flopped around my shoulders, and the sun had turned all their heads one way, following its trajectory in an idolatrous worship. When the wind blew among them, these Van Gogh faces shifted in a somnambulistic dance, drowsing and nodding about me at eye level. Bees were drinking at their hearts, where the fallen seeds had left black, burnt-out whorls.

South-eastward from where I walked, the valley of the Don river was muffled in islets. It gathered its strength secretly, apparently motionless, easing southward through the soft soil in long, connected lakes. Across the fields' skyline ridges of harvested hay stretched a hundred yards long each, like yellow carpets rolled back from a black floor. At first glance it was inexplicable why the harvest of this gigantic earth could not feed the whole nation, the whole world, however erratic its rainfall and brutal the winds. But the collective and state farming systems fester in chronic failure. The peasants are the serfs of Communism. Until recently they were denied even the privilege of a passport for travelling within the country. Between them and the industrial worker yawns an ancient apartheid. The townsman has long regarded them either with disdain or guilty romanticism. They are worse paid than he, worse educated, cut off.

I gave a lift to two labourers. They talked about their work without a flash of pride. They were young. The Stalinist myths and dreams of collective farming had died in them, or never been born. The old truisms were still true: that Party functionaries and accountants stultified the system even here. The collective farmer is motiveless. Thirty per cent of Russia's agricultural product is grown on just three per cent of its tended land—the private plots of the peasants. Nobody will work for an abstract concept as he will sweat for a wife or a child.

The farmers' brick houses nestled possessively among their private fruit trees, and this free enterprise had overflowed in larger markets under makeshift awnings along the road: buckets of apricots, green peas, melons, sunflower seeds, yellow-capped mushrooms. They were more expensive than collective food—they were dear by any standards—but they offered choice and a little quality. All day old peasant women would sit before a jar or two of plums or a handful of sourish grapes—yet such markets were more varied than in any northern town.

I stopped for a woman hitch-hiking. She looked almost sixty. Five days a week she hitch-hiked twenty miles to work in a fabrics factory. The return bus fare cost a rouble, she said, and she couldn't afford it.

It was already eleven o'clock. What time should she be at work?

'Ten, eleven, twelve! What does it matter?'

Had she no family?

'Ach!' She waved them away. She lived alone in a tiny flat. In four years' time she'd receive a pension of forty-five roubles a month. It wasn't enough to live on, but she looked forward to it. As for her husband, she'd left him because of drink—the old, commonplace tragedy. 'He drank so much it was hopeless. We'd been married twenty-seven years, and still I put up with it. But in the end he was completely gone. He didn't understand anything, or make sense at all. My daughter said: You must leave him. And so I did.' She spoke stridently but without rancour. 'What else can a woman do?'

If the old are not protected by their families, a state pension will barely keep them alive. But the woman seemed too robust for my pity. She gossiped and laughed through gleams of silver teeth. I left her at the factory: a ramshackle building employing many hundreds. But work was better than loneliness. She offered me ten kopecks—Russian motorists ask money for lifts—but pocketed it gratefully on my refusal and marched away through the gates.

All day the country had lain in dead-flat calm, washed by a sky which paled to mist along the vast circumference of its horizons. But suddenly, north of Rostov, I was driving among the waste heaps of the Don basin coal mines. Black or pink discoloured pyramids shot up from a treeless roll of valleys. Sometimes they stood along the skyline in hazy isolation, like forgotten tumuli. More often it looked as if a titanic mole had burrowed beneath the valleys, nudging up cones and earthworks along its run. Mile after mile they continued on a scale as elemental as the land where they stood—inky scarps which loomed above miners' cottages, ventilation plants, pit-heads, mills, compressor houses. They were desolately impressive, like a poster from Russia's thirties.

So I came to Rostov-on-Don. This, too, might symbolize the march of industry over the steppes—the triumph of the new Russia over the old Cossack anarchy. It is the gateway to the Caucasus and the eastern shores of the Black Sea. Its citizens are proud of it, and the campsite authorities alighted on me—a rare, lone Westerner—with a language student as guide.

'This is Yury,' they said. 'He's a Cossack.'

I looked into a near-featureless face, its gaze as grey and unfocused as his native wilderness. I remembered my experience at Minsk, but I had not the heart to send him away. I was his first 'real Englishman', he said.

For two days he showed me round the official attractions of Rostov. He recited his facts dutifully—good and bad—in a throaty, smothered voice. He showed none of the hectic evangelism of Alexander Intourist. One skyscraper, he said, had already taken fifteen years to build—he was a child when it had been started—and nobody knew when it would be finished. It was a half-standing joke. And the huge Gorky Theatre, built in the shape of a tractor—a last shout of Constructivism from the early thirties—only faintly stirred him.

Yet Yury was touchy. And he understood nothing of the West at all; he could scarcely focus his imagination for a coherent question about it. Around him the Soviet Union was so vast and hermetic that it comprised all the conceivable world.

One thing I remember with peculiar clarity. This was when I told Yury that we in the West were afraid of Russia. For an instant he stared at me open-mouthed, then burst into disbelieving laughter. It was the only time I heard him laugh, so preposterous to him, so manifestly silly, was the idea of his country's dangerousness. This disbelief had already been echoed by other Russians along my route. Twice Yury asked me if I were not joking, then gazed at me for long moments, astonished at the depth of my delusion.

And I, in turn, became mesmerized by his enclosedness. Rostov to him was the measure of all things. He took me to the gates of the mammoth Rostelmash factory, the country's biggest producer of agricultural machinery, which had won the Order of Lenin, he said, and the Order of the Great October Socialist Revolution and the Order of the Red Banner of Labour. He chanted the orders like a liturgy. Then we went to a People's Palace of Culture. We peered into music and ballet rooms, filming and sculpture studios. They were heavy with control. Yury sensed my distaste, but he could not gauge its cause. He grew disconsolate, and redoubled his efforts. He took me to leisure centres run by trade unions on the south bank of the Don. They were compounds of tin-roofed huts, decorated by plants set in rubber tyres. Everything was violently painted. People came here in summer to escape their apartments, Yury said; the best compound had been visited by Gagarin, and displayed a commemorative fountain, which was falling to bits. No breath of proletarian jollity fired these camps. They were almost deserted. In three different compounds I saw only one netball pitch, a split table-tennis board and a billiard table whose pockets had rotted to shreds. It was the nightmare of some Marxist Butlin.

But Yury felt none of this. He liked the trees, and the sense of the river nearby. Living in a city, he was yet a countryman. He took the steppeland into the streets with him. It lumbered in his walk and filled his inarticulate gaze and hands. He typified, perhaps, the Russian whom Westerners underestimate: decent, conscientious, enduring.

His ancestry was as remote and glamorous to him as it was to me. We spent a morning at Novocherkassk, the Cossack capital—a town like any other now, he said. But two triumphal arches celebrated the entry of Platov's Cossacks into Napoleon's Paris, and the crypt of the forbidding cathedral was filled with the tombs of wild atamans. There were still a few old Cossack families living in the town, Yury said, but they kept to themselves and he did not know them. So we wandered round the Don Cossack museum, gazing at a booty of velvet, glass, carpets.

The Cossacks refuse any ideological mould. Refugees from serfdom or revolution, flamboyantly whiskered men and braided women, prodigal of life, roisterous, drunken, free—this seemingly indestructible people coalesced into unruly democracies on the frontiers of empire, pushing it forward but half independent of it, and became in turn the martyrs of peasant revolution and the brutal instruments of imperial repression. The later tsars elevated them to an élite military caste, until they formed the hardest and most reactionary regiments of the army.

All this—royalist or revolutionary—was splashed about the museum in a tempestuous duality. But their later history had been reconvened into ghostly, half-recognizable shapes. Their role in supporting the White armies had tactfully dwindled; so had those who fought for Germany in the Second World War and who were betrayed by the Treaty of Yalta; and so had Stalin's collectivization of the *kulaks*, the richer farmers, which went ahead in a welter of violence and family feuds, to end in mass arrests and mass exile.

But the drift to the towns was destroying Cossackdom more surely, and less painfully. 'You can't be a Cossack and live in a city,' Yury said, as we swallowed fish soup and beef pancakes in a self-consciously Cossack restaurant on the Don. 'You have to stay in the village, the *stanitsa*. An urban Cossack's a contradiction.'

We stared out at the river. Between its unequal banks—the northern high and tree-crowned, the southern low and merging into steppe—it flowed, rife with history, to the Sea of Azov. Over its surface a light, troubling ripple played all afternoon, but left its depths untouched, as if the great waters were scarcely moving. Upriver, said Yury, it no longer skirted the wattle-palisaded *stanitsas* of old, but emerged from a land of collectivized hamlets and forestation schemes.

'The whole society's dying,' he said. 'It's happening very fast. When I think of my grandfather, who rode with the Red cavalry in the Civil War!' And in a rare moment of evocation, he conjured this ancient warrior before my eyes: a lean, choleric, sickle-whiskered barbarian, whose hair exploded in hoary thickets from under his sheepskin cap and whose gorilla arms were laced with burns. He had died of drink.

'But what happened to him in the thirties?'

Yury kept his eyes on the grey river and announced without emotion: 'My grandparents were considered *kulak* because they owned a horse, a plough and a patch of land. They were deported to Siberia. Before they went they placed my mother—she was a girl then—with one of my aunts. Those were bad years: famine. My mother's still physically small. She came from deep Cossack country—a hundred miles north of here.' He gestured upriver. 'But she doesn't want to go back. She says they're very bitter in those villages. They wouldn't offer a stranger so much as a glass of water. And of course they hate the memory of Stalin. Three-quarters of our people loathe Stalin.'

[136]

Southward, a feeling of timelessness descends. In the west the Azov and Black Seas, where the great rivers spill, merge invisibly with the Mediterranean world. To the east stretch the cloudy steppes of the Caspian and Asia, ancient mother of half the earth's peoples, whom it has loosed in a staunchless flood since before record. Scythians, Huns, Avars, Tartars, Parthians, Magyars—a myriad barbarians grew in this fearsome womb and flung themselves west and south and east, in spasm after spasm, towards the civilizing sea.

Here and there along the roadside, where holidaymakers were returning north in cars bulging with children and tents, one of the tall Don horses stood in glossy solitude—a stilt-legged beauty, built to stare over the grasslands. The country nourished vines and sunflowers, withering now, and combine harvesters reared their brontosaurus heads from the maize fields. Once again the whole land had smoothed to an oceanic peace, as if it must pour itself away over the earth's edge.

At last, like a paler emanation of the sky, appeared a long, colourless ridge. In any other terrain it would have counted for little, but for four thousand miles I had seen nothing so high. It lifted from the flatlands like a portent, abrupt and eerie, predicting a new country. And soon I was driving along a plateau of exhausted hills which broke in waves against the highway. On milder slopes the tracks of vanished rains sliced through the fields; on others only the aluminium sheen of willows survived.

A hundred miles later the first mountains appeared. Huge but insubstantial, they shifted and overlapped like shadows thrown on the sky. At dusk, when I arrived in the campsite at Pyatigorsk, it was to find these outworks of the Caucasus hovering all around in black, refractory silhouettes. The camp was half empty. I carried my bedding to my sleeping-hut under a sky already flashing with stars. But somebody had arrived before me.

'You will please excuse me, sir'—I saw a dark man with a smooth-skinned, ingratiating face. 'May I petition your kindness to call me Misha? I was appointed here as your guide by the authorities because they consider you particularly honourable.'

I wasn't anxious to be noticed by the nameless authorities, but his whimsical English dismissed a faint disquiet. He was small and slight, with an ambivalent face: a forty-year-old boy. His head looked perfect-ly circular, and was muffled in short black hair incongruously flecked by grey. From time to time his quaint, phrase-book speech was pocked by unintentional slang.

'Tomorrow we will visit the beauties of Pyatigorsk spa. But first may I

lavish with you some booze on the occasion of your successful arrival?'
In either hand he held a bottle of Georgian champagne, and all the time
he spoke his forehead shot up and down in comical spasms and his eyes
popped, as if he were trying to keep awake.

'It is not allowed to guides to tipple alone with foreigners, neverthe-
less,' he said, then uncorked the champagne and gurgled it into two
glasses plucked from his pockets. We sat at the table in my hut, with the
curtains drawn. Misha stretched back in his chair with self-conscious
hedonism, cigarette in one hand, champagne glass poised in the other,
his face crossed by a sybaritic grin. I could not make him out. 'To tell
you the truth, there's nothing to do in Pyatigorsk spa at all,' he said,
'unless you have a stomach complaint. As for me, my own origins, sir,
are not in Pyatigorsk. According to the anthropology, I believe I have
Tartar blood. I am from the Volga. But sometimes people mistake me
for a mountain Jew, or an Italian, perhaps, because I talk too much.'

He spoke unlaughing. Sometimes his alternate pedantry and vulgar-
isms gave me the fleeting illusion of a Dickensian gentleman fallen on
evil days. He had studied English, he said, at the pedagogical institute
in Moscow. Now he was a schoolmaster and part-time guide in
Pyatigorsk. 'And what is your profession?' he suddenly asked.

I launched into an outdated story about a company directorship. He
poured out more champagne.

'You were today a long time arriving here. I have been waiting for you
since three o'clock—propping up the bar, if thus I may put it.' His
forehead performed a mazurka of spasms. I thought he was slightly
drunk. 'I feared something had befallen you.'

No, I said, nothing. He uncorked the second bottle of champagne
with a celebratory flourish. 'This is Black Label Georgian. The best!
Now this company directorship of yours. . . .'

The drink seemed to be seeping into my eyes, clouding them. I was
watching Misha through a muslin curtain. His forehead was shooting
about in self-conscious imbecility now. I wondered momentarily if he
were retarded. But his questions had become more searching. Somewhere, far back in my mind, a warning bell was sounding.

'Tomorrow,' he was saying, 'we will go into the mountains. There is
a game reserve where I have a certain buddy. I do not wish to press my
insistences upon you, but you are a sportsman are you not? I love
hunting. Do you love hunting? It is forbidden there, but neverthe-
less.'

The second bottle was draining fast. Misha refilled the glasses with
remorseless devotion, grinning at nothing. I reckoned he was drunker

than I, but my head was already swaying feebly, and to refuse the last champagne was to insult his hospitality.

He began talking politics. He was a member of the Communist Party, he said, and certainly he seemed modestly privileged: he had worked as an interpreter with Russian groups abroad; he had also read the best-known Western exposés of the Soviet way of life. 'Those books are right,' he said. 'Politics here are a farce.' He burped. 'Just propaganda. Nobody can find out anything serious except through the Party grape-vine. Do you know there are strikes going on in Poland at this moment . . . serious strikes . . . and almost nobody in this country knows about them?' And what were my politics, he asked?

I mumbled some British complacencies, gauging my own drunkenness, feeling unhappy. When he next refilled my glass, I surreptitiously emptied it into an ash tray. I did not take his news on Poland seriously; I had heard nothing.

A distant, slurring voice (my own) asked: 'How can you be a Party member when you think it's all a farce?'

He smiled, and misunderstood. 'I deserve my place in the Party. In the early sixties I was with Soviet troops in Somalia, shooting members of the Somalia resistance and so forth. Then the country's allegiances, if thus I may put it, unfortunately changed to the British, and we were chucked out.' He said the word 'British' as if it had nothing to do with me (and his history was badly garbled).

'You shot Somalis . . . but you think your politics. . . .'

In my champagne-sodden mind the idea of Misha was by now hypnotic. I foraged for some hidden rationale to his self-cancelling beliefs, but he intimated none. One moment he let drop that the whole Soviet Union was rife with corruption. The next he asked me to send him a postcard from Britain congratulating him on his country's glorious October Socialist Revolution. His talk was an obscene chiaroscuro of ideology and cynicism. It was as if his integrity had rotted away long ago, or never existed.

Suddenly he said: 'You will not refer on me to the authorities?'

'I don't know any authorities.'

He dropped his cigarette into the ash-tray. It fizzed in my discarded champagne. 'Why have you poured it away?' He stood up. 'We'll go to the camp restaurant. I have friends waiting there. We'll have a party.'

From this later, drink-fuddled celebration, which drowsed and gabbled far into the night, I retrieve only random glimpses. A gallery of inebriate faces glows in my memory, severed from time and place; their remarks surface in meaningless isolation, and whole conversations lie stranded without starts or ends. But the faces, I recall, encapsuled in miniature the Soviet empire. Opposite me a Slav suet-pudding physiognomy proposed cumbersome toasts and cracked into smiles with the slowness of a geological fault, while beside him a citron-skinned architect might have sprung from the pages of Russian folklore. On my right Misha's low brows and Tartar cheeks surrounded bright but indecipherable eyes; to my left a long-faced Armenian barman, with the creamy skin and voice of his people, offered me seductive sums for my Morris.

The architect, I thought, looked restrained, ill at ease. He talked to me ruefully. His teenage children, he said, were besotted by pop music; as for him, he wondered if I had any records of Victor Sylvester with me—he loved those. He shared the Russian passion for the countryside, and would often vanish on two-day fishing expeditions, although this upset his wife.

'Actually he fishes for women,' said the suet-pudding, fracturing into a grin. 'There aren't any in Pyatigorsk, only sanatoria.'

One by one we declaimed portentous toasts, groping to our feet with teetering solemnity. Wine, vodka and Armenian three-star brandy slopped down our throats in ceremonial debauch. With each toast the little glasses of vodka were tossed back at a gulp, so that drunkenness advanced in dazed leaps and bounds, and faculties were amputated at a stroke. On one side of me the Armenian's car-prices spiralled into fantasy, on the other Mischa kept clinking his glass against mine, chirruping 'Quite sincerely!' and spoke of himself in the third person. 'Misha needs a holiday. . . . Misha is quite fed up with being a schoolmaster. . . . Tomorrow, or perhaps the day after, we will go into the mountains and see the eternal snows. Misha loves beauty. Do you love beauty?'—glasses clashed—'Quite sincerely! . . . Misha should have been a lawyer. . . . What did your father make you do? . . . He didn't? Your fathers in the West, they're very lenient. . . . Misha's made him work at an English language institute. . . . Quite sincerely! I was only seventeen, and I wanted to do law. . . .' Snatches of pop songs droned inconsequently in his speech, then he would change the subject without warning or ask sudden questions.

'It's true there are no girls in Pyatigorsk . . . not after Moscow. Misha enjoyed himself in Moscow. But it's not a good city for the personal relationships. . . . *Bye-bye, baby, bye-bye.* . . . Russian girls, let me tell you sir, make very good wives, excellent in the home, very tender and not very sexually experienced. . . . What is your father's job?'

It struck me that Misha was not only drunk but pretending, perhaps enjoying the idea of drunkenness, I didn't know. His forehead and eyes wrinkled and popped in unison. 'Let me tell you, sir, there was a Belgian girl on the language course in Moscow . . . lovely wide hips, very woman-like . . . oh Misha! *Save all your kisses for me.* . . . How is it you are allowed on such a tour by your authorities? You must be an important person. . . .'

But a tiny, watchful fragment of myself was refusing to get drunk. I remembered a sixteenth century ambassador to Moscow writing that he could only avoid stupor by feigning it already, otherwise he was forced to continue drinking. Feigning wasn't difficult. My head had become a hydrogen balloon tethered among empty bottles and dismembered expressions. The architect, as it happened, resembled a French schoolmaster from my childhood, so that in my drugged vision the two men—the present and the imagined—nudged each other bifocally and occasionally overlapped. For all I know I began calling him 'sir' and conjugating irregular verbs.

Then the suet pudding lumbered to his feet for yet another toast. We had already pledged eternal friendship, the beauty of women, the peoples of our two countries, our families and much else, and had now entered a realm of flowery, maudlin libations which threatened to drop me senseless. 'We come like many rivers from different sources,' he intoned, 'yet we meet in the same sea, under the same sky, so let us drink. . . .'

Two or three more vodkas, I calculated, and I'd be insensible. I proposed my return toast in a babble of goodwill and mixed metaphors, and spilled my glass unseen into a vase of plastic flowers.

Soon afterwards the restaurant closed, and we were stumbling out under the stars. The air was soft and warm. Good-nights sounded in the dark. I walked gingerly to the camp gates. My feet felt numb on the path. Misha kept blundering against me. 'You can't drive home in your state,' I said.

'It doesn't matter,' he slurred. 'The police won't do . . . anything to me.'

'Why not?'

'Because I work. . . .' He floundered again, recovered; but I suddenly knew what he was going to say. 'Because I work . . . for the KGB.'

My voice sounded flat. 'What's that like?'

'Mostly rather . . . boring.'

We were approaching the gates, where porters loitered. I had time, I estimated, for one more question. 'I don't imagine they're interested in me, are they?'

An ugly silence fell. 'In you . . . especially.' Then he disappeared through the gates and into the dark.

A nineteenth century grace and leisure linger about the terraces and springs of Pyatigorsk—an aroma of Baden-Baden or Bath. Trees bloom and tumble about the lower slopes of Mount Marshuk, where the health-giving waters flow, and limestone pavilions touch its walks and arbours with a tryst-like seclusion. Once orchestras lilted in the acacia boulevards, and blue-pantalooned tsarist officers sauntered the terraces at evening, their silver epaulettes yellowed by sulphur fumes, while a chaperoned and crinolined procession of ladies, with fashionable or unmentioned diseases, fluttered by in a prattle of gossip and bad French.

But higher up, the slopes of Marshuk suddenly turn naked, and the scent of box and lime trees vanishes in a sharp air. The jagged hills lift and fall in the shadow of steeper heights, which litter the sky behind in pinnacles of snow. The feel becomes less of Bath than of Victorian Simla—a privileged sanctuary on the edge of tribal wilderness. Far into the last century Cossack pickets were still guarding the spa's outskirts, and the threat of kidnap by Circassian brigands filled the visiting ladies with pleasurable horror.

A lacework of stairs and terraces ascends to the sulphurous halls of the Elizabeth Spring, the old hub of spa society, and an elegant belvedere, whose weather-vane once plucked the strings of a suspended harp, still emits unearthly music in the wind. But the exclusive resort of a century ago has spilled over the slopes in ranks of modern sanatoria. Robust young couples in shorts and T-shirts cram the walks on health-cult holidays, and mud and carbonic baths receive the suffering bodies of a long-excluded proletariat. The sallow ghosts of nineteenth century debutantes, who once lowered little wicker-cased tumblers into the waters, have been ousted by the squat local townswomen—limbs unshaven and blond-dyed hair showing inches dark at the roots—who invade the spring-kiosks on their way to work and swill back the nauseous waters from beaked cups.

Pyatigorsk is dedicated to the Romantic poet Lermontov, who was shot here in a duel in 1841. There are Lermontov baths and statues, a Lermontov walk and grotto, Lermontov station. On the site where he was killed a commemorative obelisk is ringed by chain-hung pillars shaped like bullets; attendant vultures reverse their bronze heads into their ruffs in mourning; and a plaque declares that Lermontov's memory is cherished for ever in the hearts of the people. Yet it occurred to me how few nineteenth century writers would have survived the Soviet regime—not the Westernized Turgenev nor the God-haunted Dostoevsky. Pushkin would have been disgraced for bawdiness, and the apocalyptic Tolstoy was too like his spiritual descendant, Solzhenitsyn, for his own or anybody's comfort. As for Lermontov, he was an outspoken and cynical delinquent, out of love with men and with himself.

My wanderings round Pyatigorsk were dogged by Misha. His services as a guide were useless—he knew almost nothing—but I was afraid of estranging him. We drove up the flanks of Marshuk together, but all around us dense clouds scarfed the hills' peaks or rolled between their clefts, and on the summit we stood in a whiteness so utter that Misha turned to me, dilating his suddenly puerile eyes, and said: 'Never mind. Tomorrow we'll go into the mountains.'

For a few hours I escaped him by visiting the architect, who showed me round his spartan office. Its lobby was lined by photographs of staff members who had fought in the war, each elderly face coupled with its wartime one. The responsibility of being snapped had frozen all their expressions into the same dead gravity.

The architect was modest and direct. No foolish statistics left his lips. The building trade was undermanned, he said; speed and simplicity were vital. In the West, he knew, countless small companies made for variety, but here in Russia, where all materials were prefabricated *en masse*, new forms could only be achieved by the wholesale changing of factory moulds.

Hence the stultifying uniformity of Soviet cities.

The day became a flight from Misha. I even sought out the car-mad Armenian barman. In a month's time, he said, his name would top the waiting-list for an 8,500-rouble Zhiguli Fiat; but he had fallen in love with my old Morris. He longed, with a terrible passion, to buy it. I was glad that this was illegal, but he sank into ecstasy when I let him drive it, caressing its dashboard and steering it with such awestruck tenderness that I was amazed again by the desolate sameness of Soviet things.

Towards evening I found solitude in the largest medicinal bathhouse in Russia. I strolled through resonant waiting-halls past radon water tanks furnished with banks of control panels. I felt peacefully unnoticed. An old man and a bespectacled woman lay in gas baths under transparent covers, breathing oxygen, and gazed up at me indifferently, like mummies from sarcophagi.

I took a shower, slopped through two trays of disinfectant and into the 'simple waters' of a huge swimming-pool. Beyond its picture-window a scarp of hillside, pared to shrub and grey rocks, lifted into cloud with the frozen clarity of a Japanese garden. But the pool was bubbling like a mill-race. All along one side, in dedicated unison, a regiment of middle-aged health-addicts was bending, kicking, bouncing and dog-paddling in time to the whistle-blasts of a white-uniformed amazon striding above. They jogged and wheezed like monstrous babies. She shouted at them to stretch, leap, arch their backs. Clinging to the bar at shoulder level, they sent out tidal billows of spume and grunts of muscular accomplishment. Ageing biceps and deltoids reeled into life. Necks bulged, calves flailed. They belonged to Stalin's physical-jerks generation. Flaccid Russian backs and a polished Uzbek one lurched and wallowed in line with hirsute Georgians and Armenians. When they turned, several chests showed sprawling tattoos: patriotic sickles and stars. One man's torso was vivid with a portrait of Lenin on one side, Stalin on the other, which wobbled and shook unhappily together as he bounced, or eyed each other in stillness through a greying maquis of hair.

Just as I expected to be dragooned into line, the exercise ended and a scrum of gargantuan women burst from the dressing-rooms—cliché Soviet giantesses whose cask-like torsoes expanded downward from formless shoulders to a flood of loins and quivering thighs. They jumped shouting into the water.

I was washed against the man with the patriotic bust. Had he regretted its left-hand portrait—I asked tactlessly—after the denunciation of Stalin?

He stared at me and submerged himself. The jumping women were exploding about us like cannonballs. And I marvelled that this people, while fostering the world's finest dancers and athletes, should yet be among the least co-ordinated and graceful on earth. It was hard to look at their worn-out bodies without a pang.

The next day there was no escaping Misha. He had arranged that we drive to Mount Elbruz deep in the northern massif of the Great Caucasus. He lay back on my mattress over the flattened passenger-seat, with his thin legs stretched fastidiously in front of him, and said in a voice of smothered pain: 'Misha has a stomach ache.' From time to time he would massage his ribs and grimace, ascribing his pain to the bumpy roads or the altitude. But it seemed merely to be a bid for attention. He had an infantile need to be felt. He was neurotically sensitive to my moods, which he gauged with creepy swiftness and always related to himself (he was right) asking: 'I do not offend you in any way, sir?'

As for his own moods, I would catch the changing roles of his face in the car mirror. At some moments he appeared sly and seemed to be watching me, at others his expression slumped into a mask of simpleton candour; more often, with his look of self-conscious hedonism, he would affect sleep. But he had become irredeemably sinister to me, and now, as he leaned back with closed eyes, I felt as if the yellow membrane of his eyelids were transparent or perforated, and that he was seeing everything.

We turned west by a thin road into the mountains. The valley was steep and beautiful with trees. A young tributary of the Terek river ran beside us in grey-green spate, making for the Caspian, and spread into a stone-dimpled flood where the way eased, before descending in cold torrents again.

Misha's eyes suddenly opened. 'I was dreaming of the Belgian girl,' he said. 'I believe I will press my insistences and marry her.' He smiled secretly. 'I bedded a German woman last night, while her husband was having a drop, so to speak . . . a brunette, not a bad piece. . . .'

These transparent lies called for no reply. They belonged to the Russian mode of *vranyo* fantasy, which rampages through public as well as private life. Perhaps they were Misha's form of sex.

He pleaded to halt at each restaurant along the way. They were poor places, but after many meatless days in north Russia I was happy to eat their tough *shashlik* and burnt chunks of liver. Misha cast a pall on his own countrymen too. Always he demanded a type of food or cigarette or canned music which was not available, so that wherever we went we left behind a litter of unfulfilled demands and puzzled or insulted staff. He would ogle the better-looking girls with an insolence made subtly more repellent by his ugliness. In each restaurant he would drink a little, then praise the beauty of the mountains. But his love for them was not really that. He merely loved the idea of himself in them. They were the theatre of his eating and drinking: a synonym for luxury. He tipped back thimblefulls of vodka in windowless restaurant rooms, and sighed with affected rapture 'Oh the eternal snows!' He belonged to a generation that had read Jack London and Burns at school; he quoted *My Heart's in the Highlands*. I felt sick.

I think he never ceased to act. I simply wondered if any of his roles were real. In one restaurant he found a public telephone, and tried to dial his mother, then sat down simpering: 'My mother tries to make me marry. She praises many boring girls.' He mimicked her voice. 'She loves her only son, she loves her darling Misha.'

I hated him.

But slowly his drinking took effect, and for a long time, lounged in my car, he did not notice that the clouds had washed away from Mount Elbruz. Suspended before us in the evening sky, it shone huge above the glacier-hung valley—a great cathedral of a mountain, untouchable, solitary: the highest in Europe.

'Why don't you love the mountains?' Misha asked, rousing himself. 'You don't say anything. Why don't you say anything?'

'It's time to turn back.'

At nightfall we ate supper near Pyatigorsk, and my mind cleared. The prospect of moving into the Caucasus next day filled me with the cleansing remembrance of my freedom. I began to think of Misha more kindly. After all, I was afraid of him only because of what he represented. In himself he was only a petty informer like thousands of others.

He was also, once again, drunk. 'The authorities,' he mumbled, fingering his empty glass at the restaurant table, 'are neurotic about foreigners from the West.' He peered up at me. 'What shall I tell them? They will say: you spent two days with this man and learnt nothing. So tell me something!'

His face might have been pleading or simply engaged in *vranyo*.

But I didn't answer.

7. The Mountain of Languages

ACROSS THE CORRIDOR between the Black and Caspian Seas, the palisade of the Caucasus mountains puts a full stop to the Slavic world. With the abruptness of some divine geological decree, it severs the northern steppelands from the plateaux of Turkey and Iran, divides ancient Christendom from Islam, Europe from Asia. Here, at the Iberian Gates, the Roman Empire petered out. It was the end of the known world. Classical legends touched its mountains with an antipodean strangeness, and placed at their mist-hung limit the haunts of the Cyclops and Amazons. Here too spread the gold-bearing kingdom of Colchis; and on a remote scarp of Mount Kazbek Prometheus the fire-stealer was chained by the gods.

Persecuted peoples—a centuries-long flotsam of war or migration— filtered into these half-inaccessible valleys. The sudden declivities and enclosed pastures preserved uncouth tribal purities: relics of ancient Celts, Armenians, Circassians, mountain Jews. Pliny said that the Romans conducted their affairs here only by using a hundred and thirty interpreters. The Arabs called it 'the Mountain of Languages'. Even into the 1930s the blond tribes of the Black Aragvi, who were rumoured to descend from Crusaders, were striding about the hills in tunics of chain mail blazoned with crosses.

South from Pyatigorsk the last northern flatlands ruffled into hills. The drizzle had thinned and I was travelling almost blind. But I sensed that the mountains were gathering in front of me now, lifting formidably through the rain. The rivers which I crossed no longer wound in the patient Russian way, but clamoured down wide, shaley beds. Among the people, too, the Slavic tameness was gone, and a mountain physiognomy had appeared: mobile bodies and eagle faces; black, crisp hair. Children ran alongside the car. The women made a dark sparkle. I felt the closeness of an old Mediterranean world: high-strung, vigorous, sensual.

But this nothern Caucasus was filled, too, with an invisible sadness. The German armies which beat against the mountains in the summer of 1942 found supporters here; and for the disloyalty of these few, Stalin deported whole tribal nations to central Asia and Siberia. Their lands were all about me. The nomadic Kalmyks to the north-east, the Balkars in the foothills to my right, the Chechens and Ingush to my left, the Karachai in the mountains farther west—more than half a million people were spirited away *en masse*, and did not return for more than a decade, depleted by starvation and disease.

The German advance, and its paranoid aftermath, faded out at the Ossetian town of Ordzhonikidze, where I cut west off the main road into the mountains. The Ossetians are descended from the Alans, barbarians who pushed out of the unknown early in the first century A.D. Some of them vanished from record in faraway Spain, where they were absorbed by the Vandals and Visigoths. But others settled here.

I found myself driving beside a tributary of the Terek, past shallow floods and stranded trees. A few people were sitting on its banks in the drizzle, cooking *shashlik* on camp-fires. Then the road steepened into the wild. Crags and ridges reeled in and out of cloud, which spurted between their gulleys as if the whole land were on fire. The shoulders of the truncated mountains came barging into the river, their rock-faces grey as the rain, or poured in gentler slants under a deciduous gush of trees. Sometimes, hung with clinging outcrops of shrub, the massif closed about the Terek altogether in vertical curtains of rock, whose kestrel-wheeling summits loomed three hundred feet above, and almost snuffed out river and road together.

Then, cresting a ridge, I entered such thick cloud that I could not see fifty yards ahead, but drove along a track suspended between blurred hills on one side and a drop into silence on the other. The rain was still falling. The road had dwindled to a track. In a half-farmed valley where it descended, I rounded a spur to find dwellings like stone beehives rotting on the slope. It was an Ossetian city of the dead.

The river flowed stark and cold under its hillside. In the distant valley the village of the living, which it served, looked cheerless and ordinary. It was these outlandish sepulchres which seemed to contain the Ossetian identity, a timeless ancestor-worship. Their windowless towers were each pierced by a single shaft. The richer families lay in slate-roofed mausoleums, the poorer in stone huts half sunk beneath the ground. Their tapering roofs of alternating slate and stone gave them a weird, Hindu look. They had been here ever since the fourteenth century, perhaps longer, and were barely discontinued.

An Ossetian woman lived nearby, to guard them. She hailed me through the bitter wind on the hill. Why was I alone? Was I not cold? Where was my woman?

Nothing showed underfoot but a savage medley of stones and grass. A cold blast of wind enveloped the valley. I sheltered in one of the shafts, where sparrows flitted in and out, and peered through its dimness. Here, and in many of the taller towers, the corpses still stretched yellowing in their clothes, stacked one above the other on decaying timber floors, so that arms and legs dangled between the splitting planks and whole families and generations lay jumbled together in heaps of rotting garments and bones. The air had half mummified them; their ribs, dresses and dust-clogged intestines were stuck indissolubly together in depersonalized confusion.

The woman was at my elbow. She was heavy and dark, grossly motherly. She shepherded me into her hut away from the cold, and brewed me tea. The hut was furnished only with a bed and a stove. Her children had gone away to the cities, she said, that's where everybody went now. And the tombs? Her mouth flashed with gold teeth. 'Yes, my family's all over there.' She shook her head. 'But you see how it is, everything falling. Somebody should renovate it. It's a historical place, you see, centuries old. It's not death that's a shame. We all die. It's the indignity of it. . . .'

I could think of nothing comforting to say. The place fell into my journey like a monstrous caesura, violated, meaningless.

By noon I was going south on the Georgian Military Highway—'one of the most beautiful mountain roads in the world', says the old Baedeker—which winds across the deep heart of the Caucasus to Tbilisi, the capital of Georgia. Through the first half of the last century the Russians pushed the great artery southwards as they subdued the upland tribes, until it dropped at last into the valleys north of Turkey.

But all was invisible as I approached. Clouds and rain thrashed across the mountain wall, which engulfed me before I knew of it. Greenish streams and black shale poured and frothed between the cliffs and clattered over the road. Above my way great rock-scarps hovered for hundreds of feet, crowned with Gothic pinnacles and clinging trees. After the interminable Russian plains, they struck me almost with alarm. The road seemed scarcely to rise at all, but to penetrate deeper and deeper into the massif. Alongside, the infant Terek boiled and curdled brown-white. It was barbarously beautiful.

Then my way entered a seemingly impassable arena of cliffs which surged to a height of six thousand feet almost vertically into the sky, their summits undisclosed, adrift in cloud. In this savage place—the ancient Iberian Gates—the river rang with a mad, cold clamour and the air was moist and sunless, as if at the mouth of Hell. Pompey halted his legions here on the edge of the recorded world, and the Romans closed the ravine's mouth with colossal wooden and iron-bound gates, as if to shut out the unknown for ever. Rotted and tumbling castles clung on the rocks' shoulders or perched above the desolate stream in a prism of spray. From one, runs legend, the Georgian queen Tamara unsportingly pitched her beheaded lovers into the river after a single night. Across the canyon's face whole clouds drifted independently, or hung windless.

Then slowly, brokenly, the road levered itself out of the twilight. The Terek sank to a tormented sliver, and vanished. I could glimpse, far below, the chaotic plunge of spurs towards its torrent. The tarmac became more splintered, the peaks more austere, the shale more vertiginous. At last the way climbed so high that the clouds cracked apart and a rent of artificial-looking blue appeared. Suddenly, miraculously, I was travelling along a green upland where rivulets trickled and the hills were touched with autumn shrubs. I was in Georgia.

The name defines a land whose inhabitants are ancient to it, a people of the black-eyed Armenoid kind, the self-styled offspring of biblical giants. For at least three thousand years they have held their mountain kingdom through disunion, invasion and prodigious bursts of independence, becoming Christian early in the fourth century and surviving conquest with a native glitter and resource which never quite takes its oppressor seriously. Their villages were scattered on the meadows where the river spun itself in ten or twenty different tendrils, meandering through sward and flocks of sheep. Sturdy men and and handsome women were haymaking in the fields. Whenever I stopped they demanded if I had anything to sell, rubbing their fingers together in an age-old gesture of complicity. A cheerful anarchy reigned. Hairy pigs plodded about the village streets. The traffic police posts were abandoned. Isolated churches poked up from the ridges, sanctifying old legends, and distant outcrops of rock were spiked with castles and watch-towers blasted to stubs by the wind.

A frightened Russian lorry-driver flagged me down. 'Is this the way to Tbilisi?' He'd never been in the mountains before. He was more alien than I. 'What's the road like farther on? Have you found any petrol? These Georgians. . . .'

For hours I had driven among ranges beheaded by cloud, and had envisaged their summits thundering and looming out of sight. But now, for an instant, the whiteness peeled away from the 16,500-foot Kazbek, 'the Mountain of Christ'. It was like a religious unveiling. One moment it was obscured. The next, the shroud had slid away and the mysterious peak revealed itself, glimmering with snow and higher than anything I had imagined. It towered over the whole valley. The local tribespeople call it the seat of God, and believe it harbours Abraham's tent and the holy manger—but they say the only climber to have searched there descended stark mad. For a minute it filled the sky. Then the mists closed in again, and it was gone.

A cold wind started to blow. The afternoon was thinning away in eerie washes of light—pinks and yellows which seemed to emanate from the mountains themselves. The road ascended again, but frost and avalanche had hacked its surface to bits, and chunks were dropping off into the ravines. Even in September the gulleys were lined with snow. The overhanging scarps flared russet against their whiteness, and other slopes were flaking away as if diseased, so that the chasms beneath them were mounded with brittle scales. I was nearing the highest pass. Long, concrete tunnels, some disused, covered the road against landslide. The clatter of the car inside them sounded hoarse and old. But I had an ignorant faith in it.

By dusk I was over the watershed, descending out of volcanic ranges into wooded hills. A huge, dim perspective opened up. The road twisted and plunged above gorges where rock-flung waterfalls dangled, and streams showed in icy filaments far away. Then I was sinking to a gentler country of apple and peach orchards. It was almost night.

Even in the morning the dining-room of the hotel at Pasanauri was bursting with carousal, its tables ringed by circles of guzzling revellers and stacked with two bottles of wine apiece. They shouted at me to join them.

But I was making south for the Kura valley, which divides the northern, Greater Caucasus from the Lesser, and nurtures the veteran capitals of Mtskheta and Tbilisi. As the last hills dropped behind me, I escaped the noon sun in a huge, bare corpse of a church, enclosed by a castle in the foothills. It was empty and desanctified. A single brazier guttered before its frescoed Christ, and the muralled saints seemed to occupy their pillars apologetically, like denizens of a forgotten felicity.

A fierce-eyed Georgian youth burst in on me as I studied them. He tugged my elbow and talked in rapid, urgent tones. But I knew no Georgian. As this dawned on him, he grew frantic with frustration. His eyes bulged and threatened, his hands flew in a furious sign-language.

He started to shout. But I could only stare back at him in doltish helplessness.

He could contain himself no longer. 'Leeverepul-too-Tbilisi-tree!' he screamed. He plucked out a knife, sank on his haunches and feverishly inscribed something in the stone floor. It was a cup.

I stared at it. A chalice. Was he a member of some mystical sect? I became as maddened as him. I tried Russian, English, French, schoolboy German. But nothing worked.

For a minute he went on shouting and gesturing in despair. Then he enclosed his head in his hands for a mammoth feat of recall, and suddenly yelled: 'World Cup!' He positively danced in front of me. 'Liverpool—two! Tbilisi—three!' Then he pummelled the floor to indicate the return match in Georgia. 'Tbilisi—three! Liverpool—nought! Nought!'

I showed polite rejoicing at this news—all Georgia must have raged with it for months. Instantly his manner turned secretive, and his shoulders coalesced into the furtive hunch which precedes illicit trade. This time his English came smooth as butter: 'Have you anything'—his voice scaled down to a susurration—'anything to sell? Trousers? Magazines? Discs?' The word came in a stage whisper: *'Jeans?'*

I shook my head. His eyes pinned me like javelins. 'Nothing?'

We were crouched under a fresco of the Last Judgement, where the damned were roasting or freezing in the rather bureaucratic departments of the mediaeval Hell. He edged away from it. 'Radio? Shoes? You have *nothing?*'

But I had nothing. To Georgians, and later to Armenians, I was pure heartbreak. My commercial uselessness left them dumbfounded. Why, they seemed to ask (but were too polite) had I come all the way to the Soviet Union if not to effect some deal? They begged to buy my Morris for three times its worth in Britain. For one man the knob of its gear-handle exercised a terrible fascination. He was determined to buy it, but couldn't screw it clear. Every day I steadfastly refused to sell car parts: neither its tyres, its mirrors nor its cushioned seats. As the bids mounted, I realized a stubborn affection for it.

By the time I reached Mtskheta, Georgia's early capital, I felt as if I were back in Syria or Sicily, in the colour and caprice of the south. Brown-limbed children cavorted in the streets. Driving became an act of bravado and opportunism. Everywhere the dedicated plodding of northern crowds was replaced by a languid stalk or a crutch-tight swagger. Photographs of the half-disgraced Georgian, Stalin, stared defiantly from shops and restaurants.

[152]

Mtskheta is a small town now. The high places of its pagan idols—moon-god and fertility goddess—were exorcised by Christian churches on the encircling hills, and the foundation of its great cathedral is suffused with fables. Clenched in battlemented walls, the building is typically Georgian. Its short transepts and long aisles meet beneath a turret like a giant candle-snuffer. It is strong, handsome. It belongs to a tradition grown from the far marches of the ancient Christian world, like the churches of Armenia. Its people show a peasant attachment to it and circumambulate its walls piously in the drenching sun, fondling its blond masonry and leaving flowers at its doors. For the Georgians the Church is the expression of the nation. The Russians have tampered little with it. Stalin himself refrained from persecution because (it is said) he was frightened of his pious mother, who lived to be almost a hundred, still regretting that her son had not become a priest. Inside, the cathedral shines with the same fair stone. It is the Rheims of Georgia, where her kings were crowned and some-times buried. Under my feet the marble grave-slabs were dimpled with crests and inscriptions.

I peered into the lady-chapel, where a wedding ceremony was proceeding with majestic domesticity. Its sad-faced priest intoned in a sorcerous patter. The guests chatted and grinned. The bride, in white dress and coronet, kept brushing her eyes with one slender, silver-nailed hand, not because she was weeping, but because her mascara was smudged. Everybody seemed at home with God. The groom was dressed in shirt and trousers, but crowned outlandishly by a coronet like his bride's, dripping with glass beads and crosses. He joked as he processed round the altar, his fingers linked with hers. Meanwhile a black-clad widow took the part of choir and sacristan together, and bullied the congregated friends. 'Cross yourselves now,' she would command. 'Stand back now! Cross yourselves again!' She filled the chapel with bucolic zest, while the priest remained no more than a blaze of crimson and gold vestments, from which a disenchanted voice united the couple to God.

Then it was over. The friends swarmed forward to kiss. The bride, a hard-faced beauty, strolled away matter-of-factly down the nave, he following. The service had seemed less a sacrament than the signing of some occult register—the act of people to whom divinity was either ubiquitous or non-existent.

In the sixth century Mtskheta lost its hegemony to Tbilisi, which for more than twelve hundred years remained the precarious head of a

[153]

land ravaged by Arab, Byzantine, Mongol, Persian and Turk—a splintered mosaic of princedoms.

Squeezed between hills and river, Tbilisi spreads along nineteenth century boulevards in medleys of balconied shops and offices, restaurants, thermal baths, cafés, theatres, soda fountains. It exhales a dynamic disorder, sharpened by mountains and tinged with the orient. Its tram-rattling alleys are riven by bargaining, laughter, cheating, fights. A feeling of commercial and emotional laissez-faire is about. Contraband goods linger under many a counter. Illicit posters of Stalin, Marilyn Monroe and the Holy Family mingle in idolatrous schizophrenia. The fruit stalls are heaped with apples and peaches, and alone in a near-meatless empire the restaurants make free with lamb.

At evening the crowds along Rustaveli Prospect swell into a long, social promenade under the plane trees. The boulevard is the soul of Tbilisi and of Georgia—and is named after a poet, not a revolutionary. Raunchy youths and self-conscious girls circle and perambulate in segregated clusters as if on an Italian *corso*, showing off black market T-shirts stamped with stars and stripes or the American eagle (but this is fashion, not politics). For an hour or so before sunset, the whole Georgian nation seems to be gazing at itself in ritual narcissism, strutting and teasing through a sexual dance of shameless *machismo* or coyness. Among these dagger-bright people, the Russians appear slow and monochrome, like the British in Italy. They lumber along the pavements with a certain wistful disquiet, as if envious of what they cannot be. For the Georgian is the Russian's antithesis. He has a hugely heightened sense of self. He behaves not as a part, but as the epicentre of things. Before the Revolution, one in seven men on the streets of Tbilisi was rumoured to be a prince.

Above the east bank of the Kura the oldest Georgian quarter totters along the cliffs on wooden stilts. The Kura here is a deep, processional river which hooks around the heights in a sickle of darkness, flowing to the Caspian. A thirteenth century church rears theatrically above, and a basalt king rides his horse on the point of the bluff.

At the foot of the western bank, a veritable Babel begins. Tin-roofed houses converge in an architectural din of Tartar balconies and Persian courts. A minaret totters in the sky above the sunken domes of a Turkish bath, where old women with henna-bright hair sit in the sun. The alleys wriggle upward through a jungle of cracked plaster and splintering wood, mansions poised over nothing on wonky struts and hung with peppers, bath tubs, bags of onions. Everything betrays private loves and vanities, and the air is touched by the murmurings of courtyard intrigue, of gossipers invisible under grape-dangling trellises. While high above, dominating all else, a castle founded by Persians in the fourth century girdles the summit in massed phalanxes of towers.

It was while wandering here that I met a Tbilisi Jew. Framed in an astrakhan hat and greying locks, his fine-boned cheeks degenerated to half-shaven jowls and a fleshy mouth. It was as if he had been put together by identikit, from two different sources: prophet above, lecher below. He was wheezing and moaning with the steepness of the ascent. As we wended together along the overgrown footpaths he told me how the city's thousand-year-old community of Jews was shrivelling away. The 1970s' emigration to Israel had bitterly depleted it.

'My friends have almost all gone. Everything's different now.' He was panting like a hound. 'Tell me, are there Jews in England?' Then he slipped an arm round my waist. 'My childhood was spent here, round this castle. . . . We used to play under the walls.' His voice turned soft, maudlin. I attributed his embrace to friendly tactility, ignored it. 'Even the names of my old friends . . . I've started to forget.'

We were walking in solitude high above the city curled on its brown river. I wondered how good life was in the labyrinth of oriental houses under the hill, but thought I knew. 'The people fight each other like dogs,' the man said. 'The married girls all play with other men, in and out of bed . . . it's disgusting.' He turned to me. His patriarchal locks dribbled sadly round the dual face. 'People don't seem to like me, I don't know why. I treat everybody sincerely, but I'm always rejected. I think people should love one another.' And the next moment he was trying to kiss me.

Angrily I extricated myself and walked back down the hill. As if to obliterate this encounter by some happier meeting with his people, I lingered round the little synagogue in the old district; but nobody came. I telephoned friends of Lyudmila—a doctor and a secondary school teacher. But the day seemed to be cursed. The doctor was away, and while waiting for the teacher in a metro station that evening, I was arrested by an inquisitive policeman. I had no idea who he thought I was, or what I might be doing. But he did not believe me British. He led me into a booth-like office and made me read out a passage from an old medical treatise which he had. 'This is English,' he said. 'Can you read it?'

I was surprised to see that it was Latin, and told him so.

'It's English,' he declared.

'It's Latin.' I was becoming embittered with the whole day.

'It's English,' he repeated. Concealed under his fat, hirsute hands were parallel texts in Russian and German. 'Read it.'

I read it, appending some schoolboy fragments from Caesar's *Gallic Wars*, to annoy him. I was thoroughly angry. Then our impasse was ended by a pretty girl who looked in laughing. 'He can barely read *Georgian*,' she said, pointing at the blushing policeman. When she took up the treatise to test him, he let me go.

The teacher Malhaz turned out to be small and bookish, but even in him Georgian patriotism bubbled like the national champagne, the more explosive for being bottled up. His flat was full of friends. They congregated to the blare of pirated American pop songs, re-recorded and sold in Moscow or bought in Hungary and Poland—all bellowed out on his Estonian Hi-Fi. They spoke of the Russians with more indifference than hostility.

'They're undeveloped,' said Malhaz. 'We feel there's nothing in them. But look at us!'—and the sweep of his arm paraded a roomful of seething faces in which the Slavic dourness was exchanged for a fiery, reactive life. 'Yes, of course we want to be free. It's impossible to be Georgian and not to want freedom. Think of our country! Who says we can't be independent? We could be rich on tourism alone! As for Communism. . . .' He scratched his head in mock perplexity. 'Ah yes, Lenin . . . there's a statue in our main square. I believe he's shouting about something. . . .'

Gori is like a town of one inhabitant, and he a ghost. The cobbler's son Yosif Dzhugashvili, who called himself Stalin, was born here in 1879, and even during his lifetime the place became a mausoleum to his memory. In 1937 the hovels around his father's workshop were demolished, the cobbled street beside it encased by marble paving, and a pseudo-temple raised above, with a vast garden and Italianate museum. All through the forties and early fifties the pilgrims poured in.

But now these acres lie frozen and dead in the town's heart. Ever since Kruschev's denunciation of him in 1956, Stalin has stood in half-light: a borderland between deification and dishonour which may only be resolved after the generations which loved or loathed him have gone. I drove down Stalin Prospect through utter emptiness. In the town square, a colossal statue of the *Vozhd*, the Great Leader—the only such one left in the Soviet Union—looms over a tarmac void once filled by visiting delegations. Mine was now the only car.

In the lanes beyond the boulevard you may still sense the constricted poverty in which the cobbler's son grew up. The photographs which hang in the tiny cottage groan with the same remorseless hardship—a brutal father, a suffering mother, and the boy Joseph whose eyes are already alert.

Ten or twelve Russian tourists waited in the museum foyer. Apart from two girls, they were middle-aged, and some wore service medals. At the head of the stairway a statue of Stalin posed under muted light, and our tour began in a hush of consecration. For this was not a museum at all, but a temple to a still-worshipped god. Stained-glass windows bathed the halls in an opaque sanctity. The wooden floors were inlaid like those of a tsarist palace, and the ceilings dripped with chandeliers. Yet there was scarcely a true relic in the place. Like some monstrous and continuing *coup de théâtre*, it projected instead a glorified life-history in blown-up photographs, statuary, battle-charts and inscribed quotations. We were a captive audience. We moved from Stalin's childhood to his revolutionary youth. Martial music played from concealed microphones. I watched the pictures grow more enigmatic, the busts more prestigious, the plaudits more grandiloquent. But as time went on, the photographs of the *Vozhd* showed him peculiarly isolated. Even in a meeting, he seemed alone. Some psychic space had appeared around him, and widened, just as now no houses encroach upon the house where he was born. The boy's face had become bluff, unreadable.

I stared at my fellow-tourists. They were absorbed, devout. They whispered together. Only the girls looked rather bored.

The rooms unfolded before us like a liturgy. The god to whom they were dedicated was .the one who wrenched his country into the industrial twentieth century and hurled back the Nazi invader. For the rest, the shrine was a sightless lie. There was no hint of the horrors which beset enforced collectivization; no mention of the cynical pact signed with Hitler in August 1939, nor of the partition of Eastern Europe; no suggestion that Stalin ever had a daughter—she who defected to the West. Above all, those who died in the years-long reign of terror by torture, firing-squad, famine or sheer despair in labour-camps—the flower of Lenin's old collaborators, the cream of the Party, of the armed forces, the sciences, the arts, the secret police themselves, together with innocents whose numbers run into numbing millions—all these (and the tens of thousands who killed them) were utterly suppressed. They screamed in the silence.

We walked through the last hall into a pseudo-mortuary. It was decorated by vases holding dead, twisted branches, and seemed to reproduce Lenin's tomb-chamber in Red Square. Our feet were silenced by a scarlet carpet as we circled its arc of columns. At its centre a gold death-mask shone. The face looked old, small and exhausted. One of the girls tripped up in her high heels and burst into nervous giggles.

The next moment we were released into a gallery of the post-war years, as into paradise after the Passion—beaming miners, booming industry, clapping delegates. But in the hall there was a mingled smell of incense and latrines.

I sat in the gardens outside, drugged by nausea. A trickle of tourists was moving among the grandiose fountains now, and some cars had appeared. Two of them showed photographs of Stalin. When Russians praised him, I realized, it was of power that they spoke. He was more graspable than Lenin. Lenin preached an international workers' brotherhood—but Stalin preached Russia. He was the demiurge of her greatness, the nation transcendent. And her people were his children. He answered their yearning for a god's or parent's rule, the power which would protect them from the terror of their own disorder and that of the world, the power of Ivan the Terrible whose hand you kissed as it executed you. Beside that timeless despotism, law and the individual had no history.

The two girls emerged from the museum and passed near me. I asked them what they thought of it. 'Quite nice,' they said. And as they did so I realized that Stalin's time was as remote to them as that of Peter the Great. They were about twenty years old. They wandered chatter-ing away, discussing where to buy tights in Tbilisi. And I felt thankful for them, and for tights and for all trivia.

Even my hotel had been built to accommodate the pilgrim hordes of Stalin's day. Its coffered ceilings and rude glut of pillars topped by fat capitals—classicism in its last perversion—resembled one of the sta-tions of the Moscow metro. A repressed-looking girl sat at the reception desk. Under the painted vaults of the dining-room the tables were crammed only with men, and when I left at eight-thirty the next morning a forty-strong delegation was already downing a full-scale meal with two bottles of champagne each.

As I passed the last suburbs of Gori, I wound down my car window and let in the air. A warm wind blew from the Black Sea a hundred miles away. From the vineyards and apple orchards of the Kura valley the road twisted into hills dotted with beehives, and all the lorries seemed to be carrying animals: horses whose chestnut flanks quivered with every jolt of the road, pigs gruntingly astir, crates of gawping chickens.

Towards noon I wriggled a few miles off my prescribed route to where the huge, floating spur of Gelati monastery overhangs its valley. All about it the Caucasian mountains billow in on forest-dappled waves, then drop into the plains at its feet. Surrounded by a shambling wall black with ivy and jostled by apple trees, its churches are lifted naked to the sky and mountains.

The Church of the Nativity was the Saint-Denis of Georgia, where her kings were buried. It was built with the high walls and turret dome of all this land, solitary and confident in the beauty of its stone. I had arrived on a Sunday, and while the Russians plodded here and there in educational groups, the Georgians were enjoying themselves. All round the monastery they were drinking, picnicking and playing football, with a robust sense of what was theirs.

'Look!' boomed one, as I went inside the church. 'Our kings still live here!' Around us the nave rose in frescoed glory—a painted incantation to the hierarchies of earth and heaven. And there, sure enough, the royalty of Georgia was banked in phalanxes of canny kings and tight-lipped queens. They looked like crowned and anointed bandits. Inside their obligatory haloes the kings showed black, flinty eyes and horizontal moustaches; and even the mosaic archangels in the apse were dressed in the pearl-encrusted robes of secular princes, whose gush of wings was merely a hereditary leftover.

'There's our Bagrat! Our Giorgi! Tamara!' My self-appointed guide poured out a hoarse torrent of ownership. 'And there's David—the big one! What about *him* then?'

David and his great-granddaughter Tamara compass the apogee of Georgia's power in the twelfth century. It was they who stretched the Christian kingdom from the Black Sea to the Caspian, ravaged northern Persia and endowed at Gelati a famous philosophic academy, whose ruins were still crumbling on the valley's lip, their stone benches feathered in grass. David the Builder, prodigious soldier and statesman, at once gracious and formidable, is the quintessential Georgian folk-hero. By the end of his reign the Turks, who had contemptuously dubbed him 'a woodland king', had relinquished Tbilisi after four hundred years of Moslem rule. His life, say contemporary annals, was stained only by some youthful escapades 'which God Himself has forgotten', and he lies buried now with ostentatious humility across the deep, powerful entranceway to the monastery, where an iron gate, captured from Persia by his son, swings thin as a leaf in the wind. It is the gravestone of a titan—cracked and enormous. It spans the whole way, where every passer-by could tread it underfoot. 'This is my home for all eternity,' runs the inscription. 'Here shall I dwell, for I have willed it.'

'See what a size the man was!' My guide spread his arms as if to embrace an oak. 'There's a six-hundred-kilogram stone in one corner of the church, and this man lifted it up! Just as if it was a child!' He tossed an imaginary infant into the air. 'No problem!'

'And Queen Tamara?'

'Oh yes, she was OK too. But . . . well. . . .'—his fingers twirled in reservation—'. . . just a woman.'

There are other shrines tucked along these ridges—tiny, huge-stoned churches, built for eternity, their gravestones half drowned in the earth. But I had little time to explore them. The afternoon was fading and soon I was circling back across those western lowlands which the Georgians call Imier, 'that side', to distinguish them from the harsher 'this side' to the east. The change, beyond the Kikhi passes, is sudden. The mountains relax into peace, and watered valleys fatten in the hills. The Rioni river, the Phasis of the ancients—and the epony-mous home (they thought) of the pheasant—swells and meanders through the lush plains of Colchis, flax-rich kingdom of Roman geographers, where each verandaed house stood in a plot of sweetcorn or a bier of vines. The Mediterranean was breathing close now. Poplars and olive trees appeared. The verges cackled and bellowed with geese and cattle, and grunting pigs in makeshift halters. This was the land of a people already flourishing when the black ships of the Greeks first hove onto their horizon—Jason and his Argonauts, early traders or pirates. The natives, it is said, laid fleeces on the beds of the alluvial streams to pan for gold. But the Golden Fleece may simply have symbolized alchemy or trade, or have grown from a memory of the golden light which bathes this ample land, and which was even now dropping out of the evening sky. With every mile the fields grew denser in tea and fruit, the plains more sodden with their streams. The village gardens slopped and blazed. Cattle slumbered in the road. Palm trees and water buffalo emerged out of the dusk. And as night fell, the verge-grazing cows and pigs gathered by ones and twos at their owners' garden gates, awaiting admission like domestic pets. I had time only to glimpse a black clamber of mountains descending to the sea, before darkness came down and I was on the shore under a sky barely paler than the water.

All this brought on a voluptuous nostalgia. The shores of the Mediterranean!—or nearly. I was no longer quite alone. The history-laden sea accompanied me. I felt vaguely homesick. I settled by my car in a half-deserted campsite near Sukhumi, and began to cook a supper of scrawny chicken. It was my last night in Georgia. But I had no sooner lit my stove than a pair of trendily-jeaned legs intruded into the gaslight, followed by a saturnine face which lowered itself conspiratorially to mine. It wore a look of hard, Georgian ebullience.

'You're British aren't you? If you have any. . . .'

But the familiar litany fell into a gaping absence of jeans, and the man's hunger for the West—for all novelty and stimulus—turned into a fierce conviviality. 'The moment I saw you I thought "Ah, there's a foreigner I could like." Something about your face!'—I at once felt fraudulent—'Let's have a party! My name's Zahari. I know a place. . . .'

Five minutes later we were racing into Sukhumi with a frightened Czechoslovak girl who needed to catch a train and who said she was being followed. The lights of another car glared and wavered behind us, and as we reached the station and she ran through the ticket barrier, a car-load of youths spilled out behind us.

'You've let her get away!' The driver gaped at me. 'What did you do that for? We only wanted to fuck her.'

Even Zahari looked uncertain, split between friendship and *machismo*. I said the girl was afraid. But the youths stared at me nonplussed, wrinkling their shallow moustaches and fingering their belts. I began to feel stupid. And now the girl was gazing back from the platform with what might have been regret.

Zahari and I passed the evening in a conflagration of talk and music around a dance-floor packed by fifty-odd whirling couples. We sat with a bottle of wine each, and plates heaped with *kebab*. Every time a woman passed, Zahari would hitch his jeans ruttishly about his thighs and evaluate her figure to me in fiery, glottal Russian.

'But this is a deadly dull town, I can tell you. The mountains are beautiful, of course, but there's nothing else.'

'You'd prefer Moscow?'

'No, oh God, no.' He shuddered and hissed. I couldn't imagine him there. 'Moscow!'—he exorcized the thought with a swig of wine—'I had to live there once. Politics! The place reeks of them. It freezes you. And business is hopeless there.' But in Sukhumi his talent for banditry had found its outlet in a profitable trade from backstreet clothes factories. 'We Georgians are basically selfish. I suppose the Russians are more idealistic.' He grinned and shrugged. This idealism qualified them only for his distaste.

I asked him if he'd visited Lenin's mausoleum?

'Lenin? I've never heard of him!' He flicked a piece of gristle off his plate. 'That's for Lenin!'

He drank again, more heavily. At the thought of Moscow, Sukhumi became bearable to him. 'In summer we even get a few foreign women. I had an English girl from Hull once. God . . . I wonder if all the girls there are like that?' He jabbed at his lamb with phallic repetition. 'Women! I was married at twenty, but my wife left me because I got at other girls. Tell me, how much does a first class prostitute cost in London?'—he speared the *kebab* again—'I mean an *absolutely* first class one?'

I made an uneducated guess.

'Christ, I'd rather spend it on drink. . . . All the same, can you get me a work permit?'

We drank to women and to 'little Georgia'. Our bill came to nearly fifty roubles, two days' salary for a working Soviet man. But Zahari laughed at it. 'You think I live on a *salary*? Huh! Nobody can live on a salary here. Everyone lives on the side. But I can tell you we're not so bad as the Armenians.' He whistled with admiration. 'Even the *dogs* live on the side there. . . .'

As we tossed back the dregs of the wine, the band's singer began crooning a new melody. 'You know that?' Zahari asked. 'It's a song about Stalin.'

'What does it say?'

'It says that Stalin's ours—*ours*.' Suddenly his eyes were shining with a deep, atavistic fervour, almost with love. 'It says Stalin was born here and belongs to us. *Us!*' His hand groped for a glass and I guessed that he was about to propose a toast to Stalin. I think I turned white. I made no move. I imagined the evening's camaraderie, which was in any case built on transience—the traveller's dishonesty—plummeting into wounded national pride and breached hospitality. Yet no, I could not toast Stalin. But as Zahari's fist closed around the stem of the glass to lift it, we both saw that it was empty—my own glass empty too, and the bottles drained—and we let the song pulse and die in a forgotten river between us.

8. Armenia

THE LITTLE REPUBLIC of Armenia is the remnant of an ancient splendour which once stretched over half eastern Turkey to the Mediterranean. Spread where the Lesser Caucasus mountains break into tableland, the province now occupies a mere tenth of Armenia's historic empire. It is the refuge of a people all but annihilated by the Turks in 1915, and decimated in a second nightmare under Stalin— a people half lost in a worldwide dispersion as awesome as that of the Jews. But now this stony region, suffocated by quarter of a million refugees after 1915, has farmed and industrialized itself and achieved a modest wealth, so that its very existence helps to heal those psychic wounds which far outlast a people's physical degradation.

South from Tbilisi, crossing the north-west tip of Azerbaijan, the road travels through a premonitory barrenness. The wooded valleys and sky-splitting rocks of Georgia have gone. In their place the earth folds into volcanic hills glazed with yellow grass. They ripple into one another. Their trees drop dust. Here and there a river paints a line of green, and vineyards appear. But all around, the scarps are smeared with etiolated saffron and umber strata, or erupt in discoloured fangs as if some deep unrest in the earth were not yet allayed. The land has a seared, Asiatic beauty. It is at one with the Turkish and Iranian plateaux which bleed away from it to the south.

Then, for forty miles, the road twines among the last Caucasian mountains, and climbs through valleys soft with oak, hornbeam and beech, billowing in green ramparts from pass to pass. In their nondescript villages the people show the gentle, aquiline faces which have come down from Armenian antiquity.

But police posts multiply. In a single day's journey I was stopped eleven times and was refused permission either momentarily to turn back or to turn aside. The Turkish border was less than eighty miles away. The road became a thin ribbon through the forbidden. At evening I broke through cloud onto a stark plateau under clear sky. In front of me the horizon flattened to lunar ranges and the glassy stillness of Lake Sevan. It is one of the biggest inland lakes on earth. It cut through the hills with a clean, surgical strangeness, and shared their dead eternity.

I settled by the north-west shore in a three-year-old motel which already looked derelict. Order and conformity, even in small things, dissipate southward from the Baltic. In Riga and Tallinn cars could be parked in safety for weeks in front of the hotels; here they were locked in clanging cages and the keys entrusted to porters.

But in the huge dining-room at night, a clamour of jubilation rose. All evening people drove up from the dust-bowl of Erevan, Armenia's capital, to the lakeland air six thousand feet above sea-level, and crowded the motel dance-floor. Tables brimmed with the lake's salmon trout, and groups of swarthy, womanless men sat in gluttonous circles, talking of money, their little glasses of cognac uplifted in an endless flurry of toasts. My solitude distressed these parties; they shouted at me to join them. But the music throbbed and drowned our talk.

The Armenians danced as if they meant it, in a whirl of writhing arms and bottoms, and clapped themselves delightedly; while from their long, organized tables, fifty-strong tour-groups of Czechs and East Germans watched as if staring into a lit room which they could not enter. Only when the music quietened did they stand up and waltz slowly and gracelessly all together. In the north I had often seen Russian women dancing puritanically with one another. But here it was the Armenian men who flaunted themselves by twos, without touching, in a parade of peacock ego. They glided between the northerners like water round stones. The German girls began to flirt with them. The pop band bawled out old British numbers. It seemed as if everything which people considered important—beliefs, systems, ideals—were fatally divisive, and that the miracle of human unity was performed instead by pop songs.

Between these outbursts of sound the sad-faced Armenian beside me dropped isolated sentences. His name was Manouk . . . he was a clerk in local government . . . what did I think of The Rolling Stones? . . . his job was deathly boring. . . . His plaintive eyes flinched behind their spectacles, and his hair was already receding at the age of twenty-six. We sat in the motel's rowdy night-club together, drinking vodka, coffee and fruit juice, while he grew maudlin about women. His first love had married an Armenian living in Marseilles, and he had never got over it. He stared lugubriously into successive glasses of vodka, and his small, persecuted eyes grew moist as he remembered her.

'After she left I went on drinking-bouts with friends and pretended to be happy. But this girl still sits behind my eyes, after two years. Everything reminds me of her'—he downed a compensatory vodka—'and now she's come back to Erevan for two weeks because her father's ill. That's why I don't want to be down there. I'm staying up here.' In the semi-darkness his eyes and spectacles swam together in doleful concentric pools. Every time he went to the bar for more drinks, his legs slurred to a worse shamble. He seemed in love with his own martyr-dom—a classic Armenian, condemned to the chauvinism of suffering. He swallowed his drinks like medicine, but only sank deeper into the morass.

'I saw her husband just once, and he looked a sympathetic man. So I hope she's happy. Yes, I hope. . . .' The vodka lifted tenderly to his lips like a sacrament now. 'I hear people earn good money in Marseilles . . . they must be rich. . . .' I felt I was watching a man come up for the third time. But as he did so an ancestral resilience asserted itself, and his gaze lifted. 'Did you see that girl who just went by? What did you think of her?' The bespectacled eyes were suddenly satyr-bright. A fifth vodka vanished. A new wave of self-pity broke. 'All the same, this other girl. . . .'

Two brandies later he had decided to return to Erevan next day, and asked me to go with him. The morning found him in high spirits. He had dressed to kill, in silky black trousers and a carefully-pressed T-shirt. A heavy-stoned ring studded one finger and his wrist flashed a digital watch. I did not have to ask what plans had provoked this. While he started his clapped-out Zhiguli on the forty miles to Erevan, he crooned snatches of *First and Last Love*. A black-market Virginian cigarette dangled prestigiously from his lips, and the dashboard was littered with packets of contraband chewing-gum and Western cas-settes.

As we clattered round Lake Sevan's north-west shore, another symbol of romanticized suffering hove into view: a statue of the mediaeval princess Tamara, who was incarcerated in a convent on the peninsula there. Every night, said Manouk, she was visited by her lover who rowed to her signal-fire over the water, until a storm extinguished the light and his corpse was washed up beneath her window. Now there are Tamara cigarettes, Tamara restaurants, Tamara comic-strips. You can read, munch or smoke Tamara. She is part of the national conscious. But in fact the legend was transferred wholesale from Lake Van in Turkish Armenia. And Tamara never existed.

For three thousand feet through desert hills our road dropped into the cauldron of Erevan. The very air thickened into a fine powder as we descended. This bare country was easily desecrated. Pylons limped across its mangy hills, and power excavators were churning up flinty rock in the valleys, mining for obsidian or potash. Squat factories, visible twenty miles away, sent up wavering pillars of smoke and were echoed behind by chimney-shaped hill-peaks stacked with smoky clouds. For half an hour we went down through a planetary waste. Here and there the police had set up crashed cars on concrete pedestals as a warning to motorists, without perceptible effect. Manouk exceeded the nationwide speed-limit of a hundred kilometres an hour whenever we reached a suitable slope, and soon the land fell away beneath us far into the marl-rich lowlands of the Araxes river. Suddenly Manouk said: 'Look! Ararat!'

I followed his gaze. Luminous with snow, the mountain had appeared as if from nowhere. It hung like a spectre over the plain. It was solitary, complete, severed in the sky. Only a dirty string of lesser hills drifted away from it to the west. I had failed to notice it because haze cut it off from the alluvial valley beneath, leaving its summit to swim in solitude. Unearthly, treeless, it belonged to another time and substance from the plains. Its andesitic slopes presented themselves not for mining but for worship—the patriarchal mountain of Noah, and landfall of the Ark.

'We Armenians look at it with mixed feelings,' said Manouk. 'It's our national emblem, but it stands in Turkey. *Turkey!* I've never seen it from that side. I long to. It must be beautiful. . . .'

No, I said, two years before I had glimpsed it from the Turkish-Iranian border, where it was half obscured by other hills.

'So the Turks get a worse view?' Manouk was vindictively pleased. 'You see, Ararat speaks something peculiar to us Armenians. When *you* look at it you just see a mountain. But *I* see something else. . . .' He placed a melodramatic hand on his heart.

Half an hour later we were delving down into the inferno of Erevan, our gears crashing in eddies of traffic, rock music dinning from our cassettes. Erevan contains more cars per head than any other city in the Soviet Union. Its streets are jammed by frustrated drivers, fetid with exhaust fumes, dust-blown and clamorous with horns. It was a human labyrinth unimaginable in the north: thrustful, erratic. Manouk complained furiously about all other drivers, whose habits were precisely his own. 'Nobody looks where he's going. Everybody just does how he likes . . . look at that appalling U-turn . . . there's a pretty girl. . . .'

After the heartless sameness of most Soviet conurbations, Erevan elated me. The whole city was built in a rosy, laval stone peculiar to itself. Sixty years ago it was so poor that its children ate refuse in the streets. But it had risen again in these weirdly impressive squares and avenues, whose luxuriant decoration, fretted capitals and round-arched, secret windows, reproduced traditional Armenian motifs with an oddly moving faithfulness. Yet it was the quality of stone which personified it above all—walls of tufa and basalt, pink and black. Sunk in their airless cleft of river, they drank the light without refracting it. They looked still hot from the volcano—visceral, searing stones glinting (you might think) with minerals or blood.

This once-pitiful city is now a centre of industrial skills: electronics, machine tools, precision instruments. A feeling of human possibility is about. In their diaspora the Armenians seem gentler than others, but here, as in Israel, many of the familiar qualities of a people appeared lost or overlaid. Compared to Russians, the figures which crowded the pavements looked physically and sensually precocious. Their expressions were more varied, more explosive, more beautiful, more any-thing—the faces of brigands and concert pianists and millionaires. Their slender-boned features—some of the women's appeared fragile as birds'—could burn with a tragic intensity. The young men flaunted flared trousers and platform shoes. The air on street corners was raked by the cross-fire of their inquisition and the sight of a foreigner drew a barrage of inquiry. Yet they were shorter, darker than the Georgians, and in place of that brittle mountain dash they looked subtly older, as if beneath their exuberance there lingered, even in the young, some collective memory of horror.

To Manouk the city was a spider's-web of contacts. The whole place, he said, was riddled with secret offices and businesses. He was always stopping off at different stores to obtain free or illegal goods. Everything belonged to the state, and the state was abstract. He rushed into a foodshop managed by his brother, and emerged from the back entrance clutching a chicken; he collected some spectacle-frames mended for nothing; he bought illicit records.

But as for his old girlfriend, he prevaricated. He had lost his nerve. He suggested other things to do. Noon found us wandering over the plateau-ruins of earliest Erevan, which predated the Armenian people themselves—whoever they were, and wherever from. A scribble of stones traced temples and warehouses eight centuries before Christ, and frescoes in bold ochres and blues covered the astonishing walls with friezes of tiny gods riding lions. Manouk kept flicking dust disconsolately from his trousers. He was crumpled and silent. Shouldn't we go back into the city, I asked?

No, no he said, we'd go to the holy town of Echmiadzin fifteen kilometres farther on. An Armenian always felt better there, he added: Echmiadzin made a man proud and released, so that he walked and breathed in a different way.

The town is the seat of the Supreme Patriarch of the Armenian Church. Its cathedral was founded as long ago as 303 (for Armenia was the earliest Christian state in the world) but was restored many times during Turkish and Persian domination. No saints glowered from its walls. They were covered instead by a Koranic orchard of painted flowers and trees in tomato red, deep blues and gold. Marble divans circled the transepts, transforming them into the alcoves of Moorish palaces. Persian latticework screened the gallery, and the Patriarch's throne was inlaid with an Islamic iridescence of mother-of-pearl.

Manouk did not look proud or released at all, nor did he walk and breathe in a different way. He stared miserably at the fragment of Noah's Ark preserved in the treasury, and ignored the head of the Holy Lance lying in spurious state in a gold reliquary.

But other of the town's churches attested an old beauty. They were sombre and strong as fortresses. Their huge, cruciform bodies lifted blank and unadorned to turreted domes. This most ancient of Christianities shed pagan shadows even now. Lambs and doves were still killed in the cathedral courtyard on feast-days, said Manouk, and Easter Monday found the graveyards filled with families feasting among the tombs of their ancestors. In the enclosure of another church we found a harsh-faced priest blessing a sacrificial sheep. An anxious-looking family had dragged it before a stone altar, where the priest traced the sign of the cross over its doomed and slavering head. Blood dripped from its ritually cut ear. Then the priest emptied a packet of consecrating salt into the altar's bowl, and gave it to the animal to lick. It backed away. The family dragged it forward again, shouting uncouth orders to one another, and the priest rammed the salt into the sheep's mouth. One of the men pulled out a battered wallet and handed the priest a note, which he examined then walked away. Then the family galloped the sheep round a corner, heaved it into the back of a brand-new Zhiguli, and drove away to their village for the kill.

'That's always happening,' Manouk said. 'They probably want a child or more success in business. So they offer up a sheep.' He found this perfectly natural, and was baffled by my questions. It was merely common sense: a bargain driven with God. God was an Armenian.

It was dusk when we returned to Erevan. Manouk had combed his hair into tight little curls around his ears, and taken off his glasses. But he looked wretchedly nervous. 'She should have arrived last night,' he said. 'If she agrees to go to a restaurant or see a movie, will you join us? She won't go out alone with me. People talk. . . .'

His hands agitated on the steering-wheel. At last he stopped in the courtyard of a big apartment block, peered into the car mirror for the last time and slapped his paling cheeks. 'She may not want to know me at all. I dread her first look. It's always the first look that counts, isn't it?' Already his face wore an indefinable air of defeat. Without their glasses his eyes looked timid and small. He stumbled myopically over a tree-root in the courtyard, then vanished up the apartment stair.

Five minutes passed. Two old men who had been playing dominoes under the trees folded up their board and trudged inside. I waited. Lights flickered on behind curtained windows.

When Manouk reappeared, he was alone. I scanned his face for elation or grief or anything at all. But as he drove away he seemed only vaguely perplexed, as if he had woken from a dream whose memory was still stronger than the day. The aeroplane had only arrived that morning, he said, and she had gone to bed at midday. When he had called she was still asleep. She had come to the door, and they had spoken briefly. He shook his head. *'Her eyes were clogged up.'*

'What?'

'Her *eyes* were *clogged up.*'

His voice held bafflement and a faint, crestfallen distaste. Two films of sleepy-dust, and his passion gone. By the time the lights of Erevan had been snuffed in the night behind us, he was laughing quietly, self-mockingly, consulting his digital watch and throwing cassettes into the breach.

> *You know you can't hold me for ever,*
> *This boy's too young to be singing the blues. . . .*

I stayed five nights by Lake Sevan, and every morning its waters fascinated me again. Sometimes, shaken by wind, the whole lake would appear to be shuddering southward in foam-flecked ripples whose agitation seemed outlandish in those dead shores. But more often the water lay in a trance—less a lake than a huge, unblinking eye of glass, sated and colourless: the eye of the earth itself.

At night when I returned, usually after drinking with Manouk, the concierges chattered at ease. One woman in particular—a soft-faced Ukrainian who was married to a Russian factory-hand in Sevan—

lingered at my door. She was lonely in Armenia, she said, she wanted to return to her own people, or anywhere farther north. She spoke in a sad, musical drawl. 'You've seen so much of the Soviet Union, and I haven't been to Leningrad or even Pyatigorsk. Is Georgia as beautiful as they say? My husband hasn't a car. . . .'

She looked too young to be married—her mouth an adolescent bud, her expression stopped at seventeen—yet she talked of a ten-year-old son. For over an hour she stood in my bedroom and asked the guileless, personal questions which come naturally to many Russians. 'I thought you were Polish, because I heard you speak Russian. Why are you alone? Why aren't you married?' Her chatter held no undertone but an oddly desolating innocence. 'But my job's not so hard. Sometimes I sleep in my chair. You can't complain, it's just a job.'

The soft face and brown eyes became very appealing in my fuddled gaze. She wore no ring on her finger. I guessed her marriage was unhappy. I remembered stories of KGB prostitutes in tourist hotels, but she didn't look like anybody's idea of one. If I touched her, I thought, she might respond out of her loneliness with the same childishness as she spoke. But I was bound to another, and a little afraid; and I let her wander back down the passageway holding one of my torn shirts, which she said she would mend before dawn.

In the mornings I would drive down to Erevan alone or with Manouk. Once I stopped above the city to visit the memorial to the victims of Turkish genocide, and was glad that he was not with me. If I were to feel nothing in the presence of those million dead, I wanted to feel nothing alone. But as I took the long path to the monument, I fell in with a robust man and his two little girls. He stopped by the pathside and sliced open a watermelon with his penknife, thrusting the icy segments into my hands: 'Here, eat! Tell me, how are things in Britain? Not so good as before?' He clapped me on the shoulder. 'It's the same with us. . . . Here's more melon. . . . Things have been going downhill for over five years now.' I had grown used to this dirge about worsening conditions. So long as things had been better than before, life was bearable. But now the dogma of inevitable economic growth under Communism had faltered strangely. 'Everything gets spent on arms! America gets stronger, then Russia gets stronger, and so on. Where'll it all end? And here we are eating watermelon together!'

His daughters were staring at me excitedly, as if I might conclude peace in person. We were approaching the platform of the monument. They walked meekly on either side of me. Their golden hair betrayed a Russian mother. The elder wore the blue shirt and red neckscarf of the

Young Pioneers. But she did not like it much, she said; she preferred playing the piano. 'We haven't enough room in our flat for one,' she whispered, 'and not enough money either. We're getting our first car next month.'

'You'll probably buy a piano after that,' I said, for her father to hear.

He grunted and smiled. Then he, in turn, whispered: 'She'll end up in a language school . . . she's better at languages.'

We were walking across the memorial platform now, overlooking the whole city. Ararat's snow rose in haze beyond. At the platform's end a circle of leaning pillars enclosed a pit where muffled music rose. Its chorus was tumultuous and faint—perhaps the recording had grown thin with use, but I think this haunting was intended. It was as if the voices of those unimaginable dead were sounding from the grave. It was tragic and somehow final. There was nothing else but a flame. We stood silent. The man's bluffness had gone. He was too young to have lost his parents in 1915, and I couldn't tell what he was thinking. The little girls shuffled their feet and stared mutely into the fire and music, inheriting their people's pain. That, I supposed, was why they had been brought here. Only after a long time did they begin to fidget with the chewing-gum which I'd given them, and we tramped back down the long path, talking of language-schools and munching melon.

Manouk's family was an object-lesson in Armenian resilience. His father and elder brother had built their home with their own hands at a time when the suburbs were no more than a camp. Even now the house was reached over planks across open sewers. Its courtyard was cluttered with the concrete dividing walls of other families and with beds canopied by rotting blankets, and narrow-gauge goods trains jangled past the windows at bedroom level, so close that you could almost reach forward and pluck a package out of the trucks. But this clutter around a shared courtyard was no barometer of poverty. Beside houses all around, the battered sheds were full of shining cars.

Manouk's mother had emigrated here from Lebanon, where many Armenians fled after 1915. All her childhood had been spent on the edge of starvation. She was frail now, and I never saw her. But his father was a florid-faced old man with a mellow smile and kindly, rather simple eyes. He had been brought out of Turkey at the age of four, before the massacres, but his parents had returned and been slaughtered.

'I was reared in Erevan, in an orphanage run by Americans.' He spoke detachedly, as if about somebody else. 'They were good people.' He seemed deeply contented as he presided over a meal of chicken, grapes and brandy all together, and urged me to eat. He spoke of his parents as he might have spoken of mine. 'I don't even remember them.' He detached a twig-full of grapes and dropped it onto my chicken. 'I grew these myself on the side of the house. You can't grow anything else here. The land's dead. In Turkey we had better land, but it's deserted now. Everyone's gone.'

He constantly pressed more chicken on me, transferring it carefully, proudly on two forks. This tenderness with food was the only sign of his childhood deprivation. He was entering an old age sheltered by his own house, his own family. A colour television tyrannized the dining-room and was switched on even while we ate. 'A wonderful thing, these pictures. Do you have television in Britain? . . . Yes, I suppose you would.'

He was attended by his elder son's wife, who always cooked and served for him. He and Manouk ordered her about. When I asked why she didn't eat with us, they only said: 'She's got too much to do.'

I might have been in an Arab village. The talk was all of sons. 'My elder son drinks too much,' said the old man, dropping a grape onto his tongue, then he gazed fondly across the table: 'but this one hardly drinks at all.' Manouk shot me a warning—he drank like an elephant. 'Well, my elder son doesn't drink *too* much, but rather a lot. . . .' The old man paused, smiled, settling himself again into peace. 'I've got good sons.'

He himself had given up first drinking, then smoking. He was a Stalin-era health-addict. He would splash icy water over his head every morning, and engage in press-ups, running-on-the-spot and improvized shadow-boxing against enemies of the Socialist Motherland. Manouk said that his own generation privately ridiculed such antics, and that his father's readiness 'for Labour and Defence' (as the national fitness programme demanded) was aimed not at America, but at the Turk. When we touched on Armenia's two-and-a-half years' independence, quenched by the Russians in 1921, the old man's face turned wooden. He said sombrely: 'If the Russians hadn't come, the Turks would.'

As for Manouk, he tried to ignore politics. Only once, when we were driving past a memorial to Soviet power in Armenia, he said: 'That's a monument to our union with Russia—our freedom. It's nonsense, of course, but what can you do? We're utterly different from the Russians. They're cold, you know. If a man was dying in a ditch a Russian would leave him alone and a Turk would murder him—but an Armenian would lift him up' (and take his wallet, a Russian later suggested).

[172]

Manouk, like so many others, escaped the ubiquity of politics into an intensity of personal life. His sitting-room was a shrine to other gods. He had plastered its ceiling with black gypsum, whose stalactites gave it the feel of a night-club grotto, and two record-players and a tape-recorder detonated sentimental pop songs through enormous loud-speakers. The shelves were lined by empty *defitsitny* drink bottles kept for ornament, and the walls were studded with the posters and pendants of a plotless cultural pantheon: The Beatles, the Virgin Mary, Brigitte Bardot, Bambi, an Armenian folk-hero galloping over Ararat, Raquel Welch, six plastic cherubs.

Nostalgic and slightly drunk, he leafed through his photograph albums to the rhythms of Elton John. These albums seemed to encapsule and circumscribe his life. Their snapshots were all of picnics and outings: holidays by Lake Sevan or in the Caucasus. They were suffused by a Levantine intensity of friendship, and a love of self-enhancing things—cars, clothes, style. In these photographs Manouk always seemed to be on his back among a knot of revellers, with a buxom woman looming overhead. He lay supine and ecstatic under dripping wine or kisses—tickled, teased, made drunk. 'There's Lucy!' he groaned. 'Ooh! I remember that! When I got home I had love-bites all over my shoulders. I took off my shirt by mistake, and my mother asked what on earth had done it? Friends, I said . . .'—he lingered over the pages with eager hands on which one fingernail each had been left long as a mandarin's in the Middle Eastern way. '. . . And my mother said: What sort of friends do you have, that they hit you all over? Oh, there's Helen. . . .'

Yet the snapshots were already turning sepia, as if they had been taken long ago, of people now old or dead. Soon they were making him lugubrious. Past classmates, past girlfriends—their faces were too callow and clear. They waved bottles or guitars at the camera, or grouped themselves self-consciously in a brotherhood irreparably gone. Their oddly dated-looking faces stared out from another time. He closed them away.

He suggested a movie, a party, the circus, anything.

I chose the circus. Soviet circuses are like no other, and scarcely relate to the mendicant European bell-tents, with their friendly stench of dung and bruised grass. There are more than a hundred in the country, sixty of them working all the year. They take place in miniature palaces. The ring at Rostov is a domed and gilded opera-house-in-the-round, belted with Corinthian columns and seating two thousand. Even the one at Erevan was enfolded by a generous ambulatory, seething with smokers in the intervals, and furnished with a twenty-man band which played in a balcony under its dome. But in place of the blond, sleepy children of north Russia, its tiers were brimming with the olive skins and exclamatory hands of Armenia. Beneath their immaculate hair and feathery, strong-marked brows, three thousand eyes, circled in black lashes, filled the ring with a half-adult scrutiny.

There were as many grown-ups as children, and all the tiers were packed. What we witnessed were reckless acts of life rather than of theatre. It was as if each feat were being attempted for the first time, at the limit of its performer's strength or skill. And it was this sense of peril which kept the audience on its seats' edge. A man extinguished a candle-flame with the stroke of a ten-foot horsewhip, but the blazing lasso which he twisted round his body burst into uncontrollable fire and he had to leap through it. A tightrope artist lost her balance as she descended on her partner's shoulders, and was left dangling from her safety-belt seventy feet up, like a fish floating in light. A trapeze artist who tried to complete a quadruple somersault in mid-flight twice fell into the safety-net before angrily succeeding.

The audience itself was electrified by failure. But the performers, a troupe from Leningrad, were better than any I had seen. A pyramid of acrobats skipped on a bicycle. A contortionist folded and uncoiled herself in an invertebrate dance, gliding like a snake between repulsiveness and beauty. The clowns were conjurors, the tumblers were dancers. I felt as I had at the Kirov Ballet—that I was watching the spirit of a people unleashed under cover of make-believe. The clowns, in particular, become national heroes, spokesmen of the people's heart. A few years' ago they used to burlesque the shortcomings of Soviet bureaucracy (but not the Party) with a loved and merciless forthrightness. Perhaps they still do; or perhaps the shortcomings have become too painful for laughter, because I never saw this. I was struck how the audience responded, not to the clowns' humour, but to their pathos. The lover-clown's passionate heart revived a withered bouquet for his girl; the painter-clown fell in love with his own canvas and carried it away with him spotlit into the darkness; and all the while both children and adults followed them with anxious gaze, and greeted these sentimental exploits in a stricken and disquieting silence.

If I wanted to reach the rock-cut churches in the hills east of Erevan, there was nothing for it but to accept a guide. But I waited for him apprehensively. My image of an Intourist guide had synthesized into a blend of Misha and Alexander, barely modified by the kindlier contours of Cossack Yury. I wasn't hopeful. The Intourist office that morning was crowded by dough-faced men with badges and files, every one a likely candidate for my discomfort.

So she came as a shock. She looked a classic Armenian. In Erevan her face was almost a type—a satin sliver of features and sable eyes, divided by a long, sculptural nose. Such faces were both fragile and austere. They seemed to belong less to life than to antique bas-relief. Irina's beauty, in particular, was hieratic and superfine. I felt vainly pleased, as if a carved Assyrian princess—purely for my benefit—had detached herself from the walls of Nineveh.

But there was no underestimating Irina, she made sure of that. Her father was Armenian but her mother was Russian, and she had spent the past six years in Moscow. To her, Russia meant the future, Armenia the past. Her dyed, ash-blond hair asserted her chosen identity. The Armenians, she said, as we drove into the hills, were hopelessly patriarchal. She thoroughly disapproved of them. She had clear ideas of the things she wanted, and these did not include an Armenian husband. No, she was engaged to a Russian-Armenian like herself. 'I prefer Russian men—they're easier to boss.' She straightened her shoulders and laughed: the sound was like tinkling iron. 'I can tell you from experience that the men get better as you go north. The Georgians are less domineering than the Armenians, but the Russians are milder than either. In a Russian home, the woman can rule.' She gazed confidently ahead through the windscreen. She'd got everything worked out. Her fiancé was an airforce radio operator, but there wasn't much money in that, she said, so her father had persuaded him to train as an engineer.

'I don't know why the Armenians are so impossible. I suppose it's the climate down here. We live in a dust-hole all summer. But up there'—she waved a painted finger northwards—'everything's cooler and slower.' She not only felt that she could coerce that coolness, but that it was partly her own, through her mother's blood. 'The Russians mature slower than the Armenians. I remember that from school—feeling young, looking young. You know, flat.' She glanced down, satisfied with what had happened since. She wore her good looks like a weapon.

Decisiveness ran in her family. Her grandfather had escaped hanging by the Turks in 1915 even while the rope was being fastened round his neck. Her father had joined the Communist Party. 'But he wishes he'd had me christened now—and he wants a church wedding for me.' The Assyrian nose crinkled in disgust. 'But I can't tell you what an

[175]

Armenian wedding's like. You'd die. The groom arrives at the bride's house all dolled up, then everybody showers them with sweets to symbolize the future sweetness of their lives. Ugh! I'm refusing to go through with that. Later all the relatives dance, holding money between their fingers, to pay the orchestra—showing off how rich they are. By this time you're ready to retch. In the end the bride has to dance as well, and everybody sticks money between *her* fingers. I'm refusing to do that too, and I don't want ribbons flying all over my car as if I was somebody's yacht. They generally stuff a doll on the leading car-bonnet—that's meant to be good for babies—and a bear on the next one.'

'A Russian bear?'

'No.' She knit her brows. 'Just a . . . bear. And after that you're expected to go and live with your mother-in-law. I'm not doing that either. My friends all say: Why not, you've got a built-in babysitter? But I'd rather live my own life. That's the Russian way. Anyway, I don't want to sit at home. I'll go on working until I'm fat and unattractive.' She shot me a fierce smile. 'So I'm getting my husband to live with *my* family. We've got four bedrooms in a first-floor flat. We can live there.'

'If your husband agrees.'

Her forehead flickered only momentarily. 'Yes, of course, if he agrees.'

We were driving into the village of Garni now, where in Roman times Armenia's kings had built their temples and summer palace on a near-impregnable promontory above snow-fed rivers. We walked along a paved way between twisted trees and the walls of cities older still. But nothing prepared me for what was to come. To our left, the promontory suddenly dropped away. Far below there opened out vistas of hills tossing in a naked jumble. And in front of us, perfect and solitary on the bluff's edge, stood a Greek temple. Framed in those camel-coloured hills, so far from home, it was gently moving. Nothing intruded on it. It lifted above its wild backdrop as if flown in by a stage-designer, its sombre basalt only darkened and mottled a little after two thousand years.

Irina thoroughly approved. The shrine made a logic in the waste-land. It seemed to know its mind. But in fact the Armenian kings were only lightly Hellenized, and the place was old in fire-worship. Seen close, an oriental exuberance pervaded the temple's friezes, where whirls of stone foliage ran riot among the lion-masks, and undermined Ionic capitals.

We stared down at the splintered mosaics of a bath-house, where nereids and sea-monsters swam in the oblivion of their ruin. 'We worked, but we were not paid', runs its enigmatic inscription. Irina said that scholars still wrangled over the words' significance. But soon, with thudding predictability, a tour-leader pointed them out to his group as proof of the Capitalist oppression of mosaic-workers in the first century A.D. and shrivelled the life-loving fantasy beneath our feet to Marxist dust.

We penetrated deeper and higher into the hills, making for the cave-monastery of Gueghard up a valley suddenly empty and overbearing. On either side grey and yellow bluffs dangled above the river or tapered to the skyline in pitted organ-pipes. The monastery was a wild, secret place, enclosed in cliffs above the stream's head. A few pilgrims and tourists were about. Black-robed priests were tending beehives on a terrace, or snoring in the shade, and nearby trees were knotted with the handkerchiefs of the faithful, left there for a plea or a thanksgiving.

Irina sat down on a boulder overlooking the stream and told me to go in alone. 'I don't like these places. I like things rational.' She examined her painted toe-nails. 'These people call themselves Christian, but half of it's superstition—all that giving candles in exchange for favours!'

Above the monastery walls the memorial stones of the mediaeval dead, sculptured with a Celtic filigree of crosses and stars, are propped between crags or carved in the rock-face.

But beneath them, and pushing deep into the cliffs, a labyrinth of churches, cells and mortuary chapels burrows and winds through an intestinal darkness. The frescoes and church furniture have gone, but the chambers themselves heave and gouge with a savage, indestructible strength. They are upheld by the passive power of the whole mountain. Their subterranean pillars reach up to monolithic spans of arch and lintel. Their walls are carved with disordered crosses, repeated like an incantation, and the chiselled blazons of princes rise around their emptied tombs. The feel is of eternal dusk. The sun penetrates only in a jagged stammer of light, through a few embrasures and perforated domes, and the black-red basalt of the building-stone is of one flesh with the living rock.

I could understand why Irina shunned the place. It belonged too profoundly to her repudiated past. She would have liked to dye the darkness blond, as she had her hair.

As for me, I felt as if I were back in the Middle East. I passed Islamic-looking prayer-niches and trudged under stalactite vaults like those of Mameluke Egypt. Anonymous tombstones rang underfoot, and here and there some candle-blackened alcove betrayed continuing worship. I found a spring trickling in a cleft, where babies are still christened. A well-dressed family pushed by me and washed their faces there with pagan solemness; two old women dipped a bottle in its waters, and an imp-like boy scrambled into the grotto to light candles.

The Church, so an Armenian told me, is the people's soul. But as I emerged from that uterine blackness into the light, I found Irina pacing back and forth, wearing her intolerant look and waiting to go.

9. On the Black Sea

BY THE END of September I was back on the Black Sea at Sukhumi, near the border between Georgia and ethnic Russia. Here the mountain people begin to thin away, and their vividness is replaced again by the Slavic patience, which seems to disregard the present altogether in a long, dimly-focused concentration on something far off. Perhaps because I was alone, this tranquil quality reassured me. It didn't threaten. Even the Russian children—there were many here— would only assemble about my parked car in a cautious circle, standing a little back, and ask diffident questions about its speed and horsepower.

This Black Sea coast might have been sliced from a littoral of Provence or Istria. Sukhumi itself stands on the same latitude as Nice. Its boulevards are heady with banana palms, oleander and eucalyptus, and the slopes behind are steeped in ferns and creeper-dangling oaks. The town strikes a Mediterranean-lover with an odd, nostalgic confusion, so strange-familiar are its scents and sounds. Cypress trees rise like dark flames from the gardens, and canna·lilies blaze among parklands by the slop of a tideless sea. If you half close your eyes the lumbering Nordic holidaymakers become Germans and British on the Aegean; and the Black Sea itself is furrowed by the same remembered past—the square-rigged Greek merchantmen plying between colonies, Ottoman galleys policing the coasts, Venetian slavers bound for the Crimea. The sea is soft with history and men's change. It blurs all absolutes except itself. Along the promenades the mother-of-pearl-encrusted peep-boxes show quaintly illumined scenes of—what? Not the Twentieth Party Congress, but the Folies-Bergère and King Edward VII opening Parliament.

The blond Russians take boat-trips and choose souvenirs or turn prawn-pink on the beaches. A castle moulders by the sea, its turrets stripped to stone thumbs, and fig trees exploding through its ramparts; but hidden inside, a slum of huts decays in beaten-out tin or plaster walls, with dogs asleep in the dust. Some hint of the ancient world remains in a broken sea-tower turned into a restaurant; it rests on the ruins of Greek Dioscuria, whose acropolis lies under the waves.

An imperious old lady in a huge but faded straw hat—a lady escaped inexplicably from the pages of Chekhov or history—seated herself beside me in the restaurant. Lifting a lorgnette to unblinking blue eyes, she ordered everything expensive on the menu. She might have been dining by the Promenade des Anglais. It occurred to me, when I looked at her, how rarely in Russia I had wondered who anybody was. Everybody looked too much the same (although they were not.) But now I wondered. Was she, perhaps, a leftover Golitsyn or Shuvalov? Then the lorgnette was turned on me.

'You are Polish,' she said. It was a fact, not a question. 'We have something here which you don't have in Poland. The Institute of Experimental Pathology. It is the only interesting thing in the town. See it.'

'What's there to see?' I imagined contagious diseases.

'Baboons.'

I stared at her. But by now the lorgnette was glaring down at the flotsam of stones fallen into the sea below us. We were seated, I suppose, on all that was left of ancient Dioscuria—a vagabond British writer and a Russian *grande dame* from . . . but I never did discover. Because the next moment the waitress had returned to say that salmon was off.

The face of the ex-duchess (or whoever she was) compacted into a frown, then she struck the floor three times with her blue parasol, as if to summon a regiment of Cossacks, and announced: 'Nothing works in this absurd town. The trains don't work, the hotels don't work. And now the restaurants'—and she rose to her feet and marched away.

I took her advice about the baboons. The Institute of Pathology, where artificial sarcoma was induced in 1948, kept two thousand monkeys for experiment. They were constantly injected and studied—the helpless battlegrounds of germ and antibody—and their cages covered a whole hillside. It was their business to save human life. They broke out in artificial cancers and leukemia, and died wretchedly.

In one of the laboratories I found an assistant who showed me round—a girl with a Tartar moon-face and buttery skin. Her job tore her between distaste and dedication. She loved the animals, but her mother had died of a carcinoma. We wandered between the cages under the trees. I had never seen such a hill-load of monkeys, and was awkwardly conscious of how human they seemed. They rested their

heads gloomily in their hands, and peered back at us under shifting brows. When young they clung to their mother's teats with a raw pathos, flinching from the sun in the circle of her arms. Older, they engaged in random matings and grotesque wars. In some cages they sat on wooden benches, like criminals, each one inked with its number on a rear leg; and higher up the hill the observation rows for monkeys already injected fell suddenly quiet, or empty.

Most were baboons and macaques. But there were tiny, moss-coloured monkeys too; delicate russet and cream West African monkeys which gorged on dishes of rice and boiled eggs; and beautiful, restless death's-head apes, patrolling their bars on elastic legs. Finally we emerged on terraces where the fallen trees were stripped even of their bark; they glared like stone. The baboons had chewed away all trace of vegetation. 'It used to be luxuriant,' the girl said. 'Palms, shrubs, grass—and now look what they've done!' Now they sat in long, gloomy battalions—flea-picking, feuding, masturbating. Within two years they had turned their false paradise into desert.

We loitered opposite the blotched red faces of *macacus speciosus*. 'These ones respond well to cancer,' the girl said, 'if you can say such a thing. And the baboons and brown macaques are good for leukemia.' Her voice filled with those palatal caresses which give Russian its peculiar soulfulness. 'Poor darlings, they suffer a lot. They get treated, of course, but they die. We still haven't found the answers. But look at the sphinx mandrill! How beautiful he is! He just paces and paces. Look at his exquisite fingers!'

Cancer and heart disease were on the increase, she said, even in placid Sukhumi, where another institute was studying the Caucasian mountain people, the longest-lived on earth, some of whom reached 140 years of age. She peered unhappily into the cages. 'Sometimes a disease may not develop for years after its injection. More often it gets passed on to the babies by urine or saliva, poor souls, or perhaps by heredity.' She had no children of her own, and regarded the prettier monkeys with unashamed maternal tenderness: but they were already injected with death.

'I often spend my lunch hours here. But sometimes I'm too sad to look at them.' Her eyes moistened even as she spoke of it. 'Listen to the macaque rhesus singing! The baboons bark like dogs, but these ones are more like birds!' We listened. Alarmed by tourist groups, they emitted jungle chirrups and coos. The Georgians teased and ridiculed them, but the Russians fed them illicitly on olives, and sentimentalized over them. The women's chatter flowered into affectionate diminu-

[181]

tives, until every other word ended in a *-chik* or a *-nka*. Even the girl talked of apelets and mini-monkeys.

'The baboons always have a dominant male. I think that's beautiful! [She laughed.] He'll eat first, then the sub-dominant male, and finally the women.' It sounded like Armenia. 'But the strange thing is that they vary so much. Some dominant males even let the others eat first, which I think very courteous of them.'

So not even monkeys were collective, I teased her, let alone humans.

'You're right,' she laughed. 'We have a lot of capitalist free enterprise in these cages. Listen to that –'

A colony of macaque rhesus had burst into hullabaloo, its soft jungle cries turned to screams. Number 15179 had attacked number 15387, and the cage had become a flurry of bared teeth and blood-streaming ears. A big, roving male seized a young rival and dunked him in the water trough, then wrenched him out and bit him; now he sheltered with his mother, who touched him from time to time with long, tentative fondlings of her hand.

Occasionally an old feeling that I had never really touched this country would madden and depress me, and the urge physically to feel it—its tracks and unseen villages—became so intense that I would stop the car and tramp into the woods.

Not far north of Sukhumi, in one of these fits of impatience, I trekked towards a Roman fortress looming from trees a thousand feet up in the hills. As I trudged cross-country the coastline beneath me smoothed to a Tuscan stillness of vineyards and cypress trees. Only the haunted, Argonautic sea, twisting and glittering around its headlands, disturbed the illusion of a Florentine painting, the tended backdrop to some Renaissance madonna.

But where I climbed, the soil was peeling from the slopes, and grey-rooted trees came writhing out of the rocks. The only person I met was an imbecile youth wandering near a village which appeared abandoned. The Roman battlements vanished and reappeared above me, deep in woods. They girdled the hill in pale-stoned ramparts and towers gushing with foliage. Softened by ruin and solitude, they were more like a romantic engraving than a strategic fact. The warrior-emperor Trajan built them in the second century, and they passed painlessly into the Byzantine power and out of history. Yet they were formidable still, strangled in tree-roots, their binding courses of brick compact and firm. A Byzantine barbican loomed above the forest, the vaults of its hall broken apart and their central pillar toppled like an oak,

all of a piece, into the shadows. I climbed an entrance-ramp through the walls. Beyond them, the defended hill rose under whispering glades of trees whose leaves were already falling. It was shiveringly empty. Red squirrels rustled over the branches. Elms lifted from a soil glazed with moss, but the slopes around were stripped to rock and scree, as if the mountain's very bones were erupting through the frail earth. The air fell utterly still. But the Grimm-like trees, racked by winter gales, remained blasted and wrested askew in the silence, as if still shaken by an invisible tempest.

From the summit the fortress hovered over half Abkhazia—the land of a people older and stronger than most Caucasian tribes, and the last to be conquered by the Russians. Here they retain a small, so-called republic of their own. But the only Abkhazian I met was an elderly collective farmer who hailed me as I descended. The Abkhazians were happy with life, he declared, as he plied me with a treacherous homemade wine, with cheese from his goat and mandarins from his trees. The Russians allowed them their own language, their own magazines, their own television programmes. Perhaps it was only in my imagination that from time to time his hawk's face flickered into secrecy and slyness. Before Stalin's death there were plans to exile the whole Abkhazian populace inland, because they were thought dis-loyal.

But the farmer was living well. His two-storeyed house stood in its own grove of pear and orange trees. A television and telephone basked in the centre of his sitting-room like domestic pets, and a refrigerator monopolized the kitchen. Even his hat-stand was stuck with a museum of headware: straw, slouch, stakhanovite, homburg, pork-pie. His sons, he said, were taxi-drivers and sanatorium-warders in neighbouring Sochi, and he was proud of them. Their children's toys littered the linoleum floors of all the downstairs rooms, to the gentle despair of his wife.

'Abkhazia's good country—rich,' he said. 'Are there many Abkha-zians in England?'

'Well, I've. . . .'

'England . . . England. . . .' he mused, ransacking his memory for any fact or image. 'Ah yes! Churchill!' He poured out more wine from a huge earthenware jug. 'I've seen your Queen, Mrs Churchill, on our television. She had white hair and was very beautiful, but her head was sticking out of a tank.'

I dimly recognized Mrs Thatcher. This photograph of her visiting a tank regiment had been circulated by the Soviet news media to corroborate her belligerence. 'I don't approve,' said the farmer circumspectly, 'of women driving.'

I saw more Abkhazians next day. Lean, dark men on lean, dark horses, they were driving their cattle and proud-horned goat flocks down the savage glens beneath Lake Ritsa to winter by the sea. But at the holiday resort of Sochi these nomad freedoms died, and I was in Russia. Sochi, Sukhumi and Yalta are the choicest resorts of the country, and members of the Politburo keep discreet villas here. But in my campsite the rain thrashed in all night off the water, rocking my car so that I woke to find trees bent double above me and lightning illuming a sea broken and livid with foam.

By morning the storm had thinned to a frail, continual rain, and some of the campers trooped down and plunged into the curdling waves. By seven o'clock the washhouses were full of others lined up bare-chested in track-suit trousers before cracked shaving-mirrors, while their women, sleepy in slippers and flowered dressing-gowns, plodded fatalistically among the puddles with saucepans and towels.

Sochi was full of those titanic sanatoria so favoured in the Stalin years—grandiose Italianate palaces where approved workers are sent by their trade unions for 26-day holidays of sea-swimming, lectures and thermal baths. Like the Moscow subways, these institutions bring the trappings of luxury to the masses. Porticoed terraces lumber down through fountained gardens towards the sea, and the spartan dormitories are banked behind Corinthian colonnades. They seem to offer the grosser inconveniences of privilege without its essence, and the people themselves come and go in a dwarfed quiet, looking for the beaches.

In one of these sanatoria, half visible for cascading rain, I found a stout matron to show me the facilities. It accommodated seven hundred, but I wondered where they had all gone. The place's white-coated staff and elaborate size began to suggest something indefinably alarming to me—a lost episode from Kafka. A few men were standing under the porticoes by enormous chess-tables, slamming down outsize bishops and pawns, and four women emerged from the sanatorium's hair salon, crowned with bouffants and bird's-nests, straight into the destroying rain. It was oddly desolate. It suggested that something was happening somewhere else; but nothing was. Mornings, said the matron, could be passed in the health clinics undergoing diagnosis, massage, sulphur inhalation, roentgen or ultra-violet rays. Afternoons were spent by the sea.

The matron was inexorable. She tramped the corridors with doctrinal authority. 'Look at our lovely sea!' she cried. It was invisible for

rain. 'Look how beautiful our gardens!' They were soaked and obliter-
ated; muddy water gushed down the terraces. When we came to an
empty hall she declared: 'People are playing here.'

I stared. 'Where? When?'

'Now. All the time.' Objective fact was gossamer beside taught truth.

We passed noticeboards pinned with timetables: '7.45: physical jerks.
8.15: first gymn session. . . .' A succession of lectures was forecast: 'The
politics of the Communist Party of the Soviet Union', 'Reminiscences
of Edith Piaf', 'The Plans of the Party are those of the Country'. A
closed-up library displayed placards for the 110th anniversary of the
birth of Lenin. Dictatorial posters announced: 'A man should and must
give up smoking' above diagrams of decayed lungs. A bust of Stalin
lurked in a corner.

'Those places are death,' said Vasily, a student I met in the campsite
restaurant. 'They're only good for the old. Everyone's so serious you
want to puke. It's meant to be a privilege to go there—you have to get a
doctor's certificate—but they don't even allow discos. You just go mad.
Most young people get in at recreation centres instead, or go away
alone. I only went to a sanatorium because I got asthma.' He winced. 'In
August when the ambrosia comes out my nose blocks and my eyes
stream.'

'What's ambrosia?'

'This weed . . . it arrived with American grain imports. At least there
wasn't any twenty years ago, and now it's everywhere.' He frowned. 'I
don't mean to be critical . . . but then you're not American, are you?'

His was an aesthetic, nervous face, its eyes and mouth never still.
Perhaps his asthma had been brought on less by ambrosia than by some
private distress.

'We got the Colorado beetle through those grain sales too,' he went
on, 'and there are American butterflies everywhere here now, rather
pretty. It's strange. . . .'

Out of the starless night, rain came gusting and chattering at the
restaurant windows, but inside, and all around us, Georgian campers
were uncorking champagne with ribald whoops and jets of palomino
liquid, which made Vasily physically shudder. 'I don't like drinking.'
We sipped dry white wine together like fastidious spinsters, and
pretended the Georgians weren't there. As their songs and uncorkings
detonated around us, he lapsed into the kind of absent musing which I
had once imagined only to be a figment of Russian literature. What
would he do with his life? He was already nineteen, and filled with
hopelessness. Why was he so melancholy? He didn't know. Perhaps it

[185]

was the size of the land which made his people such a sad one. Up in Siberia, and even in western Russia, you could go for hundreds of miles and see nobody at all. Just a few snowy owls and wolves. Then you started to think. And then you became sad. Yes, the size of everything made you feel sad.

'Perhaps we even *like* feeling miserable.' He flinched at a new fusillade of champagne-corks. 'I can look at the sea forever, for instance . . . that vastness. Did you notice it last night—the waves? Waves, on and on. So I just went on looking, on and on. . . .'

Sometimes his talk would soften and drift away, as if into the emptiness of the seascape. Then the *thwop* of Georgian corks would jolt him into a wondering distaste. 'These Georgians . . . in a way I envy them. If somebody closes a door in a Russian's face, he just shrugs and goes away. But a Georgian always gets in through the back. You never actually see them doing any work; they just sit in the cafés. But us Russians, I don't think we're made for town life. . . .' The voice drifted away . . . *thwop*! *thwop*! . . . returned. 'I hate our big industrial cities, Moscow most of all. Everything gets coarsened there, uglier . . .' *thwop*! '. . . the best people are the Siberians, you know. They're honest and generous in ways we've lost here in the west. Perhaps I'll find my future in Siberia. . . .'

Now the rain was falling in a sustained, heavy flood, and Vasily's mind had seeped away with it. It is said the Russian is like an onion: the more you peel him, the more you weep. And Vasily was peeled to thin air. I had the sensation that he was physically disappearing, pouring down with the rain. His voice was a self-communing murmur. 'The rain'll stay for days now. Everything takes such a long time here. . . .'

Northward, for two hundred miles, the Caucasian foothills came down steep and lonely to the shore, and my road trickled in and out of their valleys. Sometimes the slopes were covered by a windswept gleam of birches; the sea would appear in turquoise triangles at the end of their corridors and small, untidy rivers slopped beneath the road to smear their floodwaters over the shoreline—muddy rainbows which deepened far out from sapphire to thunder-mauve.

Towards dusk I emerged above the horseshoe bay of Novorossiisk and turned inland at last across the sleepy humps and farmlands of the Don. The Arabish songs of the Caucasus faded from my radio and were replaced by news bulletins encrusted with the activities of Party dignitaries. In the outskirts of Krasnodar a haggard old man, recognizing a Western car, ran up and banged his fists on the bonnet, crying:

'We have no Capitalism! No Capitalism! Tell your people back home that in Russia there's no Capitalism!'

Ever since crossing the Polish border I had privately resolved not to argue, but to listen. Now I was dimly aware that the tensions of this self-imposed silence were piling up dangerously inside me. Ten minutes later, while repairing a puncture, a garage mechanic said: 'In the West you have tyres with tubes. In Russia we gave those up twenty years ago. We're in advance.' Beneath such pronouncements, sometimes fibs, a rankling inferiority glares. Cruelly I asked him how long he had spent in the West, that he should know such things.

Krasnodar seemed destined to dispirit me. It is one of those featureless Soviet conurbations, grown impressively from nothing in a few years, which dishearten by their sameness. In the absence of a campsite I had been assigned to a hotel, whose foyer was full of loitering men. It made me uneasy. I slipped away to take some children's books to the friend of an acquaintance in England, and was soon lost in a web of identical, tree-lined roads. When I at last found her, she turned out to be a spirited blonde schoolteacher. Her husband was away with students on one of those 'voluntary' brigades which are in fact compulsory, helping farmers to bring in the grape harvest. She launched into a laughing diatribe against Krasnodar. It was miserably boring, she said; that summer she had taken her eight-year-old son to Leningrad, simply to show him that a town could be beautiful. The idea of remaining all day with her two children in the cramped flat horrified her; instead she worked for a primary school at the other end of town. But she had no *babushka* to babysit—only a twinkle-eyed grandfather, eighty-five years old ('he can't babysit, he's a *man*')—so her two-year-old daughter had been attending nursery-school since the age of seven months, and remained there from eight in the morning until eight at night.

There was nothing unusual in this. Millions of children are brought up from the age of one, or less, to the crushing group identity of kindergarten; the teachers are maternal and intrusive, and even parents seem to guard their children from their own individuality—even from the most harmless flights of fancy—with instinctive fear. Already, for eighteen months, the two-year-old girl sulking on her mother's knee had been nursed in a regimen whose purpose, says a Soviet teaching manual, is 'the formation of a convinced collectivist'. She had been trained to sing songs to Lenin and the Motherland, and her dawning mind was already receiving fables about the October Revolution. The sight of the books which I had brought from England—bright, fanciful, strange—seemed to fill the little girl only with smothered alarm. She turned tearfully away from them against her mother's breast, cramming all her fingers into her mouth.

Back over the Don steppes to Kharkov, and south-west along the watershed of the Dnieper for three days, the road took me a thousand miles to the tip of the Crimea. Now the black earth was shaded here and there by a vivid green. The villages were all of brick, but were few and lost among collective farmlands whose entrance-gates lined the road-side blazoned with sickles and corn-sheaves and clasped hands. In this wide, Ukrainian flatness, it seemed as if nothing could ever change or happen, and when a car in front of me slithered off the road and glided down a bank into the fields, it occurred in an unreal silence. I found a small, drunk man trapped in its wreckage. His wife had been hurled through the windscreen. She lay in an incongruously sybaritic-looking heap among the black furrows, while six or seven village women were already hurrying round shaking bags of talcum powder over her. I wrenched open the car doors. The man hobbled out, grasping my shoulders, and sat down near his wife. She was covered in powder now, like a long-decomposed corpse, but she suddenly sat up and gaped at him. Neither said anything. The car was shaken to a ruin, but both seemed unscathed. Some lorry-drivers stopped and ran over, then slowed to a glum semicircle around us. Nobody asked, or offered, any explanation. Only the lorry-drivers, who had noticed my British car, glanced at me and muttered together, torn between patriotic humilia-tion and gratitude.

I spent that night at the campsite of Zaporozhye, a day's journey from the Crimea. I was the only foreigner, and sat alone in the restaurant, watching the flux of its customers.

A squat Aeroflot pilot bounced down opposite me. 'You're drinking alone?' His bulldog expression emanated eager goodwill. 'Drink alone, and you're an alcoholic! Better to drink in pairs!' His name was Albert—the kind of German name only given to Russians before 1941. Albert was my age, but a collapsed stomach was already oozing from under his flying-jacket and his thickened neck merged with his head in a single, flatulent column. He was determined to have a party. With a sinking heart I watched my vodka-glass fill up, and heard the toasts begin. The ritual was too-familiar. I reciprocated miserably. We drank to each other's countries, families, peace. He invented a wife for me, and drank to her. I drank to his.

Albert was bored. His wife and children were away on holiday in

Lvov, and he had driven over from the local airport to try his luck with the campsite girls. Some of the youth of Zaporozhye had adopted the place for the weekend, using its huts as bedrooms, and its bar was ablaze with noise and dancing. Soft, passive-bodied girls and vacant-looking youths sat around its walls on benches. Ukrainian girls, Albert declared, were bigger than the Russians (although precisely where bigger, he didn't say). He plied me with a cocktail called Troika—vodka, brandy and liqueur—which swam up into my eyes. I gazed out from behind it, feeling sick. Albert's face grinned and pulsated in the watery gloom. 'This is the drink that God loves!' We rubbed glasses. 'Three in one and one in three!' We tossed them back wholesale. Soon the floorboards under my chair were sodden with surreptitiously discarded Troikas, but drunkenness lurched forward uncontrollably.

Albert hunted for a girl. A ring of twenty-year-old students had gathered round us; their faces looked keen and sensitive. But he teetered away between the tables and spied a long-haired teenager, vapidly pretty. Grinning and thrusting out his chest in its prestigious flying-jacket, he presented himself before her—the epitome of confident but doomed middle age. His sagging stomach and hopeful face suddenly looked pathetic. She was mercilessly young. Her gaze swept over him, then without a word she turned away and stared back at the smoke-filled dance-floor. The canned music clashed and thundered.

Albert returned, full of Troikas and unabashed. 'She was too young,' he said. The next moment he'd gone again, and this time ended up dancing with a gawky brunette who overtopped him by a foot. He beamed and bumped against her breasts, and came back bursting with self-esteeem and shouting: 'I'll find you a girl!'

But I found her myself. She was a nineteen-year-old student from the local polytechnic. Her soft voice almost disappeared in the dinning music as we danced. She looked embarrassed and lost. 'You're *English*?' She jigged in my arms with her head turned away, blushing. 'You're not *really* English?' She answered my questions in rushed, flat monosyllables. The polytechnic was quite nice. Dancing was all right. Zaporozhye was quite nice. But I wasn't *really* English?

I settled with the students round our table, talking about poetry: one was eloquent on Blok, another passionate about Yesenin. Albert got fed up. He tried to join in, but he was irreversibly of the Jack London generation. In a moment, I thought, he would quote Burns. 'They're just students,' he said. 'They don't know anything. They've no experience of life.' And they seemed indeed to be a different race. Alternately my gaze focused on them and on Albert through the deepening pool of my inebriation. I was not sure if I were looking at a generation gap or at some other, deeper human division. 'You're *my* guest,' Albert mumbled, 'not theirs. . . .'

They were gentle with him, as with a child. They refused to take offence. His petty vanities and ritualized hospitality seemed to be as foreign to them as to me. When his talk turned crassly to politics, they deflected him. 'No, no, no,' they said. Politics threatened differences; they were less important than the flesh and blood of my presence. When Albert tried to force drinks on me, they tactfully dissuaded him.

I was dimly aware that I was witnessing two Russias. I hoped that one was the future and the other the past, although even in my drunkenness I realized that nothing was as simple as that. Yet Albert was typical of his deprived generation. He was practical, tough and narrow. To him these others were too pampered and easy. They were, I sensed, apolitical. He resented them; and they, in turn, looked on him not only with the old Russian respect for seniority but with a feeling that he was somehow irrelevant, and belonged to a world of absolutes which was forever past.

'They're too young,' he said.

Southward the land achieved a new nadir of flatness. Sluggish with haze, its 12,000-acre wheatfields wallowed and shimmered among interweaving lakes, where the enormous Dnieper moved in an invisible flood to the west. Glimpsed through wind-breaks along the road, the twin planes of land and water stretched level and interchangeable to a horizon which fell away like a cliff-edge into nothing. Around the neck of the Crimea the Azov Sea, so still and shallow that in winter it freezes solid, curved along rutted mud-flats where flocks of gulls swam offshore or paced over a sheen of pink-berried shrubs.

From the Crimean capital of Simferopol I flew that night to Odessa. In the Tupolev jet the seat beside mine was occupied by a Ukrainian vet. His suntanned face, grained and scored like old wood, either shut itself off from me with a look of paranoid suspicion, or crinkled into multiple smiles. There seemed nothing in between. Thickset, bald, uncomfortable in his dark suit and light mackintosh, he epitomized that haunted generation which spent its youth under Stalin. Half the things he said, however innocent, were pursued by qualification. If I questioned him too closely about himself, his face would suddenly freeze solid, but the moment I seemed disinterested and returned to reading my book, an impeccable pamphlet called *Lenin and Co-operatives*, he would begin to ask me questions—what did I think of Russia, was

America still 'ahead'?—and talk about himself. His life had been spent as a small-time vet on state farms in the southern Ukraine. He had only once been to Moscow, and his conception of anywhere else was as blurred and misshapen as of another galaxy. The tools for understanding had never been handed to him. He conceived of the West, of all the world, as an extended Ukrainian town. 'England . . .' he murmured, scouring his brain. 'England . . . fog!' He was delighted with this nugget. 'How is the fog in England?' He knit his brows at the thought of its impermanence, and rummaged through his mental lumber-room again. 'Bacon! The English like bacon. I remember that.' But here his knowledge ended. Fog, bacon.

Outside our window the moon, almost full, was beating out a bronze passage over the sea. Sometimes, far below, the lights of a boat flashed in the night, and I thought of Turkish fishermen I'd known on the southern shores, trading their sturgeon illicitly with Russian boats in mid-sea. The vet was talking about trotter disease in pigs now, cautiously saying that his job was poorly paid. 'I'm a specialist—five years' training, I call that a specialist . . . but perhaps that's going too far.' He had to feed and clothe two teenage daughters, and his wife worked in a chemist's shop to help (but his voice clouded when he spoke of her).

'And why aren't you married?' he demanded. 'You like girls? You're in love? Then why, at your age—you must be at least twenty-eight—aren't you married?' The next moment he was looking at me with an open, innocent cunning. 'I know. You can't find rooms. No apartments. We have the same problem here.' He brushed aside my denial as needless patriotism. 'I had to live with my in-laws for over a year, all of us in two rooms. Lack of space, it's the same everywhere . . . .'

Odessa blazed orange and white over the sea. We were flying above the harbour now, where liners showed in burning almonds of light. I imagined the gossipy pre-Revolutionary port which I had read about somewhere: the Greek, Jewish and Italianate cosmopolis with its polyglot interchange of wares and ideas, its tang of French architecture.

But morning disclosed a city quieter, tamer, more uniform. Its trade, once the highest in the Soviet Union, has been deflected to the satellite port of Ilyichovsk a few miles to the south, leaving Odessa becalmed among its nineteenth century streets and plane trees. It rises above the sea in terraced avenues fringed with old business houses, while at its quays the Black Sea passenger ships idle among cranes; a few tugs bustle over the water and goods trains dawdle on grass-sown tracks.

The Odessans show an old humour and entrepreneurial cunning. One in every three families is employed by the sea, and a desultory life still revolves around the cafés. I passed the Old English Club, the one-time London Hotel, the defunct Stock Exchange still adorned with its statue of Mercury, god of trade (and thieves), and descended the flight of 192 steps where Eisenstein filmed his classic sequence for *Battleship Potemkin*.

'You find a different spirit here,' a woman said. 'It's a slow city, but . . . subtle.' We had sidled into conversation while examining the gloomy faces on a board of honour. Individual workers were listed beside factories, ships and the Odessa Telegraph. ('Why don't they smile?' I ask. 'It would be frivolous,' she replies.) The woman seemed a quintessence of Russian middle-age: earthy, immobile as a windmill, but sentimental and vaguely sad. Her history, too, was common. After the German troops had evacuated Odessa in 1944, she said (in fact they were Romanian troops) her parents had come back to find only the ruins of the street where they had lived. She had stayed with them in a one-room flat until 1967, had married, divorced, and returned to her sick mother with a baby son. To her the war was a dimly-remembered horror perpetuated in her parents' distress and in the collective consciousness of the nation. She shared the national obsession with security. 'We have to be sure that it will never happen again.' We were passing the tomb of the Unknown Sailor, where Komsomol cadets rotated their vigil every fifteen minutes. 'The proof that our people love the Communist system,' she said (she was a Party member) 'is that twenty million died for it in the war.'

'They died *for their country*,' I said. Twenty million never died for a system.

The woman recognized my antagonism. Her mind was full of doctored history, and judgements strange to me. Stalin's faults were redeemed by his strengths, she said, speaking the word 'faults' with tenderness, as if his victims had perished in a moment of absent-mindedness; and she explained the invasion of Afghanistan by Russia's deep desire for peace. 'We have to defend our borders.'

'And what of *Afghanistan*'s peace?'

'We were invited in by Afghanistan's leader.'

'But you liquidated him!'

The woman grew muddled. Perhaps the Afghan people had invited Russia in, she said. I answered that the people had no voice: they were unrepresented. Besides, they were an ethnic chaos, not united at all. Her eyes dilated at this, her face puckered. An apparently simple situation was splintering into disagreeable and complicated patterns. For one instant a note of life-giving surprise and confusion coloured her voice. Then her expression cleared and she delivered a blunt statement of faith in her country's incapacity for evil. Facts were only decorative trifles in her emotional landscape. They would not shake her. The details were not really important, she said. Her country was right.

This blindness reappeared when we walked near the city's opera house, crowned by the Muse of Tragedy in her chariot of leopards, as the woman said: 'The leopards represent human passion, but the muse holds up a torch to symbolize the controlling power of civilization.'

I stared up. 'The torch has gone.'

She followed my gaze. 'It's there,' she said. 'She's holding it up.'

She was not. The uplifted hand was empty. 'The leopards are having a field day.'

'It's there,' the woman insisted. 'It stands for civilization.'

For a moment I imagined she must be short-sighted, but then I saw that her expression had retracted into a brooding stubbornness. The torch should be there, so it was there. It was an emotional fact. The Odessans loved their music, she went on, as if to buttress her claim. Gilels and David Oistrakh had trained at the city's academy. Two-and-a-half million litres of liquid glass had recently been poured into the opera house foundations to stabilize them; eleven kilograms of gold had been spent refurbishing the decorations. . . .

That afternoon the opera house put on a children's ballet choreographed on the fairy tale of 'the little hump-backed horse'. In the baroque auditorium, where lamps of clouded glass dangled like fat pearls, everybody became a momentary tsar. Immaculate ten- and twelve-year-old children, as many boys as girls, peered from the lavish boxes with their dowdy parents. The curtain rose on a fantasy contrasting so cruelly with their ordinary lives that the shock must have been dazing. Peacocks nesting in a golden shrine under the curly-domed palace of the czars; gauzy screens of humanoid flowers; a *corps de ballet* of rainbow-feathered birds which flitted and twirled through a blue and purple night—the audience froze into pin-drop stillness. It was a world of exuberant peasants and a harmless, imbecile aristocracy, and the hero was one of those prince-fools beloved by Russian folklore. In the intervals the children wandered after their mothers in stunned-looking shoals. Anybody trying to imitate the hunch-backed horse by galloping down the aisles was seized by frightened parents or dragooned into silence by bullying, middle-aged usherettes. Fantasy was not for living.

In the last act, as the stage princess danced in a gold and scarlet dress before her wedding, the small girl by my side, her hair clouded in chiffon ribbons, threw herself flat against the seat in front with a little cry, rammed her fists against her cheeks and went on gazing long after the curtain had fallen. Then her father gently pulled her away, and we all went back down the gold and marble stairway.

Outside in the harsh sunlight real brides, looking wooden and matter-of-fact, were laying their bouquets beneath a memorial to the city's heroes, and posing to be photographed beside their unsmiling grooms.

Early on Sunday morning I took a series of trams far into the suburbs, searching for Uspensky monastery, which runs one of the last three theological seminaries in the Soviet Union. The streets were almost empty. A few women holding enamel pots formed desultory queues beside milk-churns just arrived from the country, and some elderly men in track suits were wheezing round October Revolution Park. In my last tram I sat next to a man whose son had defected to the West and now played the violin in a New Orleans orchestra.

'Can he come back and see you?'

'Not until there's peace.' He looked crushed as he talked of it, and got off hurriedly at the next stop.

It was hard to believe that the ramshackle seminary—a scattering of monastic buildings under yellowing trees—nurtured so many of Russia's future priests. In its two churches, celebrants were already observing the liturgy, and old women were silently begging along its dusty paths. They kissed the monks' hands and pectoral crosses, bowed under their perfunctory blessing. It seemed a place for the blind, the unloved, the widowed.

The number of seminarists is not only brutally curtailed—there are 250 here, I heard, with thirty-eight monks—but the influx of those with too educated a background is restricted. Nobody seemed free to show me the buildings. Scurrying along the paths in their black, serf-like robes and crumpled hats, the monks met my requests with unhappiness or bemusement. Only one man, distressed by my failure to cross myself in church, seized my arm at the back of the nave. 'Touch your head for the Father, my child, then down to your belly for the Son—no, you've got it wrong—now across your shoulders. . . .' But when I asked him about the seminary, he said: 'I don't know anything. I never went to a seminary myself. I only finished third grade. . . . Some of the monks teach there, but not me. We pray, you see. We pray for men's brotherhood. You're not from our country, are you? I can tell that.' He twined his fingers in and out of his beard; he was like an ancient child. 'We pray for peace.'

On his lips the word 'peace' lost its contamination. For the first time I wanted to share it.

But the seminary, and Odessa itself, had eluded me.

Beneath the Crimean mountains, which fold the peninsula's southern shore in a tropical balm, I lazed away a week near Yalta, swimming a little, walking in the hills, sometimes forgetting that I was in Russia at all. The inhabitants call this early autumn 'the velvet season'—the whole land mellow and still, sinking with a sigh into October. A milky haze covered everything, smoothing the sky and the quiet sea together, horizonless, so the wake of a passing boat remained a wrinkle suspended in emptiness. Over the forest-brown earth of the foothills, a thicket of burnished reds and yellowing greens scattered and glowed. The vines were turning crimson in the valleys, the hazels gold. Juniper, cypress, wild apple, plum and pear trees and twisted Crimean oaks reached high up the hills, until mountain crags steepened out of their softness, flecked only by pine-trunks stark against the rock.

Even my campsite was perched precipitously above vineyards. I arrived at night to find its hundred-odd huts filled with Russian and East German tourists, but the murmur of their holidaymaking dissipated and died in the valley. Seated on a tree-stump near my camping hut, a huge, dreamy-faced man was staring up at the stars. He occupied the cabin beside mine, spoke a halting English, and chose to sit by me that night in the restaurant. I at first suspected him of being an informer.

Julian was my age, but the contrasting experience of our countries had equipped us divergently. I felt at once younger and more sophisticated than him. When we talked, his boyish face would wrinkle quaintly round its weather-creased eyes with the effort to understand or explain something, transforming him into a diligent but backward pupil. Yet beside this heavy simplicity there was something powerful too, and stubbornly independent. It was this recalcitrant independence, I think, which drew us together. In him it seemed to be the product of a masculine self-confidence, of the weight he gave to his own experience. Whereas in me, perhaps, it stemmed from a restless inner life and a distrust of belonging.

Julian worked in a collective farm near Simferopol. Ten years before, he had travelled in an agricultural delegation to Britain, and he now grew cucumbers on straw bales in the British way. But he had become impatient. He had enjoyed setting up the farm, but he was irritated by its routine. He preferred creation to maintenance. 'I tell you what I loved in England. I loved your personal farms—forty cows or so, and the small tractors and the little orchards. I call that a marvellous system!' He stopped, scenting his own heresy. 'But I suppose it wouldn't work here . . . I suppose not.' The wrinkles reconvened between his eyes. 'Those small farms, they make people independent. That's good. A man needs to be on his own. That's what I liked about you when I saw you. Alone.' He gave a deep, shy laugh.

He should have had his own work, his own cattle, his own space. Instead he owned a twenty-foot garden and a fox terrier, and bred pet rabbits with his son. Sometimes on weekends he frustratedly pruned his father-in-law's orchard of thirty fruit trees. But that was all. Big cities he regarded with distress, and Moscow he hated. 'It's a city which doesn't communicate with itself.' He preferred London, he said, because you could feel the earth amongst the stone. 'Those gardens and squares! I like that. But one thing astonished me—the open pornography. I don't know if it's good or bad, I was just amazed, knowing the British character. Perhaps I've read too much Galsworthy. . . .' The wrinkles spurted up around his eyes again. 'There's another thing that's very strange. We don't hear anything in our country about your fighting in 1940. It's as if those events don't exist for us.' Had a whole generation in Britain, he wondered, been transfixed by the war as it had in Russia? 'It's made a deep divide between my father's generation and mine. He's an old man now, over eighty. He used to drive a horse-cab in Oryol, and he fought in the Revolution. Pure history! He's absolutely definite about everything, even though his mind's going. But I care less for politics than he did. It's the same with all my contemporaries. We seem farther from those things. . . .'

'And your children?'

'My son's only twelve. How different he'll be from me, I can't tell. But the children are more pampered now than we were, so perhaps they'll be gentler than us.' His face clouded into disapproval. 'But there are so few of them! A lot of married couples can only afford one. And that one grows up surrounded by aunts and grandmothers and women teachers. We're growing soft.'

Julian wanted to nurture his son's enterprise. He seemed to be saying that Russia, contrary to appearances, was shaped by women, and that their influence inhibited individuality. He himself fiercely needed to be alone. This solitary holiday, which his wife resented, was spent fishing. He would row himself out to sea with an old sailor and sit for four or five hours at a time with his line dangled overboard. Once he caught a shark, but never much else. And he would often throw his catch back into the water. Each evening we met in the camp restaurant and discussed our different days; and mine, which started in a flurry of anxious sightseeing, became subtly infected by his, and slowed to a languorous procession of walks above the sea or in the hills.

Once these shores were the evening playground of the tsarist aristocracy. Their lush slopes gleam and bristle with the architectural fancies of western Europe and the Orient. But now the palaces have been turned into sanatoria for the people (as inscriptions on the base of every Lenin statue remind you). Confections in the Moorish or Otto-man taste, overblown Swiss chalets and Renaissance *palazzi*, sprout and ramble among parklands or botanical gardens fat with oak and arbutus. The castle of a German oil baron hangs in Rhenish fantasy on a cliff above the waves, and pastiche becomes brilliant lunacy in the Vorontsov palace, built in battle-grey dionite, where Mameluke minarets and Tudor chimneys taper above Landseer lions slumbering beside a Moghul gateway. Even Livadia palace, where the Yalta conference was held in 1945, rings the scene of the birth of the United Nations with a spurious halo of white granite and Moorish-Florentine courtyards.

The very coast seems touched with artifice. The so-called Bear headland abuts the waves in a shaggy, sea-browsing hulk; and the pine-hung declivity of Cat Mountain, its boulders clambering eight hundred feet into the sky, resembles some gargantuan tom crouched to pounce on the breakers. Yalta itself has doubled its size in twenty years; but its alleys still twine through a nineteenth century heart of parks and verandaed mansions, and its quay tinkles with a children's funfair; while higher inland, in a stone house and a garden jungly with lilies, Chekhov wrote *The Three Sisters* and *The Cherry Orchard*.

It is easy to see why artists loved this region. All along the coast the villages and little towns give out a haphazard secrecy, confusions of stucco houses scramble up slopes bright with hollyhocks, or lurch together in a sun-softened mingling of walls. Vines shade old foot-paths; buddleias are stuck with yellow bees. Courtyards have become living-rooms or kitchens, hung with onions and scattered with washing and cats. Sometimes, so intense is the feeling of a Latin land, that the sudden stridency of Russian radio songs, or the emergence of Slavic faces in place of the Mediterranean grace and agitation, produce an almost physical shock of dislocation.

But the beaches where I walked could only have been Russian. Their people lined them like convalescents, in a strange, prostrate self-surrender. They lay crowded on their towels or on penitential wooden boards, without playing or even talking, as if to absolve themselves, in these few snatched weeks of oblivion, from all thought and unrest. The older women, especially, stretched themselves out in heaps with a grotesque, peasant beatitude. Floppy cloth sun-hats sheltered peeling noses and inflamed cheeks. Beneath the big, loose breasts turning crimson in the heat, flaccid hips and Buddha stomachs tapered to legs as bruised and unshaped as old tree trunks. They changed dress in Victorian-looking beach-cubicles, then emerged to swim solemnly along the shallows in unisexual bathing-caps. Only a few of the young showed a Western slenderness, and occasionally, in this outwardly puritan land, a couple tentatively fondled, or a head rested on a nearby lap.

'Those beaches just make you want to get into the hills,' said Julian that evening, 'or go home.' We were gazing from our restaurant over the darkened valley. He had spent all day catching one fish. He looked happy, and his deep, rumbling laugh detonated at ease into the night. Then, suddenly serious, he pointed into the mountains. In the encircling range one bluff erupted from the others in a treeless solitude. The full moon picked it out from all the rest in an eerie interplay of shadow and insubstantial light. A dissident. 'I love that peak. Standing on its own. That's what I like about the English character too—at least the classic English character.' His laugh exploded again. 'I don't know why, but I like it. Too much Galsworthy! And your Queen, that's something I like too. An ideal.' Suddenly he was making almost a declaration of faith: 'It's hard to carve out your own way, isn't it? Not to be subjected to a laid-down principle, only to be governed by what you find is so? It's harder but . . . right.'

It was utterly, consciously un-Communist. I could only say 'Yes' as he pronounced this simple and absolute heresy against all he had ever been told.

The next moment a shabby, middle-aged man sat himself beside us and tapped my shoulder. Russians often reminded me of characters in their own fiction, and this one recalled those sad, petty professional men who wander the pages of nineteenth century novels. His face was all eager foolishness. He had diagnosed me as an American, and he had a question. 'Why,' he demanded incredulously, 'do you Americans say you're afraid of Russia? How can any country be afraid of Russia?'

Perhaps it was the gentling night, the wine, or the ease of conversation with Julian, but something in me softly broke. In the man's doltish, puzzled face his country's myth of innocence seemed incarnate and all at once maddening, and suddenly, with a distant, helpless dismay, I heard months of opinionated frustrations unlock themselves and barge out of my mouth. Why afraid? Because Russia, I began, dominated the last and hugest empire on earth. I invoked the invasion of Hungary in 1956, of Czechoslovakia in 1968, of Afghanistan in 1979. It was a country of evangelistic ruthlessness, of nationalism disguised as ethics; it was as materialistic and more cynical than America had ever been (I had momentarily adopted America); yet its government was too frightened to permit a free vote or even a free poem, and was headed by a clutch of privileged autocrats. Soviet Communism, I went on, was merely the art of opportunism, it had lost touch even with the dignity of an outdated Marxism. . . . Then I noticed Julian's face. It was turned away from me, whitened, towards the darkness. And when I looked back at the other man I saw that my fusillade of romantic disappointment might as well have been fired at the sky. His expression showed only a bewildered hurt.

'"Empire",' Julian repeated later. '"Ruthlessness". Strong words.' They hurt him—he was deeply patriotic—but he mulled and forgave them. We smoothed them away in wine until late in the night, talking of England, and of countries where he'd never been, until I wondered incoherently if the most useful role of governments might be to express all their people's fear and antagonism, and so release the people themselves into some precious and unexpected friendship.

That night I dreamed I was looking over the edge of the campsite into a waterlogged valley. I was surrounded by frightened people—Russians, British, Americans—who said that a mass of soldiers was advancing up the slope. As I peered over, I saw their helmets teeming below in the odd, aqueous light. Then I realized that they were only tree-stumps, and I called out: it's nothing, it's all right. And the fear around me vanished.

But I woke up.

The Crimea, like the Caucasus, is darkened by a displaced people. On a thin suspicion of collaboration with Germany, its two hundred thousand Tartars were deported *en masse* to Central Asia by Stalin in 1944, and their role in the partisan fight against Nazism was systematically distorted or suppressed. In 1967 the charges against them were withdrawn; but thousands had already died in the hardship of exile, and their efforts to filter back into the Crimea have been harassed ever since.

Sixty miles north through the mountains, the old Tartar capital of Bakhchiserai is now a tourist site. Its palace clusters under chestnut trees around secret courtyards and the slop of marble fountains. It has the subtle mutability of so many Turkic things—a nomad camp eternalized in wood and stone. In its cushioned chambers the sun enters only as a paler-than-usual shadow, leaking through vine-hung windows, or sliding beneath tiled roofs across the crimson flowering of carpet and divan. A goblin smallness touches everything. The little courts, once raked by the scrutiny of bored eyes from door or lattice, still reek of whispered conspiracy. The walls are low, for overhearing. The verandahs listen. The painted ceilings and witch-hat chimneys of the harem are redolent of tinkling headdresses and yawns and per-fumed baths. In the main court the Tartar Fountain of Tears, adorned with tiny marble cups, lets drop its watery beads unnoticeably from one little chalice into another, in symbol of recurring sorrow.

'A few Tartars are returning as farmers in the north of the penin-sula,' said Julian, 'but there don't seem to be any in the south—I don't know why.' He was genuinely perplexed. 'And there are plenty of jobs here.'

It was our last evening. He had bought a bottle of Caucasian dessert wine—we never normally drank much together—and we celebrated a sombre farewell. From time to time his gaze wandered uneasily to the restaurant television. 'You've heard the news?'

'No.'

It came non-committally from the television announcer: the out-break of war between Iran and Iraq.

We stared at one another, wondering where the Soviet and Western governments would stand, what we would be told to feel. 'It looks like Moscow and Washington are hanging back,' Julian said. 'It's not time for us to report for duty.' He tried to laugh. But we touched glasses unhappily, as if already clothed in invisible battledress. The news had momentarily reduced us.

'Sometimes I think of my father,' Julian said, 'and of that whole war generation, and I think: "Let the dead bury their dead".' He grimaced. 'Is that in the Bible or Longfellow?' Then, out of his schoolboy memory, he began to quote Burns. I suppressed a moan as *My Heart's in the Highlands* came up. But the words rolled out of him with a kind of ponderous wonder, restoring the poem to itself, and exorcized the sarcasm of Misha in the Elburz mountains.

Dusk had turned to night, and the wine glasses empty. Above us, as we wandered back to our huts, the one crag stood out in moon-streaked solitude from the concensus of the rest. 'In the Kruschev years, the golden years,' Julian said, 'I managed to buy a copy of Richard Aldington's *Death of a Hero*—the book of a pacifist. Have you read it? It had a deep influence on me.' We stopped in front of our hut doors. The noise of a radio sounded in the trees: Iraqi advance, Iranian casualties, American silence. We listened. 'I don't know how to talk about our meeting like this'—he was suddenly fumbling for phrases. 'It's important, you and I . . . like two people meeting in outer space. . . .' He ran his fingers over his face, as if to order its expression, his thoughts. Outer space. His country immaterial.

As we said goodbye, he clasped my hand and said: 'If in some future time I see you in the sights of my rifle—I'll miss.'

'And I won't fire at all.'

We laughed, but with deep emotion. I've never felt so brief a friendship more. In him I loved the Russian people. It was my last healing.

10. Kiev to the West

Back down the interminable highway northward, between farmlands green in winter wheat or clogged with blackened and dying sunflowers, through Simferopol to Zaporozhye to Kharkov, I went under a sky sagging like a rain-drenched tent from horizon to horizon. Along the roadsides, where the summer dust was melting to mud, the fruit-sellers still sat in the drizzle, as if unmoved since I had passed them long before. Around the asbestos-roofed villages old men grazed their cows, and ducks and geese basked in the puddles.

From Kharkov I cut across the north Ukraine towards Kiev. Enormous wheatfields, interspersed with sugar beet, flax and potatoes, flowed against the skyline. Along the windbreaks the birch trees were dropping yellow leaves, the maples flaming into red-gold candelabra, the elders thickened and scarlet with berries. The whole land was softening into death or sleep.

Kiev, 'the mother of Russian cities', still keeps the unrest, the size and a trace of the refinement of a great capital. From the ninth to the twelfth centuries it was the heart of a Russia which flowered in the sunlight of Byzantium, standing where the Dnieper headwaters gathered the Viking traffic before flooding south united to the Black Sea. Now, on one bank, the apartments sprawl in a colder-than-usual rhetoric—within fifteen years the population has doubled to two-and-a-half million—while opposite, where the Church of St Andrew rises like a trumpet-blast from the old city, the boulevards are plump with spaced gardens and parklands, and cobbled streets ruffle near the water.

Kiev is still the capital of the Ukraine, and was a strategic lodestar for the Germans in 1941. War memorials reach a deafening crescendo: mounds of immortality, obelisks of glory, parks of eternity. I noticed more than ten which had been built as late as the 1960s and 70s. Russians and Germans between them destroyed much of the central city, and in the rambling complex called the Monastery of the Cross, once Russia's holiest shrine, the eleventh century cathedral was reduced to a shattered body upholding a single dome. Far down the monastery's gardened slopes, a covered way plunges to a little square and a church. The place has been disused for two decades. Nothing gives you to expect what is coming. But within the church the plaster-smooth walls suddenly close around the monks' catacombs. For hundreds of yards, past dimly gleaming chapels and down water-dripping steps, the corridor beetles and bifurcates through a ghastly mausoleum. Robed in white silk, their faces covered by purple velvet or black embroidery and their feet slippered in silk, the abbots lie in their glass-topped coffins, with a single claw-like hand exposed on the breast. The cell-shrines are stacked with bones. Blackened skulls gape in their powder or leer from glass jars. Eight centuries of skeletons and mummified cadavers lie in their niches, hung with anti-religious plaques—the intolerance of Marxism hounding them even in their dust—until the defiled labyrinth washes you up again before the church's tarnished icon-screen.

This ghoulish maze prefigured my stay. The Kiev campsites had already closed down in early October, and I was assigned to the Ukraine Hotel. Louring above the city's Olympic football stadium, it was forbiddingly impressive. Its gloomy halls seemed always to be murmuring with a concourse of nondescript men, and the esplanades outside were dotted with other men, sitting by twos in cars, leafing through their briefcases, or waiting.

For several weeks I had visited nobody controversial and my vigilance had slackened. But that evening I overheard an assistant at the hotel's Intourist telephone-desk. Her tone was tense and deferential. She was answering questions. 'A lone British tourist? . . . yes . . . with his own car? . . . he arrived at 5.30. . . .'

As she put down the receiver I asked, still untroubled: 'Did somebody want me?'

She jumped. 'You're Mr Thubron? . . . yes . . . they, we. . . .' She was blushing, staring down and scrabbling furiously with her papers. When she looked up again her voice was loud and bright: 'If there's anything you want, we're absolutely at your service.'

I took a mental note of the car number-plates behind the hotel, and that evening it was one of these which framed itself in my mirror as I drove south into the suburbs: Kiev 75–86. Once it had gauged my speed, the white Volga saloon lingered back in a way which I was soon to recognize, tucked behind a lorry four cars behind. I might have shaken it off—it assumed I was unaware of it. But by now I was worried. I had no idea why I was wanted. Had they traced me back to meetings with dissidents in Moscow or Leningrad? I didn't know. Every minute or two the white shadow in my mirror would ease out as if to pass its covering lorry, then slide back. Once, in distraction, I overshot some red traffic-lights, and the Volga accelerated and did the same. A policeman tried to flag it down. It took no notice and swerved in close behind me. I saw a short, dark man seated in front, and a thin, fair driver. They fell back again instantly, concealed behind a truck.

I gave them a miserable time that evening. I was trying to find the flat of an impeccable Party member, a chance address given me in Moscow, but the sign-posting in Kiev was so erratic that I missed my way. Dusk deepened to night and the Volga turned to a pair of blazing eyes behind me, shifting among others. I became hopelessly lost. I drove in giddy rings along mud-caked side-lanes. Once I went full-circle and came up behind the Volga floundering in mire, its lights switched off. The two men were by now ridiculously exposed. They must have thought I was persecuting them on purpose.

Obsessed by my guilt in their eyes, I asked a policeman the way. He was off-duty, but he offered to drive ahead of me. So we started off, the unwitting policeman leading, and wound through a new cryptogram of half-lit streets and alleys. Five minutes later, so intent was I on the baleful lights behind me that I noticed too late when the policeman stopped. My foot crushed the brake-pedal, but the tyres choked in mid-scream and I crashed into him.

At that moment, in my mind's eye, a bureaucratic mountain amassed and suffocated me: insurance estimates, police reports, international telegrams, litigation. The policeman clambered from his car in amazement. 'What on earth were you thinking of?' he cried.

I glanced behind me. 'I'm sorry.' The Volga had pulled in among trees, its lights flashed off. 'I don't know.'

But when we inspected the cars, his own was mysteriously unscathed. We both gazed at it in disbelief, and for long minutes the kindly policeman stood in the road with his fist in his bovine mouth, staring down at damage which was unaccountably not there. Only my travel-sick Morris showed a dented wing and a smashed radiator grille and headlight.

After a long time he drove away nonplussed into the dark, and I was left with the KGB. But they didn't stir. Even now the street number, block number, and apartment numbers around me reeled in an incoherent maze. A few people were loitering outside the flats in the warm night. I entered the wrong block. When I reemerged I glimpsed the two men in the faint glow of the street lights, standing behind bushes near the entrance. I went up to them and asked them where was Block L?

When I looked into the face of the dark man, I recognized him from the hotel foyer. It was a face of tundra-like anonymity. Its tiny eyes peered over formless cheeks as if over a wall. It was not, I supposed, a cruel face, but unimaginative, dead.

'I don't know.' His voice was self-smothered. He tried to turn away from me. This reaction—he was obviously trained to avoid contact with his prey—was utterly un-Russian, and instantly remarkable. So I found the man's flat alone, and after a formal, ten-minute greeting emerged again and drove my battered Morris away. Its other headlight had already been broken by a tractor in the Crimea, so I nosed back blindly like a mole through the corridors of the dimmed streets, the Volga following, and all of us (I imagine) feeling foolish and angry, until I gained the hotel gates and my shadow drifted away to a compound of its own.

For the next four days I was followed everywhere. I came to recognize the techniques of the white Volgas (they were always white), sheltered by lorries a hundred yards behind me. Highly trained, they behaved in ways which were eventually so recognizable that by the fifth day I would pick them out at a glance. But by now I was riddled with nerves. I was afraid above all that my travel notes, compressed into the form of an illegible diary, would be discovered and taken away. Isolated, I began to partake in the condemnation of my silent spectators. I began to feel deeply, inherently guilty. A single friend might have saved me from this, but I didn't have one. I understood now the precious intensity of personal relationships among the dissidents. Because around me, as around them, the total, all-eclipsing Soviet world, which renders any other world powerless and far away, had become profoundly, morally hostile.

In the long, carpetless halls of the hotel, the walled-up faces of waiting men and the sunny voices of the Intourist girls became the scenario of nightmare. I began to behave guiltily. For a whole day I incarcerated myself in my room, illegibly writing up and disguising notes. I searched for a bugging device in vain; I did not dare even curse to myself. Then I wondered if I had implicated anybody else, and decided to destroy my list of Russian addresses and telephone numbers. The irony was that there was no person on it, dissident or other, who did not feel passionately for his country's good. But I could not decide how to destroy this paper. The problem became tortuous. If I shredded the list into my waste-paper basket, it might be recon-structed. If I went into the passage, the eyes of the concierges followed me; and all the public rooms were heavy with scrutiny. If I went out, I would be followed. So, like a cunning schoolboy, I burnt the list in my lavatory.

'Fire!' A fat laundry-maid burst in. 'Fire! Where's all this smoke from? Fire!' She had a blotched, porcine face which sloped neckless into her body. I stared at her with pure hate.

A young concierge appeared behind. Her gaze hardened and flew round the room. 'What's this?'

'I've been smoking.'

'Only smoking?'

'Yes.'

I felt angry, shaken by my own lie. The concierge marched back past her desk and descended the elevator. I imagined myself under inquisi-tion, trying to clear myself. I never smoke. But in one corner of the stairway landing stood an ash-bin where I found three cigarette-stubs. As if participating in some third-rate thriller, I took them back to my room, lit them to foil forensic tests, and left them in the lavatory. Then I walked downstairs and out into the sun, refusing to look behind me. I was shaking.

It seems foolish, in retrospect, that Kiev should be so contaminated for me. I thought it a handsome city, but it remains discoloured in my mind. I remember staring into foodshops whose stock was wretchedly little and expensive: in one only a heap of decapitated chickens, in another some crates of aubergines. And this was the capital of the Ukraine, of the Black Earth! I began to feel terribly tired, as if some unnoticed strain from the past months were finally spilling over. In the hotel that afternoon I found a Soviet Greek, an engineer from Kazakh-stan with a delicate, mobile face. I befriended him with neurotic relief. His parents had come from Istanbul to Sukhumi after Ataturk's victories in 1922, and had died in old age without ever talking a word of Russian. But he himself never spoke Greek, although he understood it; and his children could barely even understand it. I prompted him anxiously about his people's history. The Greeks, founders of freedom! Had he read Sappho, Cavafy, Herodotus? Those books were hard to get, he said. But did he still feel Greek, I demanded? Absolutely, he said. Yet I could not tell in what the feeling lay. He knew the date of Lenin's birthday, but he could not remember who had built the Parthenon. In my present state this struck me as a parable of total corruption.

I had been given other addresses in the city: those of a priest, a journalist and the wife of a poet who had recently been arrested. But all would have been compromised if I had met them. Although I did not know it at the time, the poet, a Ukrainian nationalist, was sentenced to ten years' hard labour on the day I arrived. I confined my trips to conventional tourist sites. I did not even see Babi Yar, where the Germans massacred over a hundred thousand Kievan Jews and others. ('It's discouraged to go there,' an Armenian had told me. 'I suppose they're afraid of it becoming a Jewish shrine.')

The only people I had warned of my coming were a Georgian agronomist and his Russian fiancée, who appeared by taxi one evening to take me to their home for supper. They greeted me like old friends—he a man of mercurial darkness, she motherly, blonde and Slavic-calm. I warmed to them at once. In the taxi we talked at ease of mutual friends in England. But through its back window I glimpsed the number-plate of the white Volga following us. I felt sick. But I didn't tell them. The contrast between their blithe chatter and this paranoid shadow was somehow horrific. And I, in my knowledge, was condemned to the shadow. My guilty diary bulged in my coat pocket.

The Volga drifted to a halt beyond us when we stopped, and as we ascended in the flat-block elevator, I glimpsed a man in a leather jacket enter below. His face was enclosed, leaden, and I could hear the noise of his feet keeping pace with the rickety elevator as we rose, until he knew which apartment we entered.

But the moment the door closed, we were at peace. Mehrab and Vera had both left behind broken marriages, and were palpably in love. Theirs was a timeless attraction of opposites. Mehrab had the trim, agile physique of his people. In his swarthy face, with its high forehead and prominent but rather delicate bones, the eyes glittered with a febrile restlessness. He spoke to me about his work, but was distracted by the closeness of Vera, seated heavy-breasted beside him. His gestures incorporated a tender searching of her body with the elucidation of drainage around the Black Sea. Irrigation ditches somehow found their way across her thighs; harvest failures were offset by a consoling crop of squeezes; a bumper year collected her breasts.

And all the time, framed in page-boy hair, her blue eyes and broad lips gave out a happy and uncomplicated strength. The word 'definitely' kept recurring in her talk. She was outspoken and often (said Mehrab) wrong. She had a puritan love of Siberia, where she had been born, and of all northern Russia. She preferred Leningrad to

Kiev. 'The people are more open-hearted there. Definitely. Here in Kiev they're enclosed, they live in their own circles.'

When she went into the kitchen to prepare supper, Mehrab laughed affectionately: 'She's biased. She was a child in Siberia, you see, and a student in Leningrad, living among students—but an adult only here. She looks back on those student days with nostalgia and on her childhood with love. So of course she sees the places in that order. But really, I think, the old gradations of north to south apply here too. Kiev, you know, is more casual and dirty than northern Russia, and the Ukrainians a bit more open. But Georgia is better still!'

Love, in many permutations and disguises, pervaded our evening. The flat was full of it: thumbed books, taped music, Black Sea driftwood which they had collected on holiday and lacquered in curious shapes. 'A man should love his work,' Mehrab said, 'that's the secret, but I'm not sure if the young do that any longer.' He spoke of 'the young' as if they were another race; I supposed he was about thirty-five. 'They're somehow more diffuse, perhaps more imaginative than we were at that age.'

I said I hoped so. I was thinking of peace, the trust which needs imagination.

'If real peace comes, it'll come because people are selfish,' Vera said. 'Definitely. They'll have too much to lose.'

'Yes,' I said. That sounded like life.

A storm rumbled outside. I went to the window. The rain was lashing down on the road, the darkened trees and the white car sheltered under them.

'The young have ten times as much as we had,' Vera went on. 'When I was five, I remember, I ached for a doll. I used to make wooden ones myself, but I longed for one with proper hair and a body made of something smooth, like skin, which I could dress and undress and wash.' She laughed boisterously. 'I got one when I was twenty! And I loved it just as much as if I was five! And now I see children with bicycles, radios, everything, and it hasn't improved them.' She looked puzzled and fed up. 'And you in the West, you have so much, but are you happier?'

I didn't know, I said (whatever we meant by happiness). *But we couldn't go back.*

When I returned to my hotel, I knew that something was wrong. The comfortable old concierge who had taken over duty on my floor, and

[208]

who had previously shown a maternal benignity, now gaped at me with horror.

My room, in my absence, had been searched. It had been done near-perfectly, everything repositioned almost precisely as it was. Only by the pinpoint siting of several objects before I left, and by the insertion in notebooks of tiny threads now dislodged, did I realize that everything I possessed—letters, clothes, wallet, books, documents—had been removed, scrutinized and fastidiously replaced.

But my diary was in my pocket, and my address-list ashes down the lavatory.

You would not know, from its exterior, that Kiev's cathedral of Haghia Sophia contained a pure eleventh century core, built at the zenith of Russia's early power. Octagonal turrets, gilded lanterns, trifling apses and a multiplicity of curvaceous eighteenth century domes cloud it in stucco candy-floss. From the surrounding trees, huge chestnuts thump onto the fish-bone paving to the delight of children, and a four-tiered baroque belfry looms above.

But inside, the Byzantine glory breaks like an ocean in wave upon wave of fresco and mosaic, embracing for ever the divine and earthly order of things, engulfing arches, pillars and galleries in its petrified and self-existent splendour. In the dome hovers the soft mosaic presence of Christ the Ruler. His russet hair falls to a misty rain of beard. But he looks unfit to rule. The mouth is a fat anemone. The huge, deer's eyes gaze dreamy-sad. Yet beneath him apostles and archangels circle the dome in adoration, and on the pendentives the evangelists relax in high-backed chairs, penning the secrets of eternity. Lower still, her feet balanced light in the golden cave of the apse, the Virgin Mary stands disembodied. Her face is long, dusky, other-than-human, haloed in refracted light—less a woman or a goddess than a metaphysical idea, a blue-gold geometry of intercession.

The tourist groups were attending doggedly to their guides, and were being dealt a Marxist interpretation of theocratic art. It was my last morning in Kiev. Behind one group, pretending to be attached, was a small, sallow man. He knew I knew (our eyes had met on another occasion) and he looked rather miserable. But by now I was released. In a moment of angry self-absolution I had started to ignore my persecutors and live my own life instead of theirs. I at last understood how in Moscow, that August night, Boris and Nikolai could have talked so outspokenly in his eavesdropped apartment, and had re-fused to be coerced into dishonesty. Besides, it seemed to me now, in calm, that this sudden intrusion on me sprang from pure bureaucracy. The big tourist hotels are heavily monitored by the KGB.

Around me the cathedral's dogma was as self-embalmed as theirs. Law and chaos, sin and redemption, unfolded in a golden dialectic across its walls, and fading over all the frescoed arches and pillars of the side-aisles, patriarchs and saints—ascetic and learned, hermit and militant—waved their chalices and crosses in ghostly obsolescence.

Once this Byzantine world had exercised so profound an appeal to the Russian spirit that despite all persecution its decline would be inexplicable had not its power so clearly been deflected into a new redemption on earth. Sometimes in the past months I had almost envied this entirety of vision. Now, wandering in the forest of pillars, I felt old and alienated. I harboured, I suppose, a sceptical European sense that no system could deeply alter the absurdities of human nature, whereas the Russians still indulged an ancient sense of mission. 'In every way there is something gigantic about this people,' wrote Madame de Staël, 'ordinary dimensions have no application to them.' And as I walked through these aisles of faded certainty, it seemed that after even the most tragic failings had been counted, despite the public tyranny and private dissimulation, the travestied history and the sallow men on the edge of crowds, there yet remained a bruised grandeur about this race who could still dream, however faintly, of a perfectible community on earth.

But all around me the frescoed ancestors of this foolishness were thinning away. The blemished saints and Church fathers no longer held the heart and gaze. They were draining back into the plaster, into their unimaginable centuries.

'It was just superstition,' a guide said. 'Primitive daydreams. . . .'

The next day I drove 340 miles westward to Lvov. Half a mile behind me over the wide-open land a white Volga kept pace. But it gave me up where the Kiev district stopped, and the traffic police flagrantly radioed my progress. After ten miles I passed two of them fidgeting with their truncheons in the middle of the road. Caught in my mirror, one of them turned and raised his arm, and a white Zhiguli slid out from the trees behind him. Thereafter, for two hundred miles, I was followed by Lvov 22–65, and drove through corridors of autumn trees, hung with mistletoe, and over the Carpathians. After a while, too, it dawned on me that half a mile ahead a second white Zhiguli was attending me in its own sophisticated way. If I accelerated to sixty, it did the same; if I slowed to thirty, it copied me. So all afternoon, bracketed between

Lvov 22–65 and Lvov 78–65 (and marvelling at the waste of manpower) I made for the West.

In Lvov itself, while searching for my hotel, I again became lost. I blundered in circles, so that my two escorts anxiously closed in, aligned themselves behind, and clung to me through a hundred futile alleys.

The city breathed out a dilapidated, Austro-Hungarian charm and the hotel, when I discovered it, was stately with gilt and aspidistras. Its old, gentle-mannered staff seemed to have survived inexplicably from the pre-war, cosmopolitan Lvov shattered by Stalin.

It was my last night in Russia. I lay in the bath, reading my travel diary. I was afraid I would not see it again. That night I was followed on foot through the streets. And as if a belated attempt were being made to expose me, I received a flurry of criminal proposals in the foyer of the hotel. A man introducing himself as a Polish student asked me for drugs. Another offered dollars in exchange for any pornography or underground literature I might have. A woman wanted to change my British pounds on the black market.

Next day the Zhigulis shadowed me to the Hungarian border, keeping their distance through the last, pine-dark hills. They vanished only at the final moment, where the border-post of Chop looked deceptively asleep. I did not know what to expect here. My close-written diary, an irreplaceable store of detailed memories, blazed like a beacon in my pocket.

I was met by a friendly interpreter who told me the formalities would only take twenty minutes. After the first hour he said: 'It's nothing personal.' A little later he admitted 'It's a bit long.' Then he fell silent. Other cars came and went; but mine stayed. Four hours later I was still being investigated. Five men inspected my scant luggage, item by item strewn miserably along the customs' counter. I was stripped and body-searched. My camera was emptied, my film developed. The mud-clogged Morris was driven over a dip where two mechanics probed it for two hours, then dismantled even its door panels, and lifted out its dashboard.

Finally, darkness falling, I was summoned into a room below the customs post. The officials looked vaguely nonplussed. Everything I owned had melted into innocence under inspection, except the illegible diary, which now lay in fingered sheafs on the desk of a stone-faced immigration officer. As I entered he glanced up from his magnifying glass with an expression of heavy frustration. He looked weary. He demanded: 'Have you developed this writing specially?'

He summoned the interpreter. Then, for half an hour, he pointed to

[211]

passages in the manuscript and ordered me to read them aloud: Odessa, Rostov, Riga. . . . I read them out, omitting a few ruderies, while the interpreter translated them into poetic Russian. Neither man could read what I had written. I might as well have quoted the psalms or Shakespeare. But this did not strike me as odd at the time.

Yet I read the diary like a valediction. I was sure it would be impounded. Even as I did so, I was reliving places and people half forgotten, until these descriptions seemed to be all I had to take away with me. I passionately wanted to keep them. Without them, I felt, I might not believe that I had entered the Soviet Union at all. And there are times even now when this land reverts to the enigma which hung on my classroom wall when I was a boy—Mercator's projection, its proportions distorted—until it seems to be less a physical country than an area of mingled tenderness and unease in my mind, which I call Russia.

At last the shoulders of the immigration officer (if that is what he was) heaved with a kind of dejected relief. 'It's getting late.'

'Yes.'

For a minute more he ruminated in silence, then a tiny, resigned smile opened in his face, and he handed back to me the notes from which this book has been composed.